Book of Bursztyn

(Burshtyn, Ukraine)

Translation of
Sefer Bursztyn

Original Book Edited by: S. Kanc

Originally published in Jerusalem 1960

A Publication of JewishGen
Edmond J. Safra Plaza, 36 Battery Place, New York, NY 10280
646.494.2972 | info@JewishGen.org | www.jewishgen.org

Book of Bursztyn

Translation of *Sefer Bursztyn*

Copyright © 2024 by JewishGen. All rights reserved.
First Printing: May 2024, Iyar, 5784
Editor of Original Yizkor Book: S. Kanc
Project Coordinator: Rivka Chaya Schiller
Cover Design: Irv Osterer
Layout: Jonathan Wind
Name Indexing: Jonathan Wind

JewishGen Press is not responsible for inaccuracies or omissions in the original work and makes no representations regarding the accuracy of this translation. Digital images of the original book's contents can be seen online at the New York Public Library website or the Yiddish Book Center website.

Library of Congress Control Number (LCCN): 2024934228

ISBN: 978-1-954176-96-6 (hard cover: 256 pages, alk. paper)

About JewishGen.org

JewishGen, is a Genealogical Research Division of the Museum of Jewish Heritage - A Living Memorial to the Holocaust, serves as the global home for Jewish genealogy.

Featuring unparalleled access to 30+ million records, it offers unique search tools, along with opportunities for researchers to connect with others who share similar interests. Award winning resources such as the Family Finder, Discussion Groups, and ViewMate, are relied upon by thousands each day.

In addition, JewishGen's extensive informational, educational and historical offerings, such as the Jewish Communities Database, Yizkor Book translations, InfoFiles, Family Tree of the Jewish People, and KehilaLinks, provide critical insights, first-hand accounts, and context about Jewish communal and familial life throughout the world.

Offered as a free resource, JewishGen.org has facilitated thousands of family connections and success stories, and is currently engaged in an intensive expansion effort that will bring many more records, tools, and resources to its collections.

Please visit https://www.jewishgen.org/ to learn more.

Vice President for JewishGen: Avraham Groll

About the JewishGen Yizkor Book Project

Yizkor Books (Memorial Books) were traditionally written to memorialize the names of departed family and martyrs during holiday services in the synagogue (a practice that still exists in many synagogues today).

Over the centuries, as a result of countless persecutions and horrific atrocities committed against the Jews, Yizkor Books (Sefer Zikaron in Hebrew) were expanded to include more historical information, such as biographical sketches of famous personalities and descriptions of daily town life.

Following the Holocaust, the idea of remembrance and learning took on an urgent and crucial importance. Survivors of the Holocaust sought out other surviving residents of their former towns to memorialize and document the names and way of life of those who were ruthlessly murdered by the Nazis. These remembrances were documented in Yizkor Books, hundreds of which were published in the first decades after the Holocaust.

Most of these books were published privately, or through *Landsmanshaftn* (social organizations comprised of members originating from the same European town or region) that still existed, and were often distributed free of charge. The languages used to document these crucial histories and links to our past were mostly Yiddish and Hebrew. JewishGen has undertaken the sacred responsibility of translating these books into English so that the culture and way of life of these communities will be preserved and transmitted to future generations.

In 1986, a group of farsighted JewishGenners started a project to pool their efforts together in groups based upon their ancestors' towns and donate funds to translate the Yizkor books of their ancestral towns into English. As the translated material became available, it was made accessible for free at https://www.JewishGen.org/Yizkor . Hardcover copies can be purchased by visiting https://www.jewishgen.org/Yizkor/ybip.html (see below).

It is our hope that the translation of these books into English (and other languages) will assist the countless Jewish family researchers who are so desperately seeking to forge a connection with their heritage.

Director of JewishGen Yizkor Book Project: Lance Ackerfeld

About JewishGen Press

JewishGen Press (formerly the Yizkor Books-in-Print Project) is the publishing division of JewishGen.org, and provides a venue for the publication of non-fiction books pertaining to Jewish genealogy, history, culture, and heritage.

In addition to the Yizkor Book category, publications in the Other Non-Fiction category include Shoah memoirs and research, genealogical research, collections of genealogical and historical materials, biographies, diaries and letters, studies of Jewish experience and cultural life in the past, academic theses, and other books of interest to the Jewish community.

Please visit https://www.jewishgen.org/Yizkor/ybip.html to learn more.

Director of JewishGen Press: Joel Alpert
Managing Editor - Jessica Feinstein
Publications Manager - Susan Rosin

Notes to the Reader

The images in the original book were reproduced from photographs from the time of the first edition. These reproductions were already of poor quality, being pre-war and at least 30 or more years old. As a result, the images in the book are the best achievable.

A reader can view the original scans of the book on the websites listed below.

The original book can be seen online at the Yiddish Book Center website:

https://www.yiddishbookcenter.org/collections/yizkor-books/yzk-nybc313718/sefer-burshtin

OR

at the New York Public Library Digital Collections website:

https://digitalcollections.nypl.org/items/c5c52520-63a5-0133-9867-00505686d14e

To obtain a list of Shoah victims from **Bursztyn (Burshtyn, Ukraine),** the reader should access the Yad Vashem web site listed below; one can also search for specific family names using family name option. These lists are continually updated by Yad Vashem, so it is worthwhile to periodically search them.

There is more valuable information (including the Pages of Testimony, etc.) available on this website: https://yvng.yadvashem.org/

A list of all books available from JewishGen Press along with prices is available at: https://www.jewishgen.org/Yizkor/ybip.html

Cover Photo Credits

Cover Design by: Irv Osterer

Front Cover:

"State of Israel" Association *[pp. 67 – 68]*

Back Cover:

From top clockwise:

Bursztyn's synagogue c. 1957 *[pp. 395 – 396]*
Rabbi Feivel Frankl and his wife Chaya *[pp. 287]*
The Zionist Youth ("Hanoar Hatzioni") of Bursztyn *[pp. 297 – 298]*
Rescued Torah Scroll *[pp. 405]*
Doctor Schmurek's family *[pp. 296]*
Aharon Nute Glasthal, trustee of the Tailors' Little Synagogue *[pp. 231-232]*

Geopolitical Information

Map of Ukraine showing the location of **Burshtyn**

Burshtyn

Burshtyn, Ukraine is located at 49°16' N 24°38' E and 274 miles WSW of Kyyiv

	Town	District	Province	Country
Before WWI (c. 1900):	Bursztyn	Rohatyń	Galicia	Austrian Empire
Between the wars (c. 1930):	Bursztyn	Rohatyn	Stanisławów	Poland
After WWII (c. 1950):	Burshtyn			Soviet Union
Today (c. 2000):	Burshtyn			Ukraine

Alternate Names for the Town:

Burshtyn [Ukr], Burshtin [Rus, Yid], Bursztyn [Pol], Burschtyn [Ger], Burstyn

Nearby Jewish Communities:

Bukachivtsi 6 miles W
Bilshivtsi 8 miles SE
Cherniv 8 miles W
Zhuriv 9 miles WNW
Dolzhka 10 miles SW
Rohatyn 10 miles N
Voinyliv 11 miles SSW
Kniahynychi 11 miles NW
Halych 11 miles SSE
Stratin 14 miles NNE
Zhuravno 16 miles W
Khodoriv 17 miles WNW
Yezupil' 17 miles SSE
Berezhany 19 miles NE
Zavalov 19 miles ESE
Mariyampil 19 miles SSE
Narayiv 19 miles NNE
Novi Strilyshcha 20 miles NNW
Kalush 21 miles SW
Ustya-Zelene 22 miles SE

Pidhaytsi 23 miles E
Zhydachiv 24 miles WNW
Hnizdychiv 24 miles WNW
Ivano-Frankivsk 24 miles S
Holyn 24 miles SW
Berezdivtsi 25 miles WNW
Dunayev 26 miles NNE
Kozova 26 miles ENE
Vybranivka 27 miles NW
Tysmenytsya 27 miles SSE
Monastyryska 27 miles ESE
Broshniv-Osada 27 miles SW
Lysets' 28 miles S
Peremyshlyany 28 miles N
Svirzh 28 miles NNW
Sokołów 28 miles WSW
Pomoryany 29 miles NNE
Rozdil 29 miles WNW
Svarychiv 29 miles SW
Bobrka 29 miles NNW
Nyzhniv 30 miles SE

Introduction and Acknowledgments

The following text—the translation of the Yiddish and Hebrew language, *Sefer Bursztyn*—was a decade in the making. It came about as the result of collaborative work between Lance Ackerfeld, Director of JewishGen's Yizkor Book Project; Erica S. Goldman-Brodie, Article Editor; Mira Eckhaus, Hebrew Translator; Susan Oher-Rosin, Publication Manager; Jonathan Wind, Formatter and Indexer; Irv Osterer, Cover Designer; Genia Hollander, Transcriber; Ann Harris, Transliterator; Yocheved Klausner, Editor; and me, Rivka Schiller, Yiddish and Hebrew Translator and Editor.

I would like to echo the sentiments expressed in many of the Yizkor books I have encountered over the years: May this collection of first-person, biographical, anecdotal, and historical accounts serve as a paper monument in place of the countless missing Matzevot (headstones) of Bursztyn Jews whose lives were cut down prematurely.

As a long-time Yiddish and Hebrew translator, I am proud to be able to make this text accessible to a broader, English-reading public. That having been said, I encourage all those who *are* able to read Yiddish and Hebrew to also consult the original version of this Yizkor book since translation is, to quote the famous Yiddish and Hebrew poet, Chaim Nachman Bialik (1873-1934), "like a kiss through a handkerchief."

I hope you find this commemorative work as compelling and informative as I did. In closing, please excuse any oversights in my acknowledgments or textual errors. I bear full responsibility for them.

Rivka Schiller, PhD

Table of Contents

Book of Bursztyn
(Burshtyn, Ukraine)

49°16' / 24°38'

Translation of:
Sefer Bursztyn

Editor: S. Kanc

Published in Jerusalem 1960

Acknowledgments:

Project Coordinator and Translator

Rivka Chaya Schiller

Translation Editor: Erica S. Goldman-Brodie

Our sincere appreciation to Yad Vashem
for the submission of the necrology for placement on the JewishGen web site.

Translations by Rivka Schiller unless otherwise noted.

This is a translation of: *Sefer Bursztyn* (Book of Bursztyn),
Editor: S. Kanc, Published by: The Encyclopaedia of the Jewish Diaspora, Jerusalem 1960 (H,Y 426
pages)

Note: The original book can be seen online at the NY Public Library site: Burshtyn

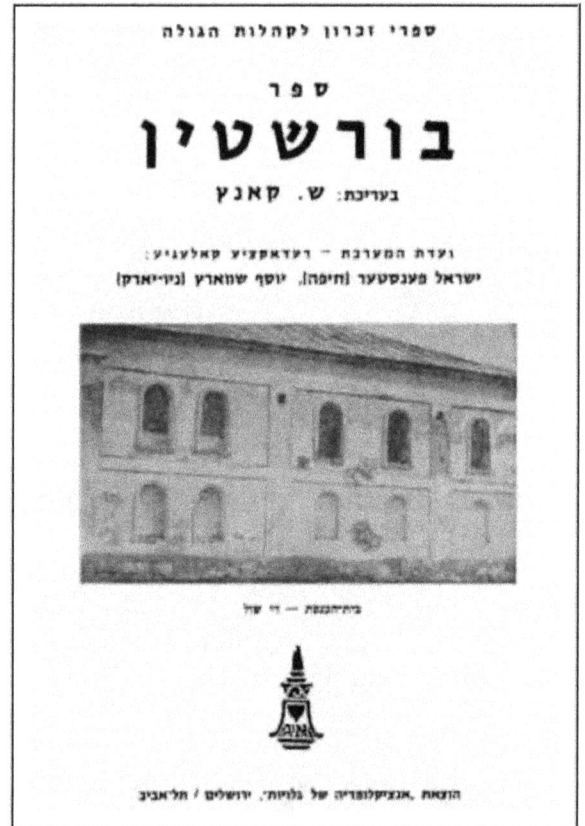

ספרי זכרון לקהלות הגולה

ס פ ר

בורשטין

בעריכת: ש. קאנץ

ועדת המערבת – רעדאקציע קאלעגיע:
ישראל פענסטער (חיפה), יוסף שווארץ (ניו־יארק)

בית־הכנסת – רי של

ספר
בורשטין

הוצאת "אנציקלופדיה של גלויות, ירושלים / תל־אביב

[pp. 9-10]

At the Gates of Tears

by Uri Zvi Grinberg

… Oh our blood in rivers and blood in the vessels of Gentiles!
Demanding blood from whom? The world is a pure crucifix:
Gentiles are cheerful, Jews the mourners.
Stand before the Western Wall and tell him!

The skies are blue, or clouds go by,
Summer rains, or white snowfalls…
At the rivers of Babylon stand my willows –
Great are my fears! Deep are my woes!

What in the world can make my bitter heart cheerful?
What should I do now with a life that remains wounded?

To bear their burden – this was given to me,
Until Jews live to see the Messiah.

May Jews live long – I among them, too.
Until – smoke ascends from the Kingdom of Edom.

Magnified and sanctified … praised be the Jews' name!
May their kingdom come … and we shall all say Amen!

(From the poem: "At the Gates of Tears Stands a Jew Remembering")

[pp. 17-18]

We will remember!

Translated by Mira Eckhaus

Edited by Rivka Schiller

We will remember **with pain and sorrow the souls of our holy and pure brothers and sisters who fell into the hands of impure murderers without the image of God.**

We will remember **the simple Jews and the chosen ones of culture, the glory of man, from old man to child, the honest and dear, those who are charitable and benevolent, the love of humanity and devotion.**

We will remember **the dreams, the hopes and the desires, the lofty ambitions, the love of the people and the love of our country, the faith and heroism, the hatred and contempt for their murderers.**

We will remember **the synagogues and Beit Midrash schools, the charity and benevolence institutions, the schools and the libraries, every Zionist and cultural organization that was sacred to the work of the people.**

We will remember **all of them, who were eradicated and cut short and destroyed and ruined by crazy evils with impure soul, we will remember – not forget!**

[pp. 21-22]

Words of the Book in Memory of Dr. Haber
At the Memorial Gathering in Haifa, on 22.10.58

Let us show respect with a lowered head for the memory of our dear friend, Dr. Mottel son of David Klirsfeld Haber, O"BM, who went to his eternal rest in his untimely passing from Israel. In his youth he left Bursztyn to acquire Torah; in our town there was no opportunity to find expression for his fermenting soul that thirsted for Torah and Avodah [literally, study and prayer]; this is a Hebrew phrase that appears frequently within the religious realm. He possessed a genteel/refined soul that was simple and full of activity [or achievements]. He would bring people closer through love and appreciation.

Dr. M. Haber

With the passing of Dr. Haber, we lost a rare type in Jewish life, from the few who go their way [who conduct their actions, activities] with modesty and devotion. He was an active and initiating youth, educated at a university in Germany. In spite of the economic difficulties, he devoted himself with all his desire toward achieving his goal, to work, to study, to help his family, and to attain an education that was suited to his spirit. A spirit of volunteering beat/pulsated within him and excited/ignited others. At our commemorative gatherings, he would speak in Yiddish: "Who from among you won't remember Bursztyn "the beautiful Jewish and beloved little town" [last quote appears in Yiddish in original text], and if you remember, do not forget it, for the honor of our martyrs demands this from us. Days and nights he wrote his essay, which included hundreds of pages, for the book, "The [Jewish] Community of Bursztyn," and once he had completed his work, he printed it and sent a copy to our brothers in America and requested of them: "Read these pages of the Shoah [Holocaust] and help us to publish the memorial book for good. There is no waiting any longer; the time is short and the work is great [the former expression is derived from the Jewish ethical work, "Ethics of the Fathers"]. Even at happy/celebratory occasions he did not forget his holy task; I will recall the wedding celebration of Moshe Matsis. I sat in my family circle, and my friend was beside the table, and here Dr. Haber approached me and asked to have a short meeting regarding the publication of the book. That was his petition at every gathering, and it is understood that he was always at the head of those volunteering for this activity. With the passing of Mottel, we lost one of Bursztyn's best sons; with his death, we lost a brother, a good friend to all of us. And he passed away before seeing the book [with his own eyes]. We, the sons/children of Bursztyn [i.e., the Jewish former residents of Bursztyn], are realizing his aspirations, with all the efforts; we will publish the book, "The [Jewish] Community of Bursztyn," in which we shall publicize the work that he composed during the final years of his life. And on the day that the labor of the memorial book is complete, we will remember/commemorate the figure of Dr. Mottel Haber Z"L. Bitter is the loss for those who hail from Bursztyn; may the members of his family be duly comforted, together with the sons/children of Bursztyn, as one.

And may we also remember Berish son of Zev, the ritual slaughterer Miller, who died in the foreign country/diaspora of the United States. Although he left our town before the First World War and settled in America, there still beat within him the Zionist spirit and love for the homeland; may his memory be blessed.

And let us also remember David Frankl, Tzvi Schumer, [and] Olek Hauselberg, who died in Israel. In the chain of generous/openhearted souls, may their souls be bound.

[pp. 23-24]

Words That Were Stated at the Commemorative Gathering
at which the decision was made to issue the book "The [Jewish] Community of Bursztyn,"
Haifa, the Pioneers' House, 17.10.1954

From Mordechai Nachwalger's words: Regarding their only crime of being Jews from birth, their honor was desecrated, and because of this simple sin, the Jews of Bursztyn were pursued, slaughtered, and burned. In the merit of the last ones who hovered between life and death within the Nazi inferno, and those who survived it, we know to [i.e., have what to] relate about them for generations.

The Jews of Bursztyn loved to live as Jews – their final cry en route to the death camps and the gas chambers resounds in our ears – do not cry about our going [to our deaths] – do not eulogize us – for there are yet millions of remaining Jews about whom one must be concerned!

And in this manner, we mourn our dear ones upon the graves of ash, and eternalize their memory by issuing the book, "The [Jewish] Community of Bursztyn." We are certain that the historians of the future will appropriately value the act of eternalizing the memory of our community, and the book will forever remain as a testament to the shame and scorn of Germany. May every single hour of our lives be imbued with the notion of remembering/memorializing; this notion will strengthen and encourage us to face tomorrow."

The gathering selected the following panel at the book council:

Among them [were]: Ben-Menachem (Breiter), Dr. Mottel Haber, Munio [Munye] Cohen; Mordechai Nachwalger; Yisrael Fenster; [and] Sarah Kessler.

It was decided to appoint members Haber, Matsis, [and] Fenster to approach former Bursztyners in the United States regarding their participation in the publication of the book and insofar as their finding funds to edit it.

At this festive occasion all the former residents of Bursztyn were invited to find manuscripts, documents, and photographs pertaining to the city of Bursztyn during the Shoah period, as well as from before and afterward, for the book council. May they fulfill their holy duty to eternalize the memory of our dear ones. May they rest in Paradise.

[pp. 63-64]

There once was a town named Bursztyn

by M. Nachwalger

Translated by Mira Eckhaus

Edited by Rivka Schiller

There once was a Bursztyn community and it is no more.

At the hands of Ukrainian German killers, it was cut short of the multi-branches of Polish Jewry.

Its memory remains in the hearts of dozens of its remnants who have been scattered all over the world, most of whom have been acclimatized in their homeland, in the country Israel.

Where is that piece of soil that soaked up their blood and in which their sacred ashes lie?

Where is the gravestone that points out that they were buried here?

Here are two rows of densely built black houses, surrounding the market square and a number of streets and alleys branch off from them to the sides. This is the town that grew slowly over hundreds of years, from a tiny settlement in ancient days, which was built next to the palace of Prince Jabłonowski.

One of the many Jewish settlements that took root on the banks of the Gnila Lipa River in eastern Poland, surrounded by villages of peasants eager for Jewish blood and property.

In the last decades before its annihilation and destruction, the Jewish community in Bursztyn reached a period of national and collective activity in all the light and shadow in which, on all the positive and the negative, which engaged in the effort for a Jewish life in the diaspora and abroad.

In this Jewish town, which was apparently dormant and silence in the great body of Polish Jewry, were reflected the sparks of our people's life in the period before the Holocaust.

Here is the wonderful figure of a typical Jew, the likes of which could only be seen hundreds of years ago in the centers of Jewish Kabbalah, in Spain or France, and here is the passionate Chasid who does not differ in his way of life from the Chasidim of the period of the Baal Shem Tov, and the fierce Mitnaged and the well versed in Shas and Poskim who are as though copied from HaRaga's time.

Who among us does not remember the small town of "Bursztyn" within its borders? On Rohatyn's side was the court, on the Demianow side – the Christian cemetery, on the Korostowice side – the beautiful Gnila Lipa River, and then the Jewish cemetery and the Catholic monastery. On all the outskirts of the city and in the center, stirred the life of Jews who were engaged in trade, crafts, and the work of the Creator.

Most of the town's Jews sometimes met in the synagogues, at celebrations, in youth organizations, in the Y. L. Peretz Cultural Center, etc., and in those meetings, they found a vent for their souls in the Diaspora. Who will not remember the Hebrew teachers: Sobel, the girl from Borysław, with energy and dedication to the teaching of the language Hebrew; Schwartz, Strohweiss and others? Each of them and all of them together, devoted their time after their hours of teaching to sow the seeds of Zionism and love of the homeland in the youth. The centers of the Zionist spirit were in the Histadruts: Hitachdut, Beitar and Hanoar Hatzioni, of which hundreds of girls and boys were members. We should note the constant concern of our parents for learning Torah, with a private "rabbi" (Hershele Strelisker and his son-in-law, Yudel Purim, the Weitz brothers, and others) or in the classes of rabbis and Torah scholars in synagogues: the Dayan Ginsburg, the Weba brothers, Yankel Shohat, Itche Gutstein, the Leibale brothers, Yeshaya Ostrower, and others. The ultra-Orthodox would gather in the house of Rabbi Landau, the Dayan Ginsburg, in the beautiful synagogue, on the walls of which pictures from the Bible shone in a pattern of colors; in the Beit Midrash, and in the "Kleislech" of the Chasidim, around the table of Reb Moshe, Baal Mofet, whose reputation preceded him.

The youth would also teach according to their spirit: Zionism, Literature, social life in an organizational framework. The youth would also attend lectures and visit the theater, which came to the town: the Goldfaden troupe, the charming troupe, as well as the foreign theater "Bestednik." There were also local play groups that presented plays directed by Mina Tobias. The youth also met at the "Sokol" building to watch films that were accompanied by the play of the Jewish violinist, Wahl.

There was a community and a "Gmiluth Chassadim" bank at the house. The community's income came, mainly, from the slaughter

[pp. 65-66]

of poultry and beef, the slips were sold to consumers at Nachman Breiter's [business]. In the course of time, the youth, who could not afford studying at schools outside the area, studied in courses in the town, a clerkship course (run by Reinhard), lessons at the Tobias brothers' [home], etc.

People with an education and degrees also lived in the town, doctors (Schumer, Katz and Sussmann lawyers (Schmarak, Ziering, Klugmann, Rohrberg, Hecker, Rosen, and others), veterinary doctor (Wattenberg), teachers (Landau, Rottenstreich and others), but they, except for a few, considered themselves "privileged," assimilated with the gentiles in a general "casino," and did not devote their knowledge to Hebrew culture.

In the last decades, all currents in the broad spectrum of the Jewish population in Poland, from the national social and political movements, stirred amidst the Jewish population in Bursztyn. As in the entire Polish Jewry, there were in Bursztyn factions of every movement, from ultra-orthodox, through assimilated and even active Zionists.

A series of characters and figures of the small and diverse group pass before our eyes. Here are the community leaders and its activists, rabbis and judges, Chovevei Tzion and Zionists, scholars of the Beit Midrash on the one hand and students of the Polish high school on the other, the "rabbi" and the court, the reformed Hebrew teacher and language learners of New Hebrew in the circles of youth movements, including socialists and communists seeking redemption among the gentiles in the foreign world, as well as pioneers and immigrants who sought their redemption in their homeland, Israel.

Many of Bursztyn's Jews were clerks, merchants, coachmen, porters, craftsmen: shoemakers, tailors, hairdressers, carpenters, tinsmiths, bakers; cattle breeders, land leasers, brokers, and laborers, who subsisted by their hard work.

In Bursztyn there were "Kloisen" institutions: we already mentioned the rabbi, the Beit Midrash, the magnificent synagogue; charitable and Gmiluth Chassadim institutions, the community, the Zionist Histadrut and its parties, youth organizations that fulfill the aspirations and ideas of national public revival.

This magnificent gallery of figures and institutions grew amidst the colorful backdrop of all strata of the community, from the impoverished people to the rich and wealthy.

Such was life within the town: seemingly quiet and sleepy; however, as a matter of fact, it was vibrant and eager for human redemption.

And our town was completely destroyed along with the rest of the holy communities.

May this memoir book be an eternal noble monument of the life and struggle of the holy Bursztyn community, so that its sons and their descendants will remember this town.

[pp. 71-72]

Beitar and Its Activities

by Munye Cohen

In the years following the First World War, most of the Jewish youth in our town joined the youth movements, "Gordonia" and "Hechalutz." Once the doctrine of Jabotinsky, for whom the ultimate goal of Zionism was the establishment of a Hebrew country, [and for whom] the youth in the diasporic lands also needed to prepare itself from a military perspective, penetrated the cities and towns of Galicia, the movement also penetrated our town of Bursztyn.

One Sabbath, when the leader of "Gordonia" was leading a discussion about the history of Zionism, and attacked and besmirched the name of Zev Jabotinsky, a portion of the people in the group, which was headed up by the young member, Gershon Ginzburg (the son of the religious law adjudicator), brought its objection/protestation, and abandoned "Gordonia."

In this group were: Gershon Ginzburg, Velvl Ostrower, Leib Schwartz, Lipa Mandelberg, Shaike Kletter, and Munye Cohen (presently in Israel), and they began right away to request a way of actualizing/realizing the ideology of Revisionism. They corresponded with two comrades/members on the spot: Yosef Kletter (today in Russia) and Hersh Breiter (resides in Vienna), who joined the youth federation, "Menorah," in Stanislawow, and through them, a connection was maintained with the headquarters of Beitar, whose moshava [i.e., agricultural colony] was then in Stanislawow, under the leadership of Adalbert Bibring.

During Shavuot of 1927, a gathering of the foundation of Beitar was held. As the overseer of the nest [or lodge] Velvl Ostrower was appointed, and as members of the headquarters: Lipa Mandelberg, Leib Schwartz, Shaike Kletter, and Munye Cohen [were appointed]. In the beginning, in the group there were [see note at end, p.10] a small number of members, only adolescents, although after a brief time, many youths joined them, male and female adolescents of every stratum, merchants, artisans and laborers, and Beitar became/turned into the largest youth movement in the city.

In the summer of 1929, 3 of the nest's members departed for the first summer camp, which the headquarters of the Lwow region in Mikulince organized. After they returned to the town, they stood at the head/helm of the physical education movement.

Group of Beitar at the time when they were founded

The teacher who came to the city, the commander/leader of the Beitar nest in Stanislawow, the medical student, Michael Frust, who organized first-aid courses and oversaw the cultural activity, also helped out a lot with the work at the nest. Bursztyn's Beitar organization penetrated the life of the movement in Poland. In the year 1930, during the time of the first Beitar convention in Poland, which took place in Warsaw, 8

[pp. 73-74]

male and female members from the Bursztyn nest participated in this. The delegates/envoys also participated in all the national and regional conferences. With the effort of nest headquarters, nests were also established in towns in the area, such as: Bolszowce, Bukaczowce, Halicz, Wojnilow, Lipica, and others. A conference was also organized in Bursztyn with the participation of 400 youths from the adjoining towns, who paraded in their uniforms through the streets of the city and made a huge impression on the city's Jewish and Christian populace. The members of the Bursztyn nest also filled positions within the central leadership of Beitar. Gershon Ginzburg was the regional leader in Lwow; and afterward, in Krakow, Velvl Ostrower – in the Stanislawow region, and Munye Cohen – in the Lwow region.

The members of Beitar were mere youths, and nonetheless, Beitar was represented in all the Zionist and general institutions in the city. During the first years, Beitar had representatives of all the political parties at the local Zionist council, and they participated in an active manner in the work of the Jewish National Fund; the representative/delegate of Beitar was the authorized deputy of the Jewish National Fund. Beitar also participated in all the Zionist enterprises, such as: the Chanukah ball/reception, Herzl festivities, etc. Beitar was also involved in elections to the Polish "Sejm" (Parliament) and fought for the election of a Zionist candidate. The members distributed Shekels to the Zionist Congress, and the Revisionist list merited second place in the Shekel enterprise.

The Beitar club/clubhouse was held in one of the rooms of the former "Baron Hirsch School." In the large [school]yard it was possible to conduct physical and intellectual education activities amongst the youth. And a great deal of attention was devoted to cultural activities. The organization was divided into units, according to age; within them, classes about the history of the [Jewish] nation and Zionism, the geography of Israel, [and] Hebrew and Yiddish literature were conducted. Every Sabbath evening there would be an evening of reading works by writers in Hebrew and Yiddish. On the Sabbaths, following lunch, there would be lectures about the events of the day concerning Jewish and Zionist issues; Saturday nights they would organize "Question Evenings," with the participation of the youths who were members of other movements. Every holiday they would organize parties with artistic programs. Once a week, they would issue a wall newspaper, whose lists that were contained therein, were written by members of the nest. A special task within the realm of cultural work was conducted by Gershon Ginzburg, who saw to this on his vacation days and on holidays; and when he was full of information about all the issues, he successfully conducted his work within this realm.

Beitar invested a great deal of toil in spreading the Hebrew language amongst the youth. The organization established a Hebrew speakers' club; and when they liquidated the Hebrew schools in the city, Beitar brought the Hebrew teacher, Strohweiss (now in Israel), and afterward, the teacher [named] Weinryb, who developed classes in Hebrew for Hanoar Haivri [i.e., a Zionist youth organization] in the city. At the same time that the danger of assimilation and of Polish literature was perceived for the Jewish youth, Beitar actively helped the I. L. Peretz Library Jewish library (which was also affiliated with the "Bund"), and also had a representative in the administration of the library. A dramatics club was also established near Beitar, which performed, among other [performances], the play, "Hard to Be a Jew" by An-ski, under the direction of V. Tobias and Y. Leib Fenster (now in Israel). The dramatics club would also frequently appear in the cities in the area, such as: Rohatyn, Bolszowce,

Bukaczowce, etc. Near Beitar a mandolin and string instrument choir was established with the success of the musician, Krigel, and so, too, that of a chorus, under the direction of the teacher, Wohl, which would appear at all the Zionist functions.

Much attention was given by Beitar to physical and military education. After one of the people from the nest completed a course for leaders in Zielonka under the guidance of the commanding officer, Jeremy Halperin, most of the nest's members passed military preparation courses. Members of the nest also participated in summer camps, and in courses that took place in the Lwow region.

Beitar began, already in 1929, to prepare the youth for Aliyah to Israel, and a portion of its members left for different Hachsharah points in Poland. On account of this, there were those from [among] them who survived, and they reside today in Israel: Yonah Bernstein, Aryeh Wieselberg, Hersh Teitler, Devorah Kimmel, Batyah Weissmann, and others. The rest of the members did not merit to make Aliyah. In 1931, a Hachsharah was founded in Bursztyn under the supervision of M. Cohen, and there, youths from towns in the area went through the Hachsharah.

Bursztyn's Beit Midrash

[pp. 75-76]

Member, Dr. Natan Meltzer, of the central Israeli office, who organized the oversight of and education at the Hachsharah point, visited there. When Beitar Aliyah permits were revoked, they began to send its illegal members "nonetheless," and this provided members of other political parties the opportunity to make Aliyah; among those in Israel, today, are: Yudel Krochmal.

Beitar raised a great deal of attention, also, among the non-Jewish populace, and brought much honor to the [Jewish] nation. At all of the national Polish celebrations, such as the 3rd of May (Polish Constitution Day), the 11th of November (the day of Polish liberation), and so forth, Beitar would march beneath the blue-white flag to the synagogue; there, they would conduct prayers, and speeches of the rabbi or the religious law adjudicator of the city, as well as the government delegate, would be delivered. The Christian populace saw that a new Hebrew [i.e., Jewish] generation had increased and proliferated.

In the later years, academic youths joined Beitar; among them was Hertz Weinert, who was a member of the Beitar administration. Nearly a majority of the Jewish youth passed through the Beitar lines/rows. Some of them who were unable to adapt themselves to the severe Beitar discipline went over to other organizations, such as "Hanoar Hatzioni" [The Zionist Youth], and these are the adult members who founded the Hatzohar [Revisionist Zionists], under the leadership of Hertz Weinert, who stood at the helm/head of the political revisionist activity in the city. Following the split/rift of Katowice, in 1933, most of the Beitar political party remained loyal to Jabotinsky; only a small portion from the Hatzohar, led by Hertz Weinert, joined the political party, "Medinat Yisrael" [the State of Israel]. From among those, Devorah Ebert and Yosef Marburg today reside in Israel.

Beitar conducted its activity up until World War Two. During the first days of the war, when the Germans began to advance toward our city, and the Ukrainians began to threaten the Jews with robbery and murder, Beitar headquarters contacted the Polish youth in the city, and along with them, established a self-defense [entity]. The Jewish youth was given a means by which to protect, during the hour of emergency, the Jewish populace in the face of attacks, murder, and robbery. When the Polish Army began its escape/flight en route to Sniatyn, and it became apparent that the end to the free lives of the Jews had been awakened, the Beitar headquarters burned, one night before Rosh Hashanah, all of its property/assets [indicated] on the lists.

After the Soviet Army had entered town, they liquidated all the Zionist political parties, and included among them was Beitar. Most of the Jewish youth perished in the hands of the Nazis, some of them were murdered by the partisans in the forests, and some of them fell in the Red Army; among them was headquarters member, Shaike Kletter. A rather small number [of them] reached, through different channels, Israel.

Members of Beitar

[pp. 77-78]

Memories of Days Past
(In Memory of My Parents and Town)

by Lusia Frifeld (Rosen)

**The small town
Where my family
And my home was**[1]

In the course of time, with our growing older, we return in our thoughts to our childhood days, and to the places in which we were born and saw the light of day for the first time.

The town in which we spent our childhoods, in which the house of our parents stood, the school, in which we had our first friends, this town became very dear to us.

Bursztyn, my town, in which the Jews numbered the majority of residents, and gave it the special appearance of a typical Jewish town, this Bursztyn was erased from the face of the earth by the hands of the Nazi troopers. The Jewish community was destroyed along with the synagogues and the religious houses of study, with the home of the rabbi and religious law adjudicator, the cheders, and the schools. The Jews, with their elderly, women, and children, were wiped out; only the name of the town, alone, remains. And in our heart there only remains a huge ache and memories of days past and of a world that was and is no more.

I was eight years old when my parents moved to Bursztyn to set down roots there. My father, Dr. Elisz Rosen, completed his course of studies in Vienna; and in 1932, he founded a law office in Bursztyn.

When I was still a little girl, I loved to observe through the small window of our house's attic, the town, and its surroundings. And this picture that appeared through the small window, remained in my memory until today.

Here is the main street, Stanislawow-Lwow. On both sides of the street, homes, and stores. In the center of the large square is the marketplace, the town's central place. Farmers from the area would come there every Tuesday of the week to sell the ground's produce.

Here is the old synagogue and the rabbi's house, and the ritual bath. From the other side, somewhat removed from them, the two churches, the Catholic one and the Protestant one, the monastery, the school, and the courthouse. In their midst rose the palace of the Polish nobleman, Jablonowski, and surrounding it, a large and pleasant garden.

From the distance a narrow and long strip could be seen; this was the "Gnila Lipa" River. The river was the boundary between the town and the adjacent villages, the single place in which we were able, during the heat wave days of burning summer, to tan in the sun, and to swim in the chilly water, to our delight.

Close to the river was a lake, and in it were small rowboats. From time to time, we sailed off in rowboats; and it appeared to us as though we were traveling far away from the town and forgetting the world and all that is in it.

Surrounding the town were fields of grain and eternal forests. The town was small, peaceful, and full of charm.

I was used to sitting for hours upon hours on the riverbank and delving into a book; there, I wove my dreams for the future. And so pleasant and beautiful were the dreams of a life of freedom and wealth, "of truth and glory, which are no more."

And here, the truth came along and removed/displaced all the pleasant dreams; and thus, it was bitter and cruel: robbery and calamity, ghetto, and concentration camps, suffering and torture, and lives of endless fear.

There is no father or mother, there is no family, an end to my childhood friends; the good and pleasant Jews of the town of Bursztyn went to their eternal resting places. All of them were killed and slaughtered, suffocated, and hanged, drowned, and burned in the concentration camps and in the gas chambers of Majdanek and Treblinka, Auschwitz, and Dachau. From the small and quiet town remained only a dream, a dream about times that had passed and would no longer return.

One of my friends, a Christian [girl] comes to memory, and her name was Renia Gwozdowicz, in whose merit I was saved from the Nazis' claws and I survived.[2] She hid me in her home, and also obtained work and papers of a non-Jew [i.e., Aryan papers] for me. May this perhaps be a small comfort that in the huge sea of suffering and torture during the days of destruction and annihilation, there were a few select individuals among the Gentiles who endangered themselves in order to rescue Jews from the Nazi inferno.

May this be a humble headstone upon the unknown graves of my beloved parents, relatives, and the entire Bursztyn Jewish community, who were annihilated, along with the rest of the Jews in Poland, not having committed a crime/an iniquity.

How good is our portion that after we had passed through the seven compartments of hell during the period of annihilation, and we had lost everything that had been dear to us, we, the children of the generation of annihilation, had merited to find our inheritance/legacy and our serenity in our renewed homeland.

Translator's Footnotes:

1.   These words, which appear in Polish in the original text, are extracted from "Miasteczko Belz," the Polish version of the Yiddish song, "Mayn shtetele Belz" ["My Little Town of Belz"] written by Jacob Jacobs and composed by Alexander Olshanetsky.
2.   There are multiple English and Polish language articles about the author's rescue with reference to Irena (i.e., Renia) Gwozdowicz, her mother, and sister. All three women helped rescue Jews during World War II and were subsequently granted recognition for their upright actions by Yad Vashem in Jerusalem. See for example the following English language article: https://jfr.org/rescuer-stories/gwozdowicz-kowalewska-helena/ (accessed 1-15-24).

[pp. 79-80]

R' Dov-Berish Gelernter Z"L

by Menachem Gelernter

R' Dov-Berish was the son of R' Shraga-Feivel and Chava Gelernter; from the family of Avraham Sharon, one of the first Zionists going back to the period of Herzl.

R' Shraga Feivel was a religious scholar of the Stratyn Chasidim, one possessing good manners and insistent upon/strict about matters concerning the interactions of people, [and] among the affluent people in the town of Bursztyn.

R' Dov-Berish Gelernter was an enormous scholar of Torah, the Mishna, and in matters of Jewish law; he was ordained as a [rabbinic] instructor but did not use the Torah as something for his own personal gain/profit, since he owned a spirits refinery. Aside from his learnedness, he acquired for himself a great deal of education in secular wisdom; he delved into Jewish philosophy and knew the German literature of his generation.

He was one of those possessing lineage in the city and within the area; his face expressed aristocracy/nobility. He was upright in his ways and little in speech; he insisted upon/was strict about the way [in which he conducted] his life and in his merchandise; his splendid clothing that never had a stain/spot – everyone would say that this was the honor of a Torah scholar.

His wife, Dreizi, the daughter of R' Yossi Lindner, the owner of a factory and refineries for spirits in the suburb of Pasieczna, nearby Stanislawow, gave him a reputation in the city and in its surroundings, on account of his uprightness, devoutness, and virtuous deeds.

R' Dov-Berish Gelernter was a Zionist all of his days. His close friend was Dr. David Maltz, a lawyer; one of the first Zionist leaders in Galicia, a gifted speaker, and sharp publicist, among those who were close to Natan Birnbaum, and among those who were devoted to Herzl (in 1900, he moved from Lwow to Bursztyn, and was a lawyer there until 1914).

R' Dov-Berish Gelernter and Dr. David Maltz were connected by ties of love that were not dependent on a [single] thing. Over the course of many years, they would meet every day to talk, and the influence of the reciprocity that existed between them, this one, from his strength in Jewish matter, and that one – from his knowledge of policy matters. They befriended R' Shalom Meltzer, the father of Dr. Natan Meltzer, one of the first founders of the "Hamizrachi" organization. From those who prepared the Hebrew school and the organization "Safa Berura" [Understandable/Clear Language] in Rohatyn.

In the year 1898, the year in which the "Treasury for Jewish Colonization" ("Jewish Colonial Bank" [in Yiddish]), R' Dov-Berish Gelernter was among the first ones to purchase stocks from it, something that was considered a very daring act at that time.

When World War I broke out in 1914, R' Dov-Berish fled with his family members to Vienna; in 1919 he returned to Bursztyn, and after a few years, he uprooted his residence from there to Lwow.

He died in Lwow in 5698 (1938).

His wife, Dreizi, [and] his daughters, Hendzi, Koina, and Esther, may God avenge their blood, perished in the Shoah [Holocaust].

[pp. 81-82]

The "Hanoar Hatzioni"[1] in Bursztyn

by Mordechai Nachwalger

The development of the Zionist movement in Galicia aroused the youths in the town to act, and they decided to prepare themselves for a national achievement, and for their goal of making Aliyah to Israel, and joining the state's builders. The organization for Hachsharah [i.e., the preparation or training for Aliyah] began in the adult clubs, of those who were 20 and above, and expanded at a fast pace, until it reached and surpassed the [number of] students in the elementary schools.

Chaim Nachwalger and his son, Yaakov Z"L

The youth movements that absorbed the students and adults as one, were Beitar and "Hanoar Hatzioni." The organization, "Hanoar Hatzioni," was founded in Bursztyn in 1928, and 164 protégés went through it. The branch alternated its location and functioned in the homes of Breiter, Mandelberg, Spitz, Grinberg, and Klirsfeld.

The goal of the organization was to educate the youths about the purity of the scouts' education (the Ten Commandments) in conjunction with the Zionist idea and the Hebrew culture of Jews in the diaspora and in Israel. The "Hanoar Hatzioni" aspired to continue its activity within the chain of branches of the "Poalei Tzion Association," which sent the first pioneers to Israel during the period of the Third Aliyah (Sarah Kessler, Bina Breiter). On the evening prior to Sarah's Kessler's departure on Aliyah, there was a party that lasted past midnight; and at dawn, all of her friends departed in song and in dance to the train station to accompany the first pioneer along the way. My young friends and I in the Noar Hatzioni were in the corridor during the party, and on that same evening we decided amongst ourselves that we would go in the paths of the pioneers: we would organize a group of youths and all make Aliyah to Israel.

The "Hanoar Hatzioni" movement brought tremendous changes in the perspectives on education. The traditional cheder could not sufficiently provide for the spiritual needs; in the "Hanoar Hatzioni" nest, another spirit prevailed; its aspiration was to provide information and knowledge in a Zionist spirit, education instituted with love of the homeland, and an aspiration for a new life, and an aspiration to reach these [goals] with forward movement, and in every way. In the nest, Hebrew classes [and] conversations about Israel were conducted; they celebrated every event in the Zionist world, and with dedication, they engaged in the collection of donations for the country's redemption, the Jewish National Fund, the United Israel Appeal [Keren Hayesod], and preparation for the Hebrew [Jewish] settlement.

In the beginning, leaders/mentors for the branch activities were lacking, but after the centers were readied and new members were brought in, this void was filled. The youth group members found them a home within the branch; they prepared to teach social studies and culture among groups. On the Sabbath they would have parties, which were a release for them from the emptiness in their life prior to their entering the nest. Aside from the activity in the local nest, members were dispatched to summer camps, to instructional courses, to regional conventions, and to farewell parties of the first pioneers from the Noar Hatzioni movement. On Sabbath evenings we would sit complete hours with open eyes, and we were like dreamers: in the beginning we read and heard stories about the events of the day. We played, sang, and danced the "Hora," and we shall not forget these experiences.

[pp. 83-84]

In a race [against] time, the mature youth made Aliyah to Israel or left the town, but the strong connection with the nest and the movement remained and was lasting. During the Shoah period, the "Hanoar Hatzioni" branch was also destroyed, but its soul and spirit did not die out among its survivors; the movement opened a new period before them.

May we always recall for good and with veneration the mentors: Dr. Wolf Schmarak and Dr. Ziering Z"L, who dedicated their valuable time to the activities of the nest. We shall remember and not forget Sholo Weinert and Kuba Bleiberg Z"L, who energetically led group activities within the branch, once a week.

The "Hanoar Hatzioni" nest in Bursztyn also received help and encouragement from the branch in Rohatyn, and it is worth praising the dedication of Yehudah Hadar and Dov Kirshen (both of them are in Israel, in Haifa); and from the members of the chief administration in Lwow – Yitzchak Steiger Z"L (who died in Israel); and may they be set apart for long and good lives: Yitzchak Golan (Goldstein), member of the Fourth Knesset [i.e., Israeli Parliament], member of Kibbutz Usha[1] David Ciment, the "Oved Hatzioni" [i.e., Zionist worker] representative at the executive committee of the Workers Organization in Israel; Shimek Bergman, chief clerk of "Malben" [i.e., Institutions for the Care of Handicapped Immigrants in Israel]; Artek Klarer, member of Kibbutz Tel-Yitzchak, and many others whom I did not mention here.

From among 70 Bursztyners in Israel, many passed through the lines of the "Hanoar Hatzioni," and in the merit of the movement, they reached this point.

These are the excerpts of memories about those days, of one the members of the institution and administration of the nest, "Hanoar Hatzioni," in Bursztyn.

Translator's Footnote:

1. The Zionist Youth
2. This was a kibbutz founded by members of the Noar Hatzioni movement and located in the western Galilee area of Israel.

[pp. 85-86]

My Adventures during World War Two
(Collection of evidence, recorded by Y. Shmulevitsh, New York, 23.3.1955)

by Dr. Lipa Schumer

Translated by Mira Eckhaus

Edited by Rivka Schiller

I grew up and was educated in my hometown of Bursztyn, in eastern Galicia, and lived there until the outbreak of World War II. I graduated from the Faculty of Medicine at the University of Vienna, became a doctor in Bursztyn and was accepted by both the Jewish and Polish residents, my wife and daughter were also with me in Bursztyn all those years.

When the Russians invaded Bursztyn on September 17, 1939, they did not discriminate in their treatment of the city's residents, Jews, and non-Jews. On the other hand, the Ukrainian residents caused incitement against the Jews, and immediately began to inform on them to the Soviet authorities: they slandered things that every Jew is a "bourgeois," that the Jews had a connection with the Polish "Pans," etc.

**The late Dr. Lipa Schumer
Passed away on 18 Cheshvan
5720,
in the United States**

As a result of this incitement, the authorities gave most of the Jewish residents passports according to Article 11, which testify that the holder of the certificate does not have permission to live in certain cities, that he is not allowed to travel from place to place, and that usually, he is a "harmful element." Mainly, "limited" passports were issued to affluent Jews, while rich Ukrainians, who were used to inform the authorities, were issued "good passports." Jews who received passports according to Article 11 were also the first on the list to be sent to Siberia.

Officially, the Soviet authorities did not adopt an anti-Semitic attitude in their actions, but regarding Jews they instituted special laws and orders. Many of the town's Jews, and Zionists among them, would say that, after all, the Red Army is a kind of salvation for Israel, and how blessed they are that they did not fall into the hands of the Nazis. In those days, bad news had already reached us from central Poland about the troubles that befell the Jews in those places by the Hitlerite occupation army. After all, it was nothing but the beginning of the persecutions. At the time, there were approximately 2,600 Jews living in Bursztyn. Only about sixty of them (and the children accompanying them) were issued "bad passports," because Bursztyn was considered a slum town, that most of its Jews were poor and destitute with only a few rich and wealthy among them.

While the Russians were in the town, the Jews were afraid to engage in trade, which involved the risk of imprisonment. In those days, the authorities banned young Jews who were the leaders of the Zionist youth movements. Those who were caught and imprisoned were taken to Lwów, where they were executed together with the Ukrainian nationalists, or sent to the Siberian steppes. Wealthy Jews and public activists were also banned and sent away. At that time, I worked as a doctor at the hospital established by the authorities. There was a lot of work to be done each day, about 20 hours a day, and my pay was little, but I was content with my lot and that I was not harassed. My wife and I sold all the items that were left in the house and that was our livelihood. Before the war, I also had a flour mill and the authorities confiscated and expropriated my property, and I even had to sign a certificate, that I give them everything as a gift, voluntarily.

The Ukrainian informants would hand over to the authorities wealthy Jews, who would be sent to Siberia, so that they could rob their property, since those who were dispatched were not allowed to take any property with them on the road. The Ukrainians slandered me that I collaborated with the Poles and advised them to oppress

[pp. 87-88]

the Ukrainian population. Indeed, for the time being the authorities did not harm me, because I was needed by them as a doctor. And the situation did not change until June 22, 1941, the day the war between Germany and Russia broke out.

The Red Army left our town in great panic. On the outskirts of the city, the battles with the Germans' vanguard took place, and the bridges were bombed. In the retreat of the Soviet army, some of the local Jews joined it. Most of them were people who served in jobs in the Soviet government, and they were afraid to stay in the town out of fear of both the Ukrainians and the Germans. During the battles, German pilots were hit by Russian bullets, and they were brought to me, and as a doctor I treated these wounded.

From the time the Soviet troops retreated, and by the time the Germans arrived in the town, a Ukrainian militia had been established there. The Ukrainians were waiting for the arrival of the Hitlerian soldiers. In the Ukrainian militia there were also people who had been with them during the Soviet occupation and even cheered: "Long live Stalin." However, after the withdrawal of the Soviet army, those Ukrainians turned their backs and cheered: "Long live Hitler."

Few of the Jews who joined the Soviet army during its withdrawal returned to the town. The Ukrainian militiamen hit them on the way, robbed and beat them, and many of them were killed and did not reach their goal. Even before the Hitlerian soldiers entered Bursztyn, the Ukrainians sent a delegation of twelve dignitaries to the district governor in Rohatyn and told him that the Jews of Bursztyn were rich, and that their houses were full of silver and gold and stores of food, tea, and coffee, which were not available. The delegation also informed the district governor about the Jews of Bursztyn, that they hurt Hitler's honor, and something should be done to prevent this insolence of the Jews.

The next day, on Tuesday, July 20, 1941, while I was at the clinic, wearing a white robe and taking care of a sick Ukrainian, a Jew named Mina Tobias, from Bursztyn, approached me, his face was as pale as plaster, in his hand he held a note, and he turned to me: "Doctor, I am very sorry, you must come with me to the public office, people are waiting for you there, this is an order."

The same Mina Tobias was one of the city's activists, and he had a small estate and a bakery. The Ukrainian militia appointed him as a liaison between them and the Jews and through him they arranged all matters and he was considered the representative of the Jews in the city.

I was rather surprised at the news he gave me and I followed him. Several militiamen were standing in front of my house, and one of them approached me and ordered me to run fast. At the moment I tried to run from the place, he attacked me with a broom, in front of my wife and daughter. My daughter screamed towards the policeman:

- Aren't you ashamed to hit an old and devoted doctor, who saved thousands of Ukrainian mothers from death in childbirth?

The Ukrainian immediately pulled out his gun and wanted to shoot her, but my wife managed to bring my daughter into the house and close the door behind her. When the Ukrainian began to beat me with his whip, I tore off my shirt and begged him not to torture me but shoot me. He repeated his order to run and continued beating me. And while running and [receiving] beatings I arrived at the town hall.

When I entered the municipal office, I found there the dignitaries of the city, judges and lawyers, and the notary, whom I used to heal in sickness and who were my friends. They pretended as if they did not see me. I was forcefully pushed into one of the rooms, and immediately I heard screams of terror emanating from it. The door was opened and Bursztyn's rabbi, Rabbi Hirtz Landau, was rushed in, beaten, and wounded and bleeding. Only a few moments passed and into the room was thrown Reb Yoel Ginzburg, an old and respected teacher in the city. The scene repeated itself in front of us several times, about eight to ten of the city's dignitaries were thrown forcefully into the room at the municipality office.

Seeing the number of beaten and wounded Jews, I turned to them and said to them:

- Jews, behave as Jews would behave in Kiddush HaShem; do not give pleasure to our haters!

The Jews huddled around me, as if I had the strength to protect them; however, I felt my helplessness.

The door opened and into the room entered a German lieutenant officer who was in charge of the Ukrainian militia before the regular army arrived in the city. He was accompanied by some Ukrainians, and all of them were armed with whips.

One of the Ukrainians approached the elderly Dayan, cut his white beard, and threw the hair on his face, and in doing so he said to the old man: "Leprous Jew, the time has come for us to get rid of you and pay you your reward." Tears flowed from the elderly Dayan's eyes but he did not answer. At that time, I approached the German officer and told him:

- I studied at a German university; I am Jewish, but

[pp. 89-90]

I was educated in the spirit of German education and all my teachers were German. In the First World War I fought together with German soldiers, worked with German doctors, and treated German and Austrian patients. I address you as a German and I do not speak to the Ukrainians; do not torture innocent people. As a doctor there are useful things in my house and I also know what is in the houses of the Jews, and all these things are no longer worthwhile to us. We will give you fine liquor and a good Leica camera. Everything will be given to you but let me go out and bring it to you.

The German pondered a bit and said that I was free to go out and bring the things I promised. I answered him that I could not do anything on my own, and I could not leave the rest of the Jews. Please let them also go out with me and collect all the things. The lieutenant officer answered me that the other Jews were also allowed to go with me, but that I must guarantee them with my life; if one of them was absent, he would kill me, and he added that we must return one hour later with all the things I promised to bring. Then he would search my house and the houses of the other people, and if he found anything, he would shoot us. The rabbi and the Dayan were not allowed to go with me, and he banned them until we returned.

When we left the room, we saw the Ukrainians tying the rabbi and the teacher with ropes around their necks to the iron bars of the window. I asked to go back to the room, but the people begged me not to leave them, because the Ukrainians would kill them when they were alone. I told them to stand in one place and

I promised them to come back right away. I returned to the city hall rooms, approached the deputy German officer, and begged him not to let the rabbi and the teacher be tortured. The German ordered me to go, "the rabbis will not be tortured to the point of death." I asked the young man to allow me to approach the two Jews and talk to them, and he agreed. When I approached the corner of the room where the rabbi and the teacher were tied to the window bar, I saw that they were terrified and praying silently. I told them: "May God be with you, in a little while I will return to you."

My friends and I went to the city. I went into my apartment to collect all the rest of my possessions, and I sent the rest of the Jews across the town to inform all the Jews, that they should bring to the municipality everything they could find: jam and liquor, sugar and pickles, coffee and tea, and anything edible. The Jews followed my advice and the young men as well as the elders went to the municipality and brought the groceries. However, on the way, they were attacked by the Ukrainians, who beat and wounded them brutally.

When I was at home, I took a sack and filled it with all [sorts of] good things, a camera, bottles of good wine, jam, sugar, and tea, etc., until the sack was too heavy to carry. I loaded the sack onto my shoulder and turned toward the city hall. Ukrainians and Poles stood on the side of the road, my patients for years, teenagers at whose birth I was present, and they laughed at me. They looked at me with joy, as if they did not know me at all. The other Jews and I took the luggage to the municipality office and I asked the German officer to stop beating the Jews.

In the meantime, the Ukrainian dignitaries in the town, the judges, lawyers, and common residents, rioted against the Jews. This was on July 20 or 21, 1941. At that time, I was standing near the city hall, and a Ukrainian doctor, the son of a pastor, my longtime neighbor, his name was Dr. Komariatsky, came to the city hall in a yellow-blue car. Along with Dr. Komariatsky, there was also judge Kalisz, who was my friend and a patient of mine, and a few other dignitaries of the place. The car in which they arrived parked next to me and they came out happy and cheerful.

A young Ukrainian from the militia approached me, about sixteen or seventeen years old, with a whip in his hand. I was dressed as a doctor, in a white robe. When I left my clinic that morning, the young Ukrainian turned to me and said: "Cursed Jew, what are you doing here?" I answered that the German officer's lieutenant had ordered me to make sure the Jews bring the necessary items. The young Ukrainian took the whip and started beating me. He whipped me five or six times. I stood upright, without moving. This probably surprised them, and he left me.

My former friends, the educated Ukrainians, stood there and watched the incident. I approached Dr. Komariatsky and said to him: "Maybe you know why I'm being beaten?" He replied that he did not see that I was beaten. I left the gang and went home to see what happened to my family.

My daughter went to a place far away from Bursztyn and hid there among Christians. When I entered the house, I found my wife crying, she prayed for my safety and did not know whether I was still alive. I never returned to the community office. I went up to the attic of a Christian neighbor's house, without him knowing it, and huddled in a corner without knowing what would be done to me. I lay all night in my corner, and my ears hurt from the sound of the shots and the shouts

[pp. 91-92]

of the Jews being tortured. On the other hand, I heard the sound of laughter and melodies of the reveling Ukrainians.

The next day I went to see the rabbi and the Dayan. Both of them were in their apartments, they were lying in their beds, wrapped in tallit and tefillin, beaten and injured. I looked at their wounds and showed them my wounds. They told me, and I even heard it from others later, about what was done on the night of the terrors, while I was in hiding. They rioted against the Jews, they ordered everyone to gather in the synagogue. They were chased to the synagogue like sheep to the slaughter. On the way, they were brutally beaten. The German lieutenant officer, together with twelve to fifteen Ukrainian militiamen, were armed with machine guns, and they ordered the Jews who had gathered there to pray loudly. The Jews prayed Maariv, and the German and his assistants beat them because they did not pray loudly enough; they began to raise their voices in prayer and were ordered to raise their hands. Some of the Jews who gathered were weak, tired, and broken, and asked to lean against the wall. The Ukrainians beat them brutally and did not let them lean and hold on. The rabbi was ordered to go up to the stage, and if someone in the crowd did anything that was not to the liking of the German officer or the militiamen, both he and the rabbi were beaten severely.

At that time, the deputy officer noticed that I, Dr. Schumer, was absent from the crowd gathered in the synagogue. Immediately he was filled with murderous rage and ordered that I be brought before him. One of the militiamen told him that a Ukrainian woman was about to give birth and her life was in danger, so he sent me to the village to rescue her. The deputy officer issued an order that I be brought to him immediately upon my return. Indeed, as mentioned, I then hid in the attic of the farmer's house, and yet he did not know this.

At the same time that they were torturing the Jews in the synagogue with severe anguish, the Ukrainians celebrated in the town. The ball was attended by educated Ukrainians, officials, peasants as well as common people, old and young, they danced and sang and sipped from the liquor that the Jews brought that day to the municipality office. Late at night they sent the Jews out of the synagogue and ordered them to return home. While on the way, the gentiles attacked them and beat them brutally. The Jews, therefore, were forced to return to the synagogue and wait there until morning. In the meantime, the Ukrainians robbed and looted the empty houses.

The Ukrainians in the town started talking amongst themselves, that an injustice was done to me when they beat me, because I had never done harm to a person, and everyone knew me as the doctor of their patients. The next day, two representatives of the educated Ukrainians in the town, the attorneys Skolski and Taratash, came to me. They apologized to me and said that I was beaten "by mistake." The two asked me not to flee from the town and said they would protect me.

The Ukrainian priest Vatsov, from the nearby village of Bouszow, heard about the beatings I received and in his sermon at the village church he said that I did not deserve such treatment, and that he wanted to bequeath his share to me after his death. The priest's words made a strong impression on the farmers.

About two weeks passed, after the Ukrainians had behaved in such an unrestrained manner in the town, and the regular German army companies arrived. In the meantime, until the Germans came, the Ukrainians expelled the Jews from the villages to Bursztyn. Many of them were killed on the road, and only a few of the deportees reached the town. They arrived naked and barefoot, everything was robbed and looted from them on the way. We learned that the leader of the Ukrainian nationalists, Bandera, issued an order to kill and exterminate the Jews, as much as they could, before the arrival of the Germans, to occupy their towns.

The Nazi occupiers entered Bursztyn at the beginning of August 1941. An order was immediately issued, that all Jews must be counted and registered. They were ordered to wear light blue and white bands with a Star of David on their arm, they were forbidden to leave the city, the Christians received instructions to avoid any negotiations with Jews. An order was given to establish a "Jewish council" (Judenrat) of eight people, who would be responsible for fulfilling all the instructions of the German government. I was also one of the eight members of the "Judenrat" and became chairman of the council. I received the appointment by force because I was threatened with expulsion from the town. However, I stayed in my position only for a short time. I ran away, as I will describe later. Other participants in the "Judenrat" were: attorney Philip Tobias, Mina Tobias, Yehuda Hersh Fischmann, and other dignitaries of the town.

Three days after the founding of the "Judenrat" in Bursztyn, a message was received from the "Judenrat" in Rohatyn, according to the order of the German authorities, that three representatives from all the towns in the district should come to the council in Rohatyn. Philip and Mina Tobias and I were members of the Judenrat's delegation in Bursztyn. When we arrived in Rohatyn, the representatives of the "Judenrat" from each town within the Rohatyn district, were already there.

[pp. 93-94]

At the assembly of representatives of the "Judenrat" from the surrounding cities, Amarant, the elder of the community in Rohatyn, spoke and read an order received from the German authorities, who imposed a compensation tax of eight to ten million rubles on the Jews, for the damage they caused. The order did not explain to whom and how the Jews had caused damage. A quota of two to three million rubles was imposed on our town of Bursztyn. Depression fell upon me when I heard this, because our town was poor, without any means, a potato was priceless, if found. And how could I go and tell the poor and destitute, to collect millions! I cried and begged to reduce the tax quota from the unfortunate Bursztyn Jews. However, I was told that the decision was final and if the amount imposed on us was not brought, all the Bursztyn Jews expected to be killed and exterminated.

Broken and devastated, Philip and Mina Tobias and I returned home on the same day. We gathered all the Jews into the Beit Midrash and brought them this bad news. The next day, a committee was appointed and a list of all the Jews in the town was compiled, and an appropriate amount to be paid was imposed on everyone according to their financial status.

The list of amounts imposed on everybody made a terrible impression on everyone, because all the Jews were extremely poor. The Jews sold everything they owned in order to collect the money imposed on them. The gentiles were happy to buy the Jews' property for a few pennies, and the Jews still thanked them because according to the order of the Nazi authorities, it was forbidden to buy anything from a Jew. We passed from house to house several times to collect the full tax quota, and then we sent it to the council in Rohatyn.

However, day by day the decrees and persecutions increased. One day, on Saturday, two Gestapo officers came to the town and issued an order to bring them within two hours: one hundred silver spoons, silverware, silver teapots, two hundred liters of coffee, one hundred liters of tea, one hundred and fifty blankets, sheets, pillowcases, and maps. And once again the Jews parted with the rest of their possessions, accumulated the few jewels and money they had left, and bought from the gentiles all the supplies that the Gestapo demanded be brought to them. Besides the farmers, the Russian priest, Gutkowski, also sold supplies looted from the Jews that the farmers gave him and that he had in abundance. The same Gutkowski was known as a quintessential hater of Israel. The required supplies were handed over to the two Gestapo men. The visits and demands of the Gestapo men were frequent in Bursztyn.

Our lives were unstable. The Germans did not establish a ghetto in Bursztyn, but all the Jewish neighborhoods became one ghetto. The Jews were ordered to leave the houses on the main streets and were forbidden to live among Christians. In their places of residence, there was little room for the Jews, and about twenty people lived in one room. The Jews were not allowed to go outside their area, they were forbidden to walk on the sidewalks and were ordered to walk in the middle of the street like cattle, they were not allowed to enter the stores in the town, even if they were owned by Jews, and gentiles came into their stores. Horrible and terrible was the sight of the Jews bloated with hunger, the children with skinny legs and stomachs from hunger. I was the doctor for both the Jews and the gentiles in the whole town, and I was given permission to leave the area where the Jews lived, and even travel to the villages to visit the sick. However, on my arm I wore a light blue and white band with a Star of David, by law.

When I would come to sick farmers to heal them, I would not take money from them, but food that I would distribute among the Jews. The Germans would often send Jews out to work in the camps, but none of those who left returned home. The camps that the Jews were taken to were in the vicinity of Zborów, near Lwów, and no one could live there for more than two or three weeks. The Germans sent demands to the "Judenrat" to send Jews to work for them, in groups, women and children. At first it was believed that the Jews were actually going to work; they were brought to the train station, placed inside the cars in groups

Dr. Eliyahu and Zhenya Rosen and daughters Mila and Lucia

[pp. 95-96]

of 120 and set off on their way. Many of those going to work suffocated and died amidst the stress inside the cars or died of hunger and thirst. The Jews were taken to the Bełżec camp, where they were killed in crematoria.

In one of the convoys that waited at the Chodorów station, a Jew handed a gold watch through the rail of the car to a gentile who passed by, in exchange for a little water. That gentile took a bottle that had been emptied of oil and filled it with cloudy water from the gutter and served it to the Jew in the car. The Jews gathered in the car and fought over the bottle with cloudy water, and many of them were killed on the spot.

The next day, after the train with the shipment of Jews left the station, Drucker, the Jewish tailor in the town, came to me and told me that in the attic of his house there was a naked Jewish doctor from Kosów who had jumped from the car on the way. The Jewish doctor arrived in the morning from the village naked, without clothes. I sent a suit with the tailor and went to visit the doctor. He told me that he jumped from the car on the way because he wanted to die, and thought he would be killed by jumping, but he fell on the grass, licked the dew with his thirst, got up and walked until he reached the town.

On October 15, 1942, the Germans issued an order that all the Jews in Bursztyn must leave the place and go to Bukaczowce, a town near the train station. All the Jews went there and were placed inside the huts of the farmers. Only about thirty Jews, who worked on the road, remained in our town. A camp was set up for them and they were all together, including two doctors: Dr. Shmuel Katz and I, as well as the head of the "Judenrat," Philip Tobias, and two more of its members. A month later, Gestapo men came to the camp and led all thirty Jews to the ghetto in Rohatyn.

On October 26, the Germans gathered together the Jews of Bursztyn, who were sent to Bukaczowce, the residents of Bukaczowce themselves and the refugees who came from Bołszowce, loaded them onto wagons and sent them to the Bełżec camp. Many of the Jews managed to escape and sought to hide, but the Ukrainian militiamen searched and found the escapees and killed them on the spot. The Germans pursued the Bursztyn Jews and brought them to Bukaczowce with the other Jews of the nearby towns, because there was a train station there, and it was easier to load them onto wagons and send them to Bełżec.

After the Gestapo evacuated the camp with the thirty Jews from Bursztyn and deported them to the Rohatyn ghetto, my daughter hid at the house of a Christian family. I was not at home at that time, and one of the boys came to tell my wife that they were preparing to evacuate the camp. My wife immediately left the place and went to the village, where she hid in the home of a Christian family, our acquaintances.

The Gestapo men came to me and asked me about my wife and daughter who had disappeared. They came to take me because the camp had been evacuated. I asked them to wait for me until I got dressed and went out, because I was wearing a white robe. When I entered the next room, I took a bottle of liqueur and handed the drink to the Gestapo people who were waiting for me until I changed my clothes. They sat and sipped the drink, and at that time I escaped through the other door, and entered the home of my neighbor, a Ukrainian, and asked him to hide me in his house. He was afraid to hide me in his home. I hurried and went up to the roof, curled up in a pile of hay, the cold was extraordinarily strong, and I stayed there for eight hours, until the day dawned.

At night I crawled and came down from my hiding place to find out what had been done to my wife. I came to the garden of my house, crawled, and entered the house of a Ukrainian farmer named Berla, who was known as a hater of Israel. I asked if my wife was still alive and he told me to run away quickly. I went up to the roof of his house and hid there and he did not know about my hiding place.

The participants in the "Mendele Ball"

First from the left, the seated – Mundzia Fischmann – who fell with his weapon in hand, in a heroic battle with the Germans and the Ukrainians in the streets of Bursztyn

My hiding place. The Gestapo men entered immediately and told him that they saw a human figure crawling about in the garden, and that he should hand the Jew over to them. The farmer replied that there was no Jew in his house, maybe he was in the attic, but he did not know that. The Gestapo men went up to the attic and found me there; and when I was taken down from my hiding place, they asked me where is my wife? I answered that I do not know; as a response, one of them pulled out his pistol and aimed it at my heart, and ordered me to say

[pp. 97-98]

where my wife was, or else he would kill me on the spot. I said to him: Please, do me a favor and kill me!

The Gestapo man put his pistol back in his holster and slapped me forcefully on the cheek. He took me to prison. There I found a Jewish woman, her name was Fischmann, who was in hiding and the Germans captured her. I asked the Gestapo people to shoot me because I preferred death.

While in prison, I knocked on the door, hoping that by doing so I would annoy the guards and they would shoot me and free me of the tortures. However, they did not respond to my knocks. They sat in the rooms above me and engaged in conversation. For a moment I leaned against the door, and it opened, and the lock fell to the ground. None of the guards came toward the noise. I passed the narrow prison corridor and there was no one in sight. I went outside and started running along the road. It was night, and on the way, I went to the house of a Christian miller I knew, where I hid for three consecutive days, and I was also given food.

I lay in the attic, and asked the miller to inform a Polish acquaintance, Staborowski, a former policeman, about me. He came to me, to the attic, took me out and led me to the house of his brother-in-law, Josef Lask, where my wife was hidden in a flower nursery, in Bursztyn proper. The farmer's situation was extremely dangerous, because the Gestapo men were angry about the disappearance of the Jewish doctor from their hands twice in one day.

The night I escaped from prison, the Gestapo sent soldiers to search the roads, they looked for me everywhere, and an announcement was made that the house in which I had taken refuge would be destroyed and its occupants killed. They even promised anyone who brought me before them, dead or alive, a reward of 25,000 gold and two logs of liquor, which in those days was priceless.

Indeed, despite the danger, he hid my wife and me in his house for many months. We were in separate places, my wife and I, until we left and went to the forest to hide in it.

We entered the forest near the village of Czahrow on July 9, 1943, and there we heard loud shots. The Germans liquidated the ghetto in Rohatyn and shot every Jew, wherever found. We built caves (bunkers) in the forest and hid there, and even changed places every time, so as not to fall into the trap. Finally, we dug a hole in the field, in the grain, and hid in it. We were hungry and thirsty, we lay in the moss and were full of lice, until farmers we knew started bringing us food. They were, for the most part, people of the "Baptist" Christian faction.

We lived in the forests and fields for about two-and-a-half years. The farmers who brought us food told us that another group of seventy-six Jews were hiding in those forests, we knew about them and they also knew about us, but we never met. Later, those Jews were caught while they were on the way to the villages to find food and water.

We gave everything we had, even the shoes and clothes we wore, to the farmers who brought us food. With us was a Jewish butcher from Bursztyn, Yekl Feldman, whom we met in the field where we were hiding, and he helped my wife and me a lot. Knowing the roads in the area and being bold and brave, he would go to the farmers and exchange things with them for bread. The farmers knew he was hiding with us, and therefore they protected him and did not inform on him.

We hid until May 1944, when the Russians arrived and expelled the Germans from that place.

After the liberation, my wife and I, and also my daughter, who lived as a Christian throughout the years of the war without us even knowing that she was alive – went to Poland, from there we moved to Germany and arrived as far as Ranshofen, near Braunau, where we lived in a Jewish refugee camp until we immigrated in 1946 to America. We arrived in New York in July 1946, on the ship "Marine Perch," and we have lived here ever since then.

We are content with our lot, even though at first, we had hard times in America as well, as we came here without anything. I passed the exams, and I am engaged in medicine, as an independent physician.

My wife and I are sick and broke, and we have no free time to deal with public needs and to belong to parties, except for the "community center" in our neighborhood. From time to time, we gather with the people of our town, and they come to our house. They know that it is difficult for us to come to them.

Our daughter is married and lives in another city; she is a social worker and her husband is studying medicine. I read the newspapers the "Forverts" and "Times" every day. In my spare time I read the books of the Zohar, Talmud, Gemara and Kabbalah.

[pp. 99-100]

Memories and Adventures
(Collection of evidence, recorded by Y. Fenster, 14.2.1956)

by Yakov Feldman

Translated by Mira Eckhaus

Edited by Rivka Schiller

I will not tell you all the adventures that befell Bursztyn in the first days of the occupation of the town by the Germans, as Dr. Schumer and others have already described them in their records. I would like to mention here the "Judenrat" people of Bursztyn, the cruelest of whom were Philip Tobias and Yehuda Hirsch Fischmann.

I want to mention some events that happened in those terrible days in the town, and it is appropriate to record them.

Our portion of bread was given to us in a ration by the "Judenrat": a quarter of the loaf. Those who worked hard received the portion of bread, and the rest would wait for a slice of bread near the office, until they almost died. They gave bread to those who pleased them and those who did not please them, starved. They treated us like dogs. The director of the labor camp was Yehuda Hirsch Fischmann, and those who did not go to work as he wished were beaten until they collapsed. And if he fell and got sick, he was carried to work. Few escaped safely from the hands of the oppressors; I experienced it myself.

The engineer Baranowski established a special work department for road construction for the purposes of the army. He chose about thirty Jews, strong, who of course had personal connections, and they all received Gestapo certificates from him. I was also among them. The "Judenrat" no longer had any right to supervise them, but once the "Judenrat" people stopped us on our way back from work. We thought that they wanted to hand us over to the Germans to destroy us. They took us and informed us that tonight they had to bring forty young Jews, whom they had not been able to catch for a long time. I immediately informed everyone I could run away and escape.

Those days were terrible for the tortured Jews of Bursztyn: many of them died of hunger; what remained of their possessions after the Germans robbed them, they sold for a slice of bread or some potatoes; they would go out into the forest, a walk of four to five kilometers, to gather twigs to burn to warm themselves a little, and usually the gentiles would snatch the twigs from their hands on the way, and even beat them. When everything ran out, the Jews of Bursztyn were hungry and they would fall down with their bloated bellies and die. The dead would remain in the streets for days, as there was no one who could bury them, and the rest were exhausted with no strength at all.

At the time of Yom Kippur in 1942, an Aktion broke out in Rohatyn, where there were no longer many Jews, and Bursztyn was ordered to send two cars full of Jews for extermination.

Yakov Feldman and his wife Dazia

I will never forget that Yom Kippur. Rabbi Yoel Ginzburg of blessed memory, a teacher of the town, asked the people to pray together on the holy day. A number of Jews gathered at Shmuel Mastel's house. The Dayan prayed all day while crying, he comforted the congregation to accept the judgment against them without fear, to walk proudly towards death. It is a wonder that that tortured and starving Jew had the strength and courage to exhort consolation.

A day after Yom Kippur, the Germans entered the city and began shooting Jews in the streets, and many were caught and taken to Rohatyn. My mother, Pearl, was also taken from me that day. The "Judenrat" knew about the Aktion, and they hid their wives and children.

[pp. 101-102]

At the same time, Bursztyn was emptied of its Jews and they were taken to Bukaczowce, where they were loaded into cars and taken to the extermination camp of Bełżec. Reb Yoel, the teacher, was shot to death in Bukaczowce while marching among the Jews, trying to comfort them, and saying confession with them. He was buried in the cemetery. The rest of the refugee population of the district's Jews were deported together to the ghetto of Rohatyn.

In those days, Baranowski's work department still existed. The few that remained were kept in Yossi Feffer's house. Once, Germans entered the house, expelled us, and started shooting at us. I suffered minor injuries and escaped with my life. Shimon and Shlomo Pfeffer from Sarnaki were among the dead.

I spent the night at Skolski's house, where I left behind some belongings. I moved to the Rohatyn ghetto, where my wife and daughter were still alive. They immediately gathered all the young men and sent them to the labor camps of Brzeżany and Tarnopol, from which not a single person returned. Many of Bursztyn's people were led there; among them was Shlomo Mandelberg who left while saying to me: "I know that I am going towards death; how terrible it is, I returned from the Land of Israel to fall into the hands of the murderers."

The Jewish police offered me to join their ranks and save my life. I absolutely refused, just as I also did in Bursztyn, even though I was brutally beaten and they took everything I had.

They placed me in the supply department. The Jewish police in the ghetto secretly sold meat, for which the death penalty was expected. Indeed, even here they looked for ways to make money, in the hope that there would be salvation in this. I worked in the meat business and helped many people from Bursztyn.

Once a detective came, a German resident (Volksdeutscher) who wanted to investigate and know where our meat came from. Seeing that we had fallen into a trap, we caught him and stabbed him, and that was his burial place.

At the edge of the ghetto stood a house, where some of Bursztyn's people lived: Pitziye Schneeweiss, Feier's wife, Rivka Haber, and Dazia, my current wife, and other people lived there. In the opposite house, across the street, lived the Gestapo men's girls, who would stand and shoot every Jew who came out of the opposite house. At night I would bring our people everything I could.

One day the murderers deceitfully assembled hundreds of children and murdered them. They announced the distribution of bread to the children at a set hour. Because the children were hungry for a loaf of bread, they came in masses, and all of them were murdered with savage cruelty.

After the liquidation of the Rohatyn ghetto, I got myself a weapon. I dug a cave (bunker) near a gentile's house in the forest, Jankiv was his name. I set out to look for my wife and children, who had escaped from the ghetto. They went to the fields, but unfortunately were not found anymore, they were killed by the murderers.

On my return to the bunker in the forest, I found Dr. Schumer and his wife there. They were broken and devastated, and wanted to commit suicide, and I had a hard time dissuading them from it. Together we expanded the hidden cave, where we lived for about half the year. At the risk of my life, I would go out at night to Bursztyn, to Lask, to bring some food. Lask was the photographer from Bursztyn, who also received letters from Dr. Schumer's daughter, who survived and had "Aryan certificates."

After the killers discovered many of the hiding places of the remnants of Bursztyn Jews – among them: Mundzia Fischmann, Wolf Ostrower, Loti Bernstein who died a heroic death, and also Berel Lundner – Jankiv came to us and expelled us from the domain of his house.

We moved to the Polish village of Ludwikowka, where we found shelter in the home of the Polish Kochman, where we dug a bunker. After a while, that gentile was saved from death because of us, and here is the story: In February 1944, the Ukrainian nationalists attacked the village of Ludwikowka and set it on fire and did not let the residents of the village escape from the burning and killed everyone who tried to flee. A few of the "Mausers," as they were called in Bursztyn, remained alive. We, Dr. Schumer, and his wife, as well as the Kochman family, stayed inside the bunker. The Germans came and gathered all those who remained alive and led them from the village. It was extremely cold; we all wrapped ourselves in rags, and together with the Poles who remained alive, we were also led from the village, and they did not recognize us.

It was evening; we dropped into the snow and lay down. At night we went to the priest Maricki in Korostowice, and he let us spend the night at his home. After severe hardships, I returned to Jankiv's house, at the edge of Bursztyn's forest. In the forest were more Jews from Bursztyn with whom we established contact.

We received a letter from Dazia Haber, to come and save her. She was hidden in the ruins, on the way to Demianow. Her clothes were worn out, and she looked terrible. Unfortunately, German soldiers roamed around the house; at the same time their withdrawal from Russia began.

[pp. 103-104]

With great effort I was able to get her out of there, and bring her back to the home of Jankiv, the good gentile, our savior.

The horrors of life in the forests and fields, in the attics of gentile houses, in caves and cellars, came upon us. It was terrible to go out at night to ask for food, to be in constant danger that the gentiles would hand us over to the Germans; however, the will to live prevailed over everything.

My wife Dazia, the daughter of Rivka and Pinia Haber and the granddaughter of Avraham Yosel Yona's, remained alive after the Jews of Bursztyn were taken out and brought to Bukaczowce for extermination. She was hiding there. Her parents were taken to the ghetto of Rohatyn and they left her money as well as gold. She went to Lwów and bought her "Aryan certificates." However, in Lwów at that time they would catch Christian women and send them to Germany to work. One day she was also caught for work, and they immediately suspected her of being Jewish, and took her for questioning. She managed to jump from the tram car, and arrived in the Lwów ghetto, where her uncle, Itzik Feldbau was still alive. At the same time, her father died in the Rohatyn ghetto. Her mother sent one of the farmers from the village of Martynow, and he brought her to the Rohatyn ghetto, where she remained until its liquidation, in June 1943. She hid in a cave, returned to Bursztyn, and hid in the houses of the gentiles Wynski, Jankiv and other familiar gentiles. I helped her as much as I could, and only God helped us both, saved us from the murderers, and brought us to Eretz Yisrael. We had three children, and we live a comfortable life.

Indeed, I will continue to talk about a number of events: the heroic deaths of Mundzia Fischmann, Wolf Ostrower, and Loti Bernstein.

When Bursztyn was already "free of Jews," there were still in its surroundings several Jews who hid at farmers' houses and in the forests. Mundzia, Wolf, and Loti dug a bunker for them in the stables of the prince's palace. They had a gun and several bullets. Rafał, the lame cobbler, who was the yard keeper, helped them, and gave them a little food. This was in the summer of 1943.

I often met with Mundzia and Wolf, and Mundzia told me that Wolf had a lot of money.

One Saturday, the stable was raided by Ukrainian policemen under the command of a German. The bunker was strong, but the chimney sweep's son, Fed Boban, tipped them off. The policemen called to the people hiding in the bunker to come out of the bunker as they had surrounded it. When Mundzia felt that there was no escape, he came out with his gun in hand and shot the German commander and seriously wounded him. He also shot and wounded the policeman who shot with a machine gun. Mundzia and Loti were killed. Wolf grabbed the gun, went back down to the bunker, and came out the other side, facing

Deichsler's garden. The murderers pursued him, Wolf Ostrower fought like a hero; not far from Dr. Schmarak's house, he also hit a Ukrainian policeman. Being wounded and bleeding, he continued to shoot the murderers who pursued him. He was killed out of town, Fed's son hit him.

Honor to their memory! In their deaths, the deaths of heroes, they brought a ray of light into the darkness of destruction and the Holocaust of our entire town.

Our Revenge

Fed Boban, the chimney sweep, was a cruel accomplice in the extermination of Bursztyn's Jews. His son was a collaborator of the Germans. They handed over to the slaughter many of the Bursztyn Jews that were hiding in the forests, and they also killed Jews with their own hands, among them: Shmuel Mastel and his son, and Yeshaya Granwitter.

We, a group of Jews in the forest, decided to take revenge on them. We disguised ourselves in peasant clothes and at night we came to the city, caught the night watchman, a gentile we encountered on the street, and forced him to accompany us, until we came to Fed's house. A night guard was ordered to knock on the door and call for Fed to come out of the house. And so he did. As soon as Fed came out of the house, we caught him and killed him on the spot. His wife also came out of the house and received what she deserved. We did not find the murderous son at that time, and after a while we learned that he was hiding in the chimney. And we greatly regretted that. Kalman, the son of Sara the baker, and two Jews from Bukaczowce, also participated in their killing.

Fed's son left Bursztyn. The gentiles in the town learned a lesson from our revenge. Our situation in the forests improved, and they stopped harassing us after that act.

Kalman, the Son of Sarah the Baker

Even during the existence of the Rohatyn ghetto, Kalman fought with weapons against Germans. He and a group of Jews attacked Germans on the way to Koniuszki. Some of the Germans were killed, but they were outnumbered. They caught Kalman and three other Jews with him and brought them to the ghetto in Rohatyn, and all of them were killed. Their bodies were given to the Jews for burial. The Jews noticed that Kalman was still alive and was only gravely wounded in the head. They took him and hid him, and in his place, they buried another deceased person;

[pp. 105-106]

there was no shortage of deceased individuals. Dozens died of typhus every day in town.

Kalman recovered from his wounds, fled to the forests, and lived there for a long time. As the days of liberation approached, Russian prisoners, who went over to the side of the Germans, attacked the Jews in the forests. The Germans sent them to kill the remaining Jews who were running around in the forests.

In those days, the Jews bought some weapons and resisted the brutal murderers. The Germans did not want to risk themselves in battle and sent the Russian prisoners into the forest. In one of the battles Kalman was killed with a weapon in hand. He died a heroic death.

Honored and revered be his name.

A Miracle

A long time before the extermination of the Bursztyn Jews, we learned about the Germans' plot to exterminate Galician Jewry completely. Trains full of Jews who were close to death, who were taken to the cremation camps, often passed the Bursztyn station. Many Jews jumped from the cars as the train sped by, some of them were killed on the spot, some of them were captured. Few among them managed to escape and reach the forest or to a place where Jews still lived.

The Jews who were caught were shot and killed. Once, eleven of the Jews who jumped from the cars near Bursztyn were caught; they were brought to the city. There was one German whose hobby was to shoot those unfortunate people, and he showed extreme cruelty towards children. And he chose the eleven Jews to be shot. He killed nine of them and left a single mother with a seven-year-old child. The killer ordered the boy to turn his face, and pulled out his gun to shoot him, and here a wonderful thing happened: the boy stood in front of the German and smiled. The killer remained standing, gun in hand, as if petrified. The same executioner who murdered a hundred people, among them many children, the same beast who did not have mercy for children who knelt before him and begged for mercy, and his hand did not tremble when he killed them, suddenly stood embarrassed at the innocent child's smile. His gun fell from his hand and he fell to the ground and fainted. When he recovered, he ordered the Ukrainian policeman Shtyk, who shot ten Bursztyn Jews, to take the boy to the "Judenrat," and he made him responsible for the boy's life. For many days, the German lay sick in the house of Tenka Moskvitin, and he ordered the Jewish boy in whose presence he was comforted, to be brought before him.

When the Bursztyn Jews were exterminated, the child disappeared together with his mother, and it is not known what happened to them.

[pp. 109-110]

Bursztyn – History and Destruction

[pp. 111-112] [Blank] [pp. 113-114]

And You Shall Tell It to Your Children
– Our Eternal Obligation

The Editors

This memorial book is the only headstone that we can erect for the victims/martyrs of our town, whose ashes were dispersed by the wind. So long as there are still living witnesses, our holiest obligation is to amass all possible materials, everything that we remember, know, and feel about our town.

We are not professional writers, not historians. Only the shocking anguish in the appearance of the horrifying holocaust opened up our mute lips and made them speak. Every single note, when it is even recorded with a mild smile and light humor, is indeed an expression of concentrated feelings of trouble. Furthermore, every line, every memory, has its place of worth/value in this headstone-book, as a remembrance of our nearest and dearest.

Only a few Jews from Bursztyn were saved from the Nazi murderers; several only remained alive so as to relate about this holocaust. In Bursztyn, just as in hundreds of other cities and towns in Poland and Galicia, there are no more Jews. Furthermore, it took so many years following the Hitlerist flood, until we had found the strength within ourselves to gird ourselves and muster the strength to erect this monument, the memorial book of our town, Bursztyn.

It is clear and understandable that in most of the descriptions and accounts, which are contained within this book, one hears the lament of mourners; in the memoirs, everyone will hear the tone of eulogy and elegy, the lament of the horrible holocaust, as with the general tragedy of European Jewry, bound up with personal tragedy, with sorrow for our own and near ones. Here and there, there are perhaps repetitions of descriptions and of reference to the same matters, events, and people. But each one completes the other, and creates a picture of the way of life, of the disappointments and achievements. Everything together tells us how much we lost, how great, and literally, how incomprehensible the loss is!

Also mentioned in this book are Jews and Jewish life of the neighboring towns and villages, such as: Rohatyn, Bukaczowce, Bolszowce, Halicz, Jezupol [Pol.]/Azipoli [Yid.], Uscie Zielone, Tysmienica, Mariampol, Demianow, and other towns, which were brothers of Bursztyn, and benefited from it

[pp. 115-116]

socially and culturally. May the kinsmen from these truncated and decimated Jewish towns, like rescued Holocaust survivors, wherever they presently find themselves, consider this Bursztyn memorial book as a monument to their most beloved and dearest ones.

With downcast heads and broken hands we stand before the modest monument for our annihilated Jewish community of Bursztyn. We unite with the holy remembrance of the murdered victims/martyrs. Sadly lost and not forgotten!

May this memorial book be an eternal reminder for generations to come, which will see in this very book, a document and a mirror of a rich way of life, which is no more.

May this lament, which ascends from this book, not be silenced and not stop demanding one's due for generations to come.

[pp. 117-118] [pp. 25-52 - Hebrew]

On the History of the Jews in Bursztyn

Dr. N. M. Gelber

The town of Bursztyn was built along the shores of the river, Gnila Lipa. On a large part of land there were pools of fish. The town lay beside the shore of the river, along the Rohatyn-Lemberg route. In the 16th and 17th centuries Bursztyn played an important role in the commercial import and export of Ruthenia. Through Bursztyn, the merchandise was delivered from Lemberg to the lowlands. It was there that the road split into two directions: one to Zloczew-Zaleszczyki, and from there, by way of Walachia, to Constantinople. The second – to Przemyslany, via Rohatyn – Bursztyn – Kalusz, Stanislawow, Kolomyja, [all the way] to Hungary.

In the 17th century, Bursztyn was a small town and belonged to the district head of Halicz. It was called Nowe Sioto. It was the property of Mikolaj Sieniawski. In 1505, 104 peasants lived there. At the top stood a "Wojt" [a high administrative officer of a Polish community]. In the same year, Zygmunt-August, the King of Poland, bequeathed estates to the brothers of Mikolaj: Prokop – the town of Ostrow, and Aleksander – Dolfojew [Dolzhka?]. Mikolaj received the entire district of Kaniuszki and the town of Bursztyn, and all the surrounding villages.

It is difficult to determine whether there was a Jewish settlement there at that time. There are no signs [of this], such as: privileges and documents to verify this. The Jews settled in Bursztyn at a later period, when the Jews of the district of Lemberg dispersed into the eastern parts of Poland.

In the 17th century Bursztyn suffered from the Tatar occupations. In October 1629, Stefan Chmielewski overtook the Tatars, drove them out from the area, and grabbed all the spoils, which they had stolen from there.

In the 17th century the economic situation sharpened in Ruthenia, so much so that the council of the district of Halicz, to which Bursztyn belonged, decided during a meeting on the 29th of July, 1681, to free the towns of Bohorodczany and Bursztyn, from paying taxes.

In the beginning of the 18th century, Bursztyn and its environs belonged to Castellan [i.e., the governor of a castle] Pawel Benoi of Warsaw; who was the castellan who built the Church of the Trinitarian Order. He took upon himself the task of liberating captives, who had been captured by the Turks. His daughter married Marshal Franciszek Rzewuski, and he received the town of Bursztyn as a dowry. From then on, Bursztyn was the property of the Rzewuski family – until the beginning of the 19th century. From the Rzewuskis, Bursztyn was handed over to Count Skarbek. And later on, it became the estate of his grandson, Prince Jablonowski.

In the middle of the 17th century, the Jewish settlement in Bursztyn was established upon the foundations, according to the model of noble towns [towns belonging to noblemen] of that time: the majority earned their livelihood by petty trade, village peddlers, tavern owners, and only a small portion took up artisanship. The leadership of the community was organized in the same manner as in all the communities in Ruthenia: at the peak stood the "Kahal" [official, designated Jewish community, recognized also by Gentile society], which was elected according to the statute that was enacted in 1630 in Kulikow, via 6 voters, in the following manner: in one of the election

[pp. 119-120]

ballot boxes, were [voting] slips with the names of the distinguished landlords/proprietors and trustees; in the second ballot box were the names of the officials and members of the commissions; in the third ballot box – the names of all the tax payers. Afterwards, two slips were removed from the first ballot box, and the rest of the slips were thrown into the second ballot box; then, they withdrew from the second ballot box two slips, and the remaining ones were thrown into the third ballot box; from there, two more slips were withdrawn; all six were those of the voters, and they nominated the new "Kahal."

At the head of the Jewish community stood 3-5 elected heads of the community, who needed to be approved by the lord of the town. The elected heads carried out their functions every month, each one according to his place in the queue. During the time that he served officially, he was called the "month's elected head." A portion of the elected heads would govern and carry out their functions with power/influence. In the Jewish community of Bursztyn, however, there were none as powerful/influential as Zalmen, the son of Wolf from Drohobicz, who was known for his cruelty, during the years 1750-1760. Up until the final years of the First World War, special songs were sung about him in the Ukrainian villages.

Aside from the elected heads, there were 5-7 distinguished landlords/proprietors in the Jewish community council, and for specific functions, special trustees were elected: "trustees of the great charity," who concerned themselves with charity and the poorhouse, hospitals/infirmaries and the free burial society; oversaw the accounts and marketplace, weight, and hygiene; trustees of the Talmud Torah and the synagogue.

During times of exceptional circumstances, such as wars, Tatar and Ukrainian takeovers, from which this eastern town greatly suffered, trustees were elected who concerned themselves with the liberation of captives.

In practically every Jewish community, money was collected for the impoverished of Israel, which was sent to the "Mara D'Atra Kadisha" [i.e., a title of honor bestowed upon a Torah scholar and Jewish community figurehead] of Lemberg. Aside from the city's rabbi, there was a religious court of law of rabbinic judges.

The communal matters lay in the hands of a religious scribe and beadle, and in the smaller Jewish communities there was merely a lobbyist/intermediary.

Within the Jewish community there were various societies for good deeds and the study of Torah.

The synagogue was built in the first half of the 18th century, in accordance with the tradition of the Jews of Bursztyn in the old Jewish cemetery, founded more than 400 years ago. The cantor, R' Itzik-Dovid told Rabbi Meir Landau, many years prior to the First World War, that he had seen a headstone in the Jewish cemetery with the engraved name of the deceased: the son of the Gaon Mahar"m [Maharam] of Lublin. Rabbi Landau deduced from this that the Jewish cemetery had already existed 400 years earlier.

The conclusion that the Jewish community had existed, already at the end of the 16th century, is, however, not acceptable. First, in the archival documents, which refer to the old East Galician Jewish communities, Bursztyn does not figure in at all: second, [the notion that] Rabbi Meir, son of Gedalia

(Mahar"m) of Lublin, lived during the years 1558-1616, is indeed not possible, if his son died 400 years ago.

To the Jewish community of Bursztyn also belonged the Jews who lived in the villages: Nastaszczyn, Junaskow, Sarnku, Ozieran, Kuropatniki, and Tenetniki.

According to the accounts that remained among the Jews of Bursztyn, the Jewish community suffered greatly from the Cossack attacks of 1658.

The Jewish populace grew, not only in number, but it also respectfully sustained the Jewish autonomous institutions. The Jewish community representatives took an active part in the regional council.

In 1714, the assembly of the "Council of the Land of Reissen" was convened in Bursztyn.

[pp. 121-122]

From this, one may derive how important and significant the Jewish community was.

The major Hetman Adam Michal Sieniawski called together on 27 July, 1713 in Bursztyn, the council of Jewish communities of the district of Ruthenia, Podolia, [and] Pokucja, so as to – as is stated in the order of the assembly – "The Jews from the [afore]mentioned places shall in an urgent/pressing manner uphold an assembly on my estate of Bursztyn of the council of the land with the goal of distributing the contributions and receiving an assignation of payment, which was issued to them, according to the lists of the appraisers and their chief writer."

Bursztyn stood opposite the cities of Rohatyn and Podhajce, the main points of the Shabbetai Tzvi movement, and later on, of Jacob Frank. Their missionaries also attempted in Bursztyn to sway people.

Elisha Schorr, one of Shabbetai Tzvi's leading believers, along with his three sons – Shlomo-Natan, Lipman, and Lieb – dispersed the belief in Sabbatianism and Frankism from Rohatyn. They moved about among all the Jewish communities in the area, and preached their [own version of the] Torah.

It is not known whether they had any influence upon the Jews of Bursztyn, and they succeeded in capturing people there, but the fact is that in the Frankist lists of converted [apostate] Jews following the dispute, which took place in Lemberg from 17 July – 10 September 1759, not a single Jew from Bursztyn was found; this demonstrates the complete failure [of the Sabbatians].

At that time, there was a rabbi in Bursztyn, Rabbi Tzvi son of Natan. Along with two Jewish community leaders and a beadle, he verified by way of an oath [taken] at a census on 15 February, 1765, "We recorded [accounted for] all the Jews from big to small, in their residences, in the villages [that stand] opposite, which are included as part of the Bursztyn Jewish community; as well as those situated along the way; we did not exclude anyone."

At the time of the census, which was taken for a head-tax, there were in Bursztyn, proper, 438 adult Jews and 154 children. In seven villages that belonged to the Jewish community of Bursztyn – 43 [adult] Jews and 5 children.

On account of the dearth of believable/reliable documents and sources, we lack information regarding the development of the Jewish community of Bursztyn. It is only known that the influence of Chasidism grew stronger with time, among the [Jewish] residents of Bursztyn, and also lasted into the periods of Austrian rule.

The owner of the city – the Rzewuski family needed the Jewish residents, who, with their merchandise, improved the economic situation in the area. Therefore, they gave the Jews separate privileges: they built stone houses for them, some of which still remained until the end of the Second World War. Economically, the situation of the Jews of Bursztyn was very good. Their livelihood supported/aided them against the peasants in the area. They mainly took up merchandise pertaining to agriculture/farming and tavern-keeping. However, they suffered heavily from the taxes that were then placed on Jews. Aside from the head-tax, they still had to pay various other taxes.

II.[1]

Following the first partition of Poland, major changes took place in the land and in Galicia, from which Bursztyn also greatly suffered.

Until the year 1785, the Jews of Galicia were organized according to the Jewish law of Queen Maria Theresa, of 1776, in a separate body: the main leadership of the Jews of Galicia, which stood at the highest point. The organization was initiated in 1785, and no other institution was founded in its place. In average-sized and small Jewish communities like Bursztyn, stood three community leaders at the peak. Their task was to take care of Jewish community matters. At that time, Bursztyn belonged to the province of Brzezhany. The Jewish community did not have a rabbi,

[pp. 123-124]

only an adjudicator of Jewish law, who did not receive a salary, merely a residence. In the provincial city of Brzezhany, there was a rabbi of the province. His annual upkeep came to 200 florins and an official residence.

In all the cities of the Bursztyn area: Bobrka, Chodorow, Strelisk, Przemyslany, Podhajce, [and] Rohatyn, there were no rabbis, only religious law adjudicators.

Just as in all the Jewish communities of Galicia, aside from the standard taxes, a "bowing fee" and a "concession fee" were also placed upon the Jews of Bursztyn. For permission to marry off a son – one had to pay according to the family's earnings. Whoever married off his children without the [controlling] power's permission, was seriously punished – even to the point of seizing his property.

At that time, the Jews of Bursztyn suffered greatly from postmaster Röttel [i.e., presumably a non-Jew], who would inform on them. For every "transmission" regarding a non-official marriage, he would receive a reward from the authorities.

King Joseph II gave an order in 1782 that Jewish land workers only needed to pay half of the marriage tax. He also promised them that in a short time he would totally free them from this tax. The government wanted to give the Jews strength, so that they would invest themselves in agriculture/farming.

The [ruling] power also prepared a plan to establish economic settlements/colonies for Jews. In the spring of 1786, the first Jewish settlement was established in the village of Dabrowka, near Nowy Sacz (Santz), and later, "New Babel" (New Babylow), near Bolechow. There were also a number of other small settlements that did not exist for long.

The government's plan confirmed that from the general number of 1,400 families, which the Jewish communities had to mobilize for the agricultural settlement, the province of Brzezhany (10 Jewish communities) must give [this to] 69 Jewish families, who had intended to settle on 49 tracts of land. They were supposed to receive 66 homes, 66 granaries, and stalls, 66 work machinery, 124 horses, 88 oxen, [and] 147 cows. At the distribution, the Jewish community of Bursztyn offered up 7 families, together: 9 men, 9 women, 2 girls, and 8 boys – they received 7 portions of land, 7 homes, 7 granaries, and stalls, 7 work machines, 14 horses, 20 oxen, and 23 cows.

According to the official report of the [ruling] powers, these families settled upon their privately owned land until the end of 1793.

In 1822, from among the 60 [Jewish] families of the district of Brzezhany, 40 of them remained in agriculture. –Thereby, it is not known how many of them hailed from Bursztyn.

The budget of the Jewish agricultural settlement was placed upon [assigned to] the local Jewish communities. The settlement expenditure account for one family reached a sum of 200 florins.

As mentioned, the Jews of Bursztyn, just like those of other Jewish communities in Galicia, suffered from the heavy taxes, which led them to economic collapse.

Aside from the "Tolerance Tax" (Toleranz-Steuer), the Jews paid various other taxes, such as: the cost of kosher meat, for lighting candles.

Aside from tavern-keeping, the Jews of Bursztyn were involved in petty trade and village peddling, [and] in the sale of agricultural products. The geographical position of Bursztyn, which lay along the main highway, created economic opportunities to concentrate various branches of trade in Jewish hands.

"The Order Concerning Jews" of King Joseph II (of 20 March 1785) forced the Jews to create their own schools. In the district of Brzezhany, during the years 1788-1792, schools were created among the Jewish communities: Brzezhany, Rohatyn, Podhajce, Bobrka, [and]

[pp. 125-126]

Rozdal. Bursztyn, a small Jewish community with a small number of residents, did not merit a general Jewish school.

In 1812, the [ruling] power of eastern Galicia carried out a census. It is understood that the census was made with the purpose of collecting taxes. The census revealed that in Bursztyn there were 100 Jewish families, among them – 197 men, 216 women – in total, 413 people. In comparison to the last census of 1765, (453 people) [this] was, according to the census of 1812, a decrease of 40 people (10%) from the Jewish population of Bursztyn.

III.

In the second half of the 18th century, one of the famous rabbis of the Jewish community was Rabbi Tzvi-Hirsh son of Natan Ashkenazi, who in 1765 had signed the census list.

Rabbi Tzvi-Hirsh son of Natan Ashkenazi was the grandson of "Chacham Tzvi" and the brother of Rabbi Yabetz. His father was a large figure in Torah, one of the wise men of the religious house of study in Brody.

He would give sermons about Halacha [Jewish law] and Aggadah [rabbinic homilies of various sources] before the wise men of the study house; his commentaries appeared in the booklet, "Imrei Noam" (compilations from the great men of that generation).

His mother was the daughter of R. Moshe of Brody.

Rabbi Natan had three sons: R. Ephraim, one of the wise men of the study house and a religious preacher in Brody, R. Moshe, the head of the religious court of law of the Jewish community of Zborow – the father of R. Yaakov of Lissa (Lorberbaum), the author of "Chavat Daat" and "Netivot Hamishpat" – and R. Tzvi Hirsh, the head of the religious court of law of the Jewish community of Bursztyn.

When R. Tzvi-Hirsh son of Natan died, his son-in-law, R. Yosef Teomim, was elected the rabbi of Bursztyn (R. Yaakov of Lissa was his student).

Following R. Yosef Teomim, R. Yosef Schwartz, a student of R. Yaakov of Lissa, inherited the rabbinate seat. He led the rabbinate for many years in the city. When he was elderly, in the year 1857, he made Aliyah to Israel.

R. Meir Landau (1830-1907), [was] the son of Rabbi Mordechai Ziskind Segal-Landau, the head of the religious court of Stryj (along with the head of the religious court of law, R. Enziel). His mother, Hinda, was the daughter of the rich man, R. Hirsh Hirtzman of Bursztyn, having been born in Grodek-Jagielonski. He moved to Bursztyn and became one of the wealthiest individuals in the area.

Rabi Meir Landau was born in Bursztyn. At the age of 20, he was already rabbi of the town of Knihinicz, not far from Rohatyn. In 1857, he became rabbi of his town of birth, Bursztyn. (The Chasidic rabbi of Stratyn, R. Avraham son of Yehudah-Tzvi, wrote to his followers in Bursztyn, and ordered them to be on his side). For 40 years he oversaw the rabbinate, until 1898, when his son was elected the rabbi of Bursztyn, while his father was still living. Rabbi Meir Landau died 10 Nisan 5667 [25 March 1907]. His son, R. Moshe-David Landau, took his place. R. Moshe-David's wife was the daughter of Rabbi Naphtali-Hirtz Landau of Strelisk, the grandson of R. Yoel-Moshe. During his time, the well-known religious judges were: R. Leizer Yaakov, R. Chaim-Yudl Deichsler, [and] R. Leibl Jupiter.

R. Moshe-David was rabbi in Bursztyn until 1927, when he died.

In 1910, following the initiative of R. Shmuel, the son of the Preacher of Strelisk, R. Yoel Ginzburg, the head of the Mesivta of the Brzezhany Yeshiva of the Gaon, R. Shalom-Mordechai Schwadron, was invited to Bursztyn. Following his sermon, he was taken up as the city's adjudicator of religious law, and filled this position until the annihilation of the Jewish community.

Prior to the revolution of 1848 in Austria, there was a difficult struggle during the lifetime of Galician Jewry between the religious and Chasidim from one side and the Maskilim [the Enlightened Ones] from the other side. The Jewish community of Bursztyn

[pp. 127-128]

did not appreciate the flavor of this struggle. Its inner life was entirely influenced by Chasidism.

Already in the beginning of the 19th century, Chasidism set down roots in Bursztyn. The founder was R. Yehuda-Tzvi-Hirsh Brandwein from Stratyn, a student of R. Uri Strelisker, known by the name "Saraf," a student of R. Shlomo of Karlin. His eldest son, R. Avraham, inherited the rabbinic seat from his father. His brother, R. Eliezer (Leizerl) was the Chasidic rabbi of Jezupol. He had two sons: R. Uri, his successor in Jezupol, and R. Nachum.

R. Nachum became the rabbi of Stratyn in 1865, when he was 18 years old. A few years later he relocated to Bursztyn, and was rabbi there until 1914; he was a diligent Torah scholar and a Kabbalist. He wrote 4 books regarding the Kabbalah: 1) "Imrei Tov," 2) "Imrei Chaim," 3) "Imrei Bracha," 4) "Imrei Ratzon." R. Nachum established a stunning [rabbinic] court in Bursztyn. There was always a large number of "residents" whom the rabbi supported. In the Bursztyn and Rohatyn area there were many of his followers, who formed local "Bursztyn study houses" – in Rohatyn, Bukaczowce, Bolszowce, Halicz, Bukaczowce, Bolszowce, Jezupol, Monasterzyska, Nizniow, Nadworny, Łysiec, Tysmienica, Stanislawow, Uscie-Zielone, Mariampol, and Podhajce.

The rabbi's court and the large number of arriving Chasidim/followers contributed to the economic existence of the Jewish community of Bursztyn.

In the summer of 1914, while the Chasidic rabbi was at his country house in the mountains, a fire broke out in Bursztyn, which destroyed half of the town, and the rabbi's court was also consumed. At that time, R. Nachumtze left Bursztyn and moved to Stanislawow. He died there in 1915. He left behind a son and four daughters.

His son, Leizerl, took his place in Stanislawow. His sons-in-law: 1) R. Aizikl of Podhajce, 2) R. Ephraim Horwicz, rabbi of Uscie, 3) R. Leib, the Chasidic rabbi of Olyka, 4) R. Moshe-Lieb, the Chasidic rabbi of Schatz [i.e., the city of Suceava, situated in the historical regions of Bukovina and Moldavia].

Following R. Nachum's death, his followers [or Chasidim] broke into three "courts": one – of R. Leizerl, the second – of his son-in-law, R. Aizikl of Podhajce.[2]

In the beginning of the 1930s, R. Moshe, R. Leizerl's son, renewed his grandfather's court in Bursztyn. He led the rabbinate until he was murdered, along with his wife and three sons, during the murderous Nazi period. Aside from the Stratyner Chasidim, there were Belzer and Czortkower Chasidim in Bursztyn. Their influence was apparent in the life of the Jewish community until the outbreak of the Second World War.

Rabbi Reb Moyshe'le (Brandwein) of blessed memory, the Rebbe of Bursztyn, the son of Rabbi Reb Leizer'l of blessed memory, the Rebbe of Stanisławów and grandson of Rabbi Nachum'tshe, founder of the rabbinic dynasty of Bursztyn. Rabbi Reb Moyshe'le was famous throughout Poland and Galicia and he had many Chasidim. The Nazis caught him and tortured him severely and he died in 1942 in Stanisławów.

During the years 1846-1847, the council of the Jewish community was in a difficult financial situation, and was unable to cover its expenses. The Jewish community asked for a permit from the regional leadership to increase the price of kosher meat, so as to cover the needs of the Jewish community. At the end of 1847, the regional leadership of Brzezhany allowed the Jewish community of Bursztyn to add an additional tax to the cost of [kosher] meat, so as to cover the expenses.

As is known, in 1850, Jews were permitted to purchase immoveable properties. From all the Galician cities, Jews submitted requests to the Minister of the Interior in Vienna, regarding permits to purchase immoveable property.

From the Jews of Bursztyn, there were three who submitted requests in 1864: B. Blauer, Mehrberg, and Feldklein. In 1866, Erdstein and Kimmel, major grain dealers in eastern Galicia, requested a permit to record their places and houses, in the registry of property estates. A few months later they received the permit.

At that time, there were already two Jewish physicians residing in Bursztyn: Dr. Goldscheider and the surgeon, Rittner. In 1845, Rittner did something that shook up the

[pp. 129-130]

Jewish community of Bursztyn: Rittner had a son, Edward, and when he was yet a small child, his father had him converted to Christianity. Insofar as the query why he had done such a thing, the father replied – that he had done it, due to a conviction in belief. He was asked: "Since when are you interested in religious matters, and when did you come to the conviction that Christianity is more desirable than Judaism?" Here he admitted that he did this, not because of conviction, but knowing that his son, who was very capable, would climb in life as a Catholic, and that if he were to remain a Jew – he would barely be able to become a lawyer, or a doctor with a good practice in the province.

Edward Rittner did indeed make a great career [for himself]: he joined the government service and became a lecturer in laws of the Church at the University of Lemberg. And when he turned 31, he was made a full professor. Later on, during the years 1896-1897, he became, in the government of Count Kazimierz Badeni, Minister of Galician Matters.

Dr. Rittner had a major influence in government circles, and was one of the confidantes of Kaiser Franz Joseph I; when the Crown Prince Frederick grew very ill, and his brother Otto was elected to temporarily take his place, Kaiser Franz Joseph ordered Rittner that he broaden [i.e., educate] him for his forthcoming position.

When Professor Dr. Rittner died on 26 September 1899, the marshal of Galicia, Count Stanislaw Badeni, eulogized him, saying: "Rittner, the researcher, the shining jurist, possessed exceptional abilities and a show of politics, and with every matter that he oversaw, he was a loyal servant of the country" --- His son, Tadeusz Rittner, 1873-1921, was a well-known writer and dramatist.

Another case of Jewish apostasy took place in Bursztyn in 1858: a Jew by the name of Finkel took his child, Ludwik, to be converted. Ludwik Finkel, 1858-1930, was one of the founders of the new Polish bibliography and historiography. He studied philosophy in Berlin and Paris, and was appointed lecturer of history at the Agricultural Institute of Dublany – and in 1886 – in Lemberg.

In 1892, he was appointed a full professor at the University of Lemberg, and he was a lecturer there until 1927. Dr. Finkel was well-known as an historian among Polish historians; he wrote many studies and books about the history of Poland during the Jagiellonian period. His bibliography regarding the history of Poland (2 volumes, 1891-1914) is a foundational book, following lengthy research work, based on primary sources.

It is worth mentioning that Polish society did not know anything about his Jewish heritage.

Later on, in Bursztyn, there arose private teachers who began teaching the children of the wealthier families, general studies and also languages, German, and Polish.

To the important families belonged: Hammer, Raphael; the head of the family was the in-law of Naphtali-Hirtz Hirtzman, the city's wealthy man and son-in-law of Rabbi Mordechai Ziskind Landau from Stryj; the families: Breiter, Feldbau, Kleinfeld, Gelernter, [and] Friedlander. Along with Rabbi Landau's family, the economic and social life of the Bursztyn Jewish community was concentrated within their hands. In the city there were already progressive Jews: Maskilim, such as Shevach Klarberg, [and] the Hammer family.

[pp. 131-132]

At the end of the 19th century, there stood at the head of the Jewish community: Moshe Hammer, Yonah Feldbau, [and] Shevach Klarberg. In 1903, the Austrian ruling powers oversaw elections for the cultural council. Elected were 12 members of the council, among them: Moshe Hammer, Yonah Feldbau, [and] Shevach Klarberg. Elected as the representative of the Jewish community council was the pharmacist, Tierhaus; his position representative – Zelig Hammer.

Bursztyn's Beit Midrash

Little by little, the aspiration toward the Haskalah [i.e., the Jewish Enlightenment] penetrated the Chasidic town of Bursztyn, into the upbringing of the youth, in the spirit of the times.

In 1898, there opened in Bursztyn – as demonstrated by the efforts of a small group of Maskilim, at whose peak [stood] Shevach Klarberg and Dr. David Maltz – a Jewish school for boys, founded by the "Baron Hirsch Foundation," which initiated educational activities in Galicia and Bukovina since 1801, and built 37 school buildings. In 1901, the number grew to 50 school buildings.

The director, Antshl Fogel, taught the students in the Baron Hirsch School farm labor.

The studies were well received, and the religious elements also sent their children to the school.

The Baron Hirsch School existed until the outbreak of the First World War, 1914. After the war, the director, Fogel, worked as the secretary of the Jewish community of Lemberg.

The Jewish community took over the school building. The Peretz Association and the People's Library were located there.

"IKO" [Jewish Colonization Organization] created loan offices in Galicia in order to provide financial aid to the artisans, petty merchants, and village peddlers. At that time, in April 1905, according to the initiative of Director Fogel, an "IKO" loan office was founded in Bursztyn. The overseers of the loan office were Antshl Fogel and Fishl Rottenstreich.

Aside from the "IKO" loan office, there also existed a cooperative bank; people called it "The Lowest [Level] Bank," because the bank was located in the cellar of Leizer Landner's house. The directors of the bank were: Zalmen Stern and Zelig Hammer. The members of the supervisory council – [were] Berish Gelernter, Berish Hornik, Avraham Eli Tobias, and Avraham Frisch.

The loan office and the cooperative bank were active until the outbreak of the First World War. In 1918, both of the institutions were consolidated into the single "Cooperative Loan Office," at whose helm stood Dr. Rurberg, Zelig Hammer, and Dr. Wolf Schmarak.

An ebullient national [way of] life began in Bursztyn with the establishment of the Zionist organization, "Chovevei Tzion." The founder was Bunem Schapira, an educated person in whose home Bursztyn's youth assembled, and Schapira would read them Bialik's poetry. Among the youths were: Tauber, Zalmen Stern, Meir Redisch, Moshe Schumer, David Frankl, Yisroel Jamper, [and] M. Tobias.

In 1900, Dr. David Maltz moved to Bursztyn and opened his legal office [practice]. With him, the city acquired a Jewish-Zionist personality, which had since 1882 carried out important functions for Galician Jewry. He was an organizer, a speaker, and a writer with a strongly sharpened quill and a lucid style.

Dr. David Maltz was born in Lwow [i.e., Lemberg] in 1862. In 1882, he joined a group of Zionist students, who were led by Dr. Avraham Kurkis, and from then on, he belonged to the Zionist activists. He was a member of "Mikra Kodesh," the first Zionist organization in Lwow,

[pp. 133-134]

founded by Yosef Kobak (1820-1913), Dr. Reuven Bierer, and Ozer Yehudah Rohatyner (1849-1889).

Dr. Yehoshua Thon, along with his brother-in-law, Dr. Mordechai Ehrenpreis, Adolph Stand, and Dr. Mordechai Brode, founded the organization "Tzion" (Rynek 12) in Lemberg. From there, they began to create the Zionist Federation of Galicia, several years before the appearance of Dr. Theodore Herzl.

Nearly every week, Dr. Maltz traveled to various cities to give talks and readings, propagandizing Zionist ideology, founding Zionist organizations, and societies for the Yishuv [settlement] in Israel.

In 1893, in Lwow, the first brochure [bearing] the contents of the Zionist program, entitled "What Should Be the Program of Jewish Youth?" [was issued]. Dr. Maltz wrote the chapter there concerning Israel and the colonization of the country. Even then, he was already considered one of the best Zionist writers. His articles in "Pszyszloszcz" and "Self-Emancipation" under the editorship of Dr. Natan Birnbaum made a strong impression with their ideological clarity and sharp polemic style, against the assimilationists. His articles provided a serious contribution to deepening the Zionist ideology among the Jews of Galicia.

In 1892, the first Zionist newspaper, "Pszyszloszcz" (Future), appeared in the Polish language. It was mainly dedicated to the propaganda among Polish-speaking circles. Dr. Maltz belonged to the most important writers there. Thanks to his sharp satirical style, he was the polemicist of the newspaper. There was not a single event in Jewish life to which he did not, in his own manner, respond. He came out especially sharp against the assimilationists and opponents of Zionism. He assaulted them mercilessly.

At the Zionist conference, which took place in Lemberg the 23-25 April, 1893, Maltz came out with an all-encompassing and sharp assault against the delegates who only emphasized Jewish nationalism, as though it had no connection to Israel; a national movement – according to his speech – "that did not include as part of its goal the renaissance of the Jewish nation in its [own] land, is foreign to the Jewish spirit. There are no prospects of dealing with the Jewish question upon the foundation of a national renaissance in Galicia. The national idea means a full-fledged solution to the Jewish question in Israel. The only means is to liquidate the diaspora and concentrate the nation in Israel."

For this particular outlook, Dr. Maltz fought his entire life.

From 1893, Dr. Maltz, together with Dr. Avraham Kurkis and Dr. Hescheles, was the editor of "Pszyszloszcz." During the summer months of 1893, Dr. Maltz made a big propaganda and educational advertisement trip across Galicia.

Under the influence of Dr. Herzl's "Judenstadt," Dr. Maltz wrote a drama in Polish, entitled "Dr. Moshe Blum," which, at the time, made a huge impact on the Jewish youth. He was elected a delegate to the First Zionist Congress in Basel (1897), in which he took an active part.

Following the congress, he was active insofar as propaganda and educational advertisement in the press. He took part in the Zionist conferences and congresses, and was a member of the country's administration within the Zionist Federation.

In 1899, Dr. Maltz became well-known for his sharp speech against Dr. Emil Bick,

[pp. 135-136]

the president of the Jewish community of Lwow, who had declared that the difference between the Jews and the Poles existed only in terms of religion.

At the Jewish Communities Conference, which took place May 1, 1900, Dr. Maltz, as a delegate of one of the Jewish communities, sharply assaulted this very theory that [caused the] degeneration of social life among the Jews of Galicia.

After he moved to Bursztyn, he was again Zionistically active in land surveying. At the conference, which took place on 16-17 June, 1901, he refereed the situation of the Jews of Galicia. Using rich historical and statistical material, he provided an overview in his lecture of the legal, economic, and cultural development of the Jews at the close of the 19th century. He established that Galician Jewry, particularly the intelligentsia, still did not understand the tragedy of the situation, and that there was no other solution, aside from Zionism. Insofar as the economic element, the Jewish populace became an extraneous matter. The Jews are pushed out of every realm, the Jewish intelligentsia distances itself from Judaism on account of fear, so that it will not need to worry about our future. At the conclusion of his lecture, he proposed an economic program, creating offices for employment mediation, organizing modern, social activities, [and] creating savings and loan offices. In the cultural realm, he demanded that they make an impact on the education of the youth in a national constructive spirit, spread education among the people.

At the conference, he was elected a member of the country's administration. At the Fifth Zionist Congress in Basel in 1901, he was elected a member of the large actions committee of the Zionist World Federation. He participated in the Sixth and Seventh Zionist Congress, where he belonged to the opponents of the Uganda Plan. Also, at the Eight Congress in The Hague (1907), he participated.

During the years 1901-1903, he took an active part in the establishment of the Zionist youth movement, particularly academically; he took part in the Zionist monthly journal in Polish, "Moriah," which was established according to the initiative of Dr. Yaakov Thon in 1903.

At the time of the elections for the Viennese Parliament, Dr. Maltz ran as a candidate in the province of Zolkiew-Rozdal and received 1,269 votes. He took an active part in the "election fight"; politically, he was for joint action with the Ukrainians, and during the election proceedings he would speak Ukrainian.

At the Assembly of the Jewish Communities, which took place on 28 April 1908, according to the initiative of the Viennese Jewish community, with the goal of establishing a general Jewish centralized institute, which would be able to make appearances in the name of all of Austrian Jewry, Dr. Maltz represented the Jewish community of Bursztyn. Dr. Maltz is the one who brought the Zionist spirit into the general debate. At that time, he was active in the realm of politics and land surveillance, actively participated in the political conference of the national federation, which came together in Krakow on the 15th May, 1910, under the leadership of Dr. Beno Straucher, the deputy of the Austrian Parliament.

**David Maltz in the group of leaders of the Zionist movement in Galicia
(at the end of the 19th century)**

**First row (from the right): David Schreiber, Dr. Gershon Zipper, Heinrich Gabel
Second row: David Maltz, Adolf Stand, Laufer**

Also, at the elections for the Viennese Parliament in 1911, Dr. Maltz ran as a candidate in Tarnow, where he received 1,194 votes.

At the Central Zionist Land Conference, which took place the 24th December, 1911, in Stanislawow, Dr. Maltz was

[pp. 137-138]

a presidium member, and was elected to the federation council. During the years 1911-1914, he concentrated his Zionist activities in Bursztyn.

When the First World War broke out, he fled to Vienna, where he was again active in Zionist activities, taking part in January 1914 in the assembly of the members of all the central commissions/committees in the Austrian Zionist movement. After he returned to Galicia, he again continued his Zionist activities.

However, during the war he overcame much embitterment and resignation.

In 1917, following the Russian Revolution, he did not believe that the war was close to ending. He asked: "Who can predict whether the Russian Revolution will give birth to a living tree, or to a totally poisonous plant?" Regarding the Jewish problem, he writes: "If the promise of Wilson and Lloyd George insofar as the national home in Israel is based on the truth, then the struggles [wars] and losses were worthwhile; then our children in Israel will have a worthy existence."

I have given more attention to Dr. Maltz, because he was among the [leading] figures of Galician Jewry, and it was an honor for the Jewish community of Bursztyn to have him among its residents and to take him up as an experienced leader.

The Zionist movement in Bursztyn was, until 1914, a social, cultural factor in the life of the Jewish populace. In 1909, a Hebrew school with one teacher and 29 students was founded by the local Zionists. At the time of the First World War, the Zionist movement received an active, organizational strength in the person of Dr. Wolf Schmarak, who moved to Bursztyn and worked as a lawyer.

From an economic standpoint, the professional composition of the Jewish populace in Bursztyn did not change. The majority consisted of merchants with stores, furs, wood, grain, cows, [and] horses. A certain number of Jews ran businesses with the estate holders and worked for them as administrators and advisors regarding the sale of agricultural products.

Jews were also merchants, tailors, capmakers, carpenters, barbers, blacksmiths, and shoemakers. Of the free professions, there were three Jewish doctors, lawyers, a pharmacist, and several government officials, employed by industrial enterprises, such as Friedlander's mill.

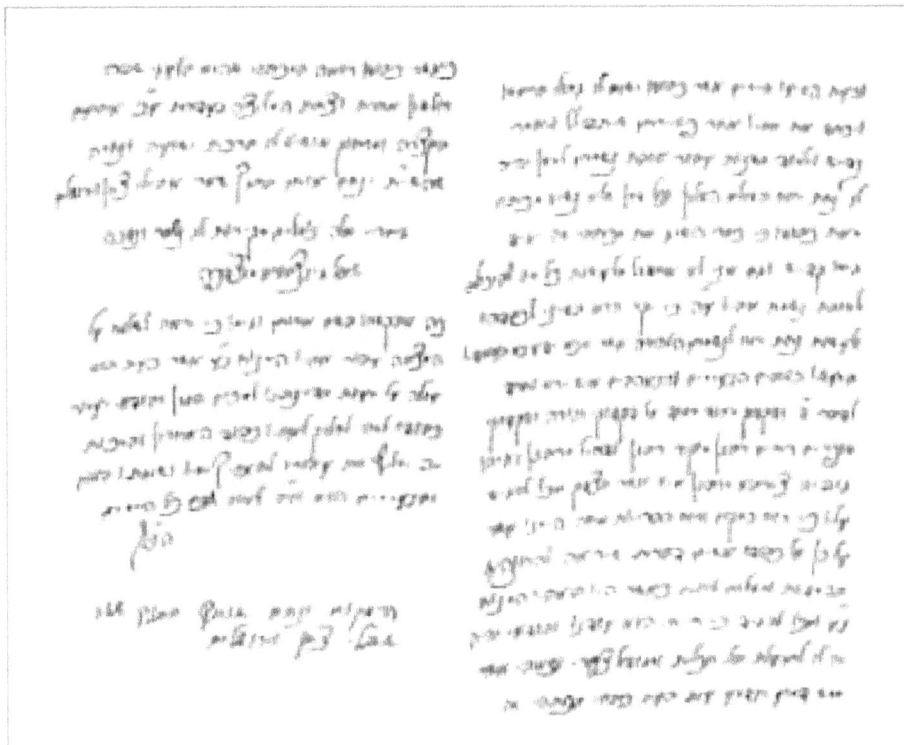

The handwriting of Rabbi Yoel Ginzburg of blessed memory, a teacher in Bursztyn

Factually, the complexion of the city was a Jewish one. Even the letter carrier, R. Ephraim Schneider, was dressed in the Jewish manner, with a beard and sidelocks, and as is understood, did not work on the Jewish Sabbath or on Jewish holidays. Even the Christian politicians spoke Yiddish.

Among the older generation, there were religiously knowledgeable people who did not cease learning Gemara or the holy books for a single day. One could always see them in the city's religious house of study and in the houses of worship.

Aside from the Great Synagogue, in the city [there] was the rabbi's little synagogue, a religious house of study, and the houses of worship of the Zydaczower Chasidim, of the Czortkower, and the Stratyner; a Halicz house of worship, a Polish house of worship, which was established by Mendl Polak, the house of worship in the religious house of study, and the "Tailors' Synagogue," which was part of the Great Synagogue.

Among the societies was the Free Burial Society, which was overseen by Yonah Geller, the Talmud Torah with Yehoshua Hammer at the helm, "Bikur Cholim" under the leadership of David Bauer; "Yad Charutzim," "Dorshei Tov," "Linat Hatzedek"

[pp. 139-140]

(an organization of artisans), the Women's Association, of which Sarah Hammer was the president.

Notwithstanding the major changes that took place in the lives of the Jews of Galicia during the years of the First World War, the majority of the Jews of Bursztyn consisted of Chasidim. Approximately 90 percent was traditionally dressed. Although in Bursztyn the rabbis of the Brandwein dynasty "reigned," many Jews were followers of our rabbis.

During the years 1912-1913, the Jewish community numbered 560 tax payers. At the peak of the Jewish community's board stood Zelig Hammer.

During the years 1880-1910, the Jewish population grew in comparison to the others [other populations], according to the following numbers:

Year	Population Number	Poles	Jews	Others
1880	3,953	522 = 13.2%	2,017 = 53.3%	----
1890	4,209	453 = 10.8%	2,174 = 51.7%	----
1900	4,438	541 = 12.2%	2,209 = 49.8%	----
1910	4,896	654 = 13.4%	2,245 = 45.8%	----
1921	3,581		1,431 = 37.4%	----

During the years 1880-1910, the number of Ruthenians grew from 1,324 in 1880 to 1,996 persons in 1910. That is, from 33.5%, it increased to 40.8%. In truth, the number of Poles increased from 522 in 1880, to 654. That is, from 13.2% to 13.4%. In contrast, the number of Jews decreased percent-wise from 53.3% in 180, to 45.8% in 1910, although the absolute number rose during the course of this period from 2,107 to

2,245 people in 1910. In 1921, there were 1,341 Jews among a population of 3,581. In contrast to 1910, the number fell from 45.8% to 37.4%.

An absolute growth both in number and in percent occurred only among the Ruthenian population.

The war during the years 1914-1918 brought with it the utter destruction of the city and of the Jewish population. Heavy battles took place around the city. A large number of Jews fled from the city, westward. A portion of them spent the war years in the refugee camps in Bremen, Moravia, and Austria. A portion managed to reach Vienna.

Following the war, a portion of the Jews of Bursztyn returned to Bursztyn.

Following the fall of the Hapsburg Monarchy and the declaration of the West Ukrainian Republic within the realm of eastern Galicia, "Jewish National Boards" were created in the cities with a Jewish population. In Bursztyn, at the head of the "Jewish National Board" stood Dr. Wolf Schmarak.

During the periods of Ukrainian rulership, the Jews suffered from the difficult economic situation and from the weakness of the central powers in western Ukraine, which could not restrain the anti-Semitism and rampages of the apparatus and military against the Jewish populace.

Before the Poles marched in, Pyetlura's military in eastern Galicia staged pogroms against the Jewish populace in the cities of Bolszowce, Bukaczowce, and Bursztyn, in which 11 Jews were killed. Also, when the Poles conquered the city, the Jews of Bursztyn still did not have any calm or peace.

Translator's Footnotes:

1. Oddly enough, there is no I. included in this original article in the actual Yiddish memorial book.
2. No third "court" is indicated here in the original Yiddish memorial book.

[pp. 141-142] [pp. 53-62 - Hebrew]

My Town of Bursztyn

Dr. Mordechai Haber

If I needed to characterize in a few words the town and its people, I would do this with a single word: readiness-to-help [in Yiddish it reads: "hilfsgreytikeyt"]. Everyone together and everyone individually was always ready to help one another.

The older generation referred to the town as: Little Jerusalem. For over four hundred years, Jews lived in this town. Generations of religious learners and common folk were raised with joint pain and joy, strange conflicts, and arguments, and yet, with so much closeness and love.

I do not know when Bursztyn received the character and name of a town [shtetl]. It is accepted that it was founded in 1654, when Count Potocki created it in the name of his son, and called it Stanislawow. At the same time, Prince Jablonowski invited Jews to come reside at the boundaries of his principality. With this, he had as his goal to develop both trade, as well as artisanship. At that time, Jews were marked as part of the Prince's property, and not as part of the general population.

From headstones in the old Jewish cemetery, we can derive that already in the 16th century Jews resided in Bursztyn. It is, however, possible that this cemetery was not the first one. Also, the old synagogue bore the seal of Romanian architecture of the 17th century. According to the legends that the old folks would relate, Bursztyn was already a large Jewish community, already four hundred years ago.

Geographically, Bursztyn lies between Lemberg and Stanislawow. With the train line it is 96 kilometers to Lemberg; to Stanislawow – 38. There is also a nicely paved highway that connects Bursztyn to these cities. Jews thoroughly resided in the center, where the businesses and shops were located. They worked in all sorts of areas: manufacture, living means, ironworks, leather [work]. There were barbers, tinsmiths, capmakers, tailors, and shoemakers.

In the middle of the circle stood a row of wooden barracks, which were designated for stores. Moshe Feld's tinsmith workshop, Mechl Drimmer's tavern, Moshe Feldbau's butcher shop, [and] the large house of the Hammers were also situated there. Beside Nachman Breiter's house stood the "cabs." This is how they referred to the carriages.

From the city to the train station it was approximately six kilometers. There was also a train station beyond the village of Demianow. In the city, people said that during the process of building the train line, Prince Jablonowski resisted, with the motive that this would disturb the peace of the populace. And he followed through [on this]. They needed to build it six kilometers further away. Beside Mechl Drimmer's tavern stood the porters with their wagons. Standing there were: Yudl Ripacz [sp.?], Moshe from the holy place [likely a reference to the Jewish cemetery], Raphael Isaac, and others. Somewhere further along, next to Nachman Breiter, stood the simple porters: Shachna-Shlomo Machnicki, the small Moshe-Leibl, Hersh Itche's brother-in-law, and others. They were heroes, always bound up in thick twine, and carried the heaviest loads upon themselves, which they carried [to their owners] for earnings of a few groschen [i.e., a pittance].

It was here that Miriam the booth keeper had her kiosk with

[pp. 143-144]

fruit and bread; Leibl, the beadle's wife and other wives who worked hard for their husbands, or widows – for their children. Every Tuesday was a market day. Farmers and traders from various surrounding towns who planted their booths in the middle of the circle came.

Jews also lived in the surrounding villages: Demianow, Martynow, Wochowka, Kuropatniki, Korostowice, Sarnki, Ludwikowka, Nastaszczyn, and others. From the three villages with the name Demianow, there was one village, in which the peasants would not allow any Jews to dwell. On Shabbat [the Jewish Sabbath] the Jews from the villages would come into the city to pray. They belonged to the Jewish community of Bursztyn.

The number of the general population in the town with the peripheries was estimated at 6-7 thousand. Of this, fifty percent were Jews.

The previous generations in the town were not involved in any politics. However, they led vivacious, social activities. There existed various welfare offices, a Linat Hatzedek, whose function was to remain vigilant about ill members. There was an organization, "Hachnasat Kallah." Every Friday, homeowners/proprietors went around collecting donations for poor brides. Every year before Pesach, the adjudicator of Jewish law, Yoel Ginzburg, Yaakov Rude/Rudy, and Yossel Mintz went around town collecting Maot Chitin for Matzot [Matzos] for poor people.

Pogroms

During the First World War, when the Russians took over the town, the Cossacks engaged in robbing Jewish homes, raping Jewish women. It so happened at the time, that a Jewish girl who had freed herself from the hands of a Cossack, fled to the Jewish study house, which was located in the home of my grandfather, Moshe Haber. The Cossack chased after her. Following the cries of the girl, my grandfather ran in. He was at the time already 75 years old, but a fit and strong person, and with force, he tore away the Cossack from the girl, who immediately took flight. The Cossack, filled with murder, attacked my grandfather with his sword, beating him up very badly. From these beatings he grew seriously ill, and a short time later, he died.

In the town there was a bank founded by IKO [i.e., Jewish Colonization Organization]. This was located in David Neiberger's [Neuberger's] house. The artisans also had their own loan office.

In this manner, the town lived calmly, [with] each one helping the other. Only when it came to electing somebody for the Jewish community, or for the [position of] a synagogue or religious study house trustee, did moods grow excited, and stormy arguments flared up.

In the synagogue building there was an anteroom in which artisans would pray. Nute the tailor was the trustee. His representative was Fishele, also a tailor. During the holidays, they all prayed in the synagogue. They would sit on the benches in the very back, not feeling as at home as in the anteroom.

The conflagration during the time of the First World War also affected both of the religious study houses. The large study house they rebuilt following the war. In contrast, the smaller one, due to a conflict with A. Breiter, was not rebuilt. Jews looked with mournfulness at the destruction.

The city had an important rabbi, a big scholar, Rabbi Moshe David Z"L [i.e., "May his memory be for a blessing."]. In his younger years he lost a leg, and walked on stilts. He benefited from the greatest respect from the entire Jewish populace, not only from the town, but also, from the entire area. Following his death, his younger son, Herzl, following another bitter argument, became the rabbi. There was also an adjudicator of Jewish law, R. Yoel Ginzburg, Z"L. His two sons and daughter all received a secular

[pp. 145-146]

education; and for this reason, he had to withstand much trouble and many insults from the Chasidim in the town. Aside from three religious slaughterers, there was also a trustee, a relative of Shalom Baumring.

At the entrance to the Jewish cemetery, there would be a lot of poor people standing, waiting for a funeral, or visitors on [the occasion of] a Yahrtzeit. One could sometimes also see a volunteer there with a plate for the Keren Kayemet for Israel.

The Jews of Bursztyn were generally calm people, but not cowards. In necessary cases, when there was some threat of danger, the Jews of Bursztyn were always prepared to defend their lives and their honor.

Prince Jablonowski, a religious Catholic, only settled Catholics upon his estates, who parted ways with the Ukrainian Protestants; this purely Polish village was called Ludwikowka. He did this with the express intention of creating a safeguard against the majority of Ukrainians, so that in a situation of need, he would have whom to support himself. He brought the new Polish peasants from eastern Poland, built huts for them in this village. Among the new transplants, were also weavers. Summertime, they worked in the prince's fields, and wintertime, they wove materials for the peasants out of linen from the surrounding area.

Prince Jablonowski always looked for a way to ease the lives of the Polish peasants. And he decided to build a water mill for this village. For this purpose, it was necessary to dig out a new bed for the stream, which would fall into the Dniester. At that time, he brought up many Tatar laborers, who were, however, poorly paid.

As customary, their wrath was taken out on the Jews, and the Tatars began preparing for a pogrom. Also joining them were Polish peasants, and they plunged down upon the town.

In the beginning there was chaos. Jews hammered up their stores and secured themselves inside of their homes. The infuriated Tatars, along with the Poles and Ukrainians, ran wildly through the streets, hitting [window] panes. However, at some point they came upon the Jewish workers of Moshe Feldbau's butcher shop, which was located in the [town's] center. Joining them were other Jews, armed with knives, hatchets, and other work tools. They threw themselves upon the Tatars, who quickly withdrew; and running from fear, they fell, one on top of the other.

On the way, they encountered a Jewish coachman who was driving from Kalisz with his horse and wagon. He was transporting salt for Yehoshua Kletter. A whole crowd of frenzied Gentiles pounced upon him. But he did not lose himself, quickly tore out a wagon shaft from the wagon, ready to defend himself. Also here, the Tatars right away, after the first blows, withdrew.

The uprising of the Jews of Bursztyn came to them unexpectedly. They knew that one can beat and murder Jews without fear of receiving any punishment. The strength and heroism of these Bursztyn Jews was for them an enormous surprise. For the first time, these pogromists felt that they were threatened with danger for their own lives, and in great panic, they fled. The town emerged with small losses. In the meantime, a gendarmerie arrived from Rohatyn. In the town there was complete calm.

This occurred at the end of the 19th century. Many years later they still spoke about this case in the area. The heroism of the Jews of Bursztyn also served as encouragement for the surrounding Jewish towns.

Jewish Heroes

In the town there were two families, which were exclusively involved in the horse trade.

[pp. 147-148]

This was the Shurkmanns and the Glotzers, who were referred to as the "chatshyuliks."[1] The Shurkmanns were an old, veteran family in the town. In contrast, Wolf Glotzer came from another place, and got married to a girl from Bursztyn. All of them were eminent heroes who bestowed fear upon the surrounding peasants.

There was a Gentile, Michajlo, who worked as a guard in the city brickyard, and lived there later on with his family. He would pick quarrels with the Jews, insult them, [and] beat them up. A tall man, a strong man, he would yet like to get drunk; and at the time, there was no limitation to his coarseness/vulgarity. Nobody wanted to go near him and avoided him, until one time when he came upon one of the horse traders, who got even with him for all the times, and beat him up so much, such that he never again attempted to bother a Jew. From that time forth, the town breathed more easily.

During the years 1917-18, at the end of the First World War, fights continued for a long time between the Ukrainians, Poles, and Bolsheviks in the Bursztyn area. Because of its strategic placement, Bursztyn sustained a key position. It is clear that the scapegoat was always the Jewish population. Everybody tore pieces from them [i.e., ganged up on them]. Whichever army went through there robbed and raped Jewish women, filling the town with wailing. The women were raped in the presence of their husbands, parents, and children. The most heavily felt in the town were the Petlyura-ists. Jewish life was utterly abandoned. In the pogroms and rapes participated both the Ukrainian peasants, as well as the intelligentsia, who demonstrated the lowest degree of animalism and sadism.

The bands of the Polish, General Haller, did not fall [far] behind. They became well-known for chopping off the beards of elderly Jews. Just as in every Jewish town, the soldiers in Bursztyn also received free reign from their general, and were permitted to do with the Jews as they pleased. The town was robbed and impoverished. Many Jewish homes were burnt at the time. In addition, there was the huge conflagration of 1921, when half of the town went up in smoke. Were it not for the help of the Joint at the time, it would have spelled the complete downfall of the Jews.

The Joint, at that time, organized a people's kitchen in Bursztyn, which was located in the building of the Baron Hirsh Synagogue. For the homeless families, temporary barracks were erected. One of these barracks was situated on the spot of R. Moyshele's burnt-down house, next door to Yosef Shlomo Rudy. Another barrack was erected next to the Great Synagogue.

Aside from the collective help with which the Jewish community dispensed, significant help also arrived for individuals from various relatives in America, which helped a lot of Jewish families get back on their feet.

These are the sad, the tragic episodes of Jewish life in Bursztyn. But each one of us also has his nice memories, firstly, of one's childhood years.

In the Glow of [One's] Radiant Childhood Years

Like a glow was the winter with its play in Bursztyn. Just as soon as the first snow fell, we immediately took out our sleds, which nearly every boy owned. Because for whomever this was purchased, he himself mastered it, for what sort of face would winter have without a sled? This was one of the greatest pleasures, to go out beyond the city, and slide down from the mountains to the valley, flushed, screaming, frolicking, without worry. The guiltless, genuine childish joy of competition, as to who would sooner reach the designated goal. It is understood that the one who won was he who had a better

[pp. 149-150]

sled. The poor, wooden sled could never catch up with the metal-forged and precision-made one.

Occasionally, one would also hitch a ride with a coachman, who would place his wagon upon wheels and harnessed his horses, wintertime, with bells around their throats, connected to the light sleigh, which literally flew across the snowy roads. When we hurriedly got onto one of those sleighs, there was nothing that was comparable to our joy at the time.

When the river, Gnila Lipa was already well frozen, with a thick layer of ice, the soda water and lemonade dealers would break up whole chunks of ice and bury them deep in the ground for the forthcoming summer. Yosef Shlomo Rudy, Chaim Stryzower, and others concerned themselves with this.

The most freezing temperatures were [felt] during the months of January and February. However, even then, it would so happen that the sun would warm things up in the middle of the day, and from the rooftops and windows it would pound down until evening time, when the sun set, and the temperatures once again dropped. All the windows and rooftops were then covered with hanging icicles, which served as playthings for the children, the following morning.

The forest, enveloped in white, empty, even in winter, did not cease attracting children and adults to it. The starlings, which did not leave the forest the entire year, echoed with their happy chirping. An exceptional event was Shabbat Shira, when father and mother would go with us to throw crumbs to the birds, and it appeared as though all of winter's nature was singing a song, praise to heaven and to life.

A beloved place for the youth to go sledding was also situated between the Christian cemetery and the home of the Malikows, who delivered bricks for my grandfather's brickyard. Here, we felt protected against the assaults of the Polish and Ukrainian hooligans.

Beautiful, Unforgettable Figures

Small and poor was our town. However, it had splendid figures. Many years have passed and I cannot precisely recall the names or lifestyles of everyone. But they stand before my eyes, and from their figures limitless, heartfelt warmth streams down upon me.

Bursztyn was a religious Jewish town. There were many Chasidim there, who followed various rabbis, who would frequently come to the town with their trustees, stayed at [the homes of] the well-off Chasidim, and led their tables[2] there. They would come in the middle of the week and remain over the Sabbath, leading the Musaf prayer at the pulpit of the large religious study house.

Following the Sabbath the rabbi would listen to all of his Chasidim [or followers], doled out advice, and granted blessings, and in addition, accepted the donations that everyone gave, according to his ability. In addition, the trustees would also receive very fat profits.

To these beautiful, unforgettable figures belongs Moyshele Rudy, who had lost a leg in his youth. He was a great religious scholar and was loved by the entire populace. He had a small factory of soda water, which the children later took over. R. Moyshele Rudy was also a Mohel in the town, for which he did not receive any money. Following his death, Berele Haber became the Mohel, who though not such a scholar as R. Moyshele, was a very religious and honest Jew. Until the time of the First World War, he lived in the village of Svitanok, next to Bursztyn. He made his livelihood from dealing in cattle. But whenever he had a Bris, he would pass up on the very best marketplace. The good deed of [performing] a Bris stood higher for him than all material profits.

Bursztyn's youth group

[pp. 151-152]

The Happiest Day of the Year

Simchat Torah was the only day when the Jews of Bursztyn allowed themselves to drink and become intoxicated. In the town, it was the happiest day of the year. People danced in the streets. Poor and rich, young and old, would break into a happy round dance and sang. Old Gentiles who had music boxes with canaries and gave concerts in the marketplace, came to the town, allowing themselves to join in the joy and play along. The blind Jewish singer, Mechl, would on that day, sing his entire repertoire.

Not far from Moshe Strickendreier and his wife, Ita, two good, honest people, lived Dovidale the cantor, a prayer leader in the large study house. From the small upkeep that he received there, he was unable to subsist, and had to earn additional [profits] by teaching boys. With him, there were already more adults learning. Notwithstanding his poverty, he was always happy, ready for everyone with an expression [and] a joke.

An important imposing figure in Bursztyn was that of Hersh Schlesinger. During the time of the various upheavals, when Bursztyn went over from one army to another, and not a single Jew could show himself in the street, the Minyan was held at Hersh Schlesinger's home, where the surrounding residents came together to pray, behind nailed down doors. With his dominating aristocratic demeanor, he also affected the other Jews. In his home everyone felt calm, full of belief and hope in better times. He was a big scholar and a beloved activist, ready to come to the aid of every needy individual.

His wife had a store of manufactured goods in the [town] center. In addition to her marketing skills, she also had the virtue of natural modesty and humility. For the men's social activities she demonstrated the warmest understanding.

Meir Walches, a poor Jew, who nonetheless, never stopped conducting himself with the utmost honesty in his relationships with people. He lived on the street that stretched all the way to the Jewish cemetery, in an old, decrepit little house. There, he had a small, compact little shop where the peasants would bring him flax, and he would sell it to other, bigger merchants, leaving for himself the smallest profits, as much as one would give a delivery boy for making a delivery. Nobody ever heard him complain about his impoverishment.

A central personality in the town was David Neuberger, the soul of the Jewish community. Much want and desolateness were alleviated by him. He blotted out many disputes. Everywhere that he got involved, he brought peace and happiness.

Following the First World War, his house became a point of aid for all needy individuals. Aside from the Joint's aid, he, too, gave from his own pockets. He was a big timber merchant and was the first in the town to give his children a secular education. His children were the first students in Bursztyn. But their son, Munye, died before completing his studies. His death broke his parents terribly; they grew indifferent to their own business, which began to go downhill.

But even in the most difficult times, the refined character of the Neubergers did not change. They still retained all their lovely manners, thanks to which their figures remain forever etched in my memory.

Moshe Yosef Tobias was an old Austrian official. In the house where he lived, outside of the city, was the post office; opposite the Ukrainian church, he built for himself prior to the First World War, a four-story house. Following the war, he sold it for Ukrainian money, which, shortly thereafter, lost its value.

[pp. 153-154]

As far as the house was concerned, later on, there were lengthy lawsuits.

Moshe Yosef Tobias' younger son, Philip, who studied law, was a legionnaire with Pilsudski; later on, a lawyer in Bursztyn, was thoroughly assimilated and had a Christian wife. During the German occupation, he was the representative of the Judenrat.

Organizations and Their Devoted Members

The Right Poalei Tzion, early on in its existence, carried out lively cultural activities among the youth. The I. L. Peretz Library was situated in the building of the Baron Hirsch School. There, courses were organized for those who could not read and write.

The library named after I. L. Peretz

Among the most active were: Yitzchak Landner, Yisroel Leib Fenster, Leib Krochmal, Fishl Schneider, [and] Heller, Nachman Geller's son-in-law. The work that they conducted at the time was exceptionally meaningful. However, it did not last for long. Soon came the fissure, which tore apart this important cultural activity.

In Yisroel Leib Fenster's barber shop, where comrades would get together, Bundist newspapers and proclamations would sometimes appear. In the midst of many youths, there existed a [state of] chaos. The constant arguments disturbed every regulated [form of] work.

The members of the "Hitachdut" Party consisted mostly of well-to-do children. Dr. Besen, a lawyer who was elected a representative in the city council, simultaneously led discussions among the youth, where Zionist problems were discussed.

In 1925, Chaim Ginzburg, the adjudicator's son who had studied in Lemberg, founded "Gordonia." Following his departure, Yisroel Weiss took over; however, shortly thereafter, he left it ["Gordonia"].

A few people remained behind after the difficult cataclysm, which hit the Jewish people, and as with hundreds of other Jewish towns, Bursztyn was likewise obliterated. Those who had the opportunity to come to Israel, feel the great obligation to write, recall, and tell future generations the history of the destruction of our most beloved and dearest. May these very lines of mine be a brick in the headstone for our town of Bursztyn.

Translator's Footnotes:

    1.   "Chatshyuliks" is quite possibly a reference to the Hutsuls, an ethno-cultural group associated with parts of the Ukraine and Romania. There is a breed of horses known as the "Hucul Pony," which may help account for the presumed reference to the Hutsuls in the above context, since there is discussion here of horse-breeding.

    2.   In Yiddish the word used here is "tish," which in this context connotes a gathering of fellow Chasidim assembled around a table in the company of their rabbi.

[pp. 155-156]

Prince Jablonowski and the Jews of Bursztyn

Yisrael Fenster, Haifa

Yisrael Fenster

A Chapter of History in the Life of the Jews of Bursztyn

Just as in all the other towns of Poland, the Jews of Bursztyn also overcame much pain and suffering. Hundreds of years of living on this soil did not extinguish the generations of prejudice, widespread [blood] libel, and the senseless hatred of the non-Jewish populace toward us. However, in this headstone that we are erecting for our town, we are also looking to immortalize, along with the pain, every light-filled moment in the history of generations of Jewish life on this very soil.

In the Bursztyn registry book, which was handed down from generation to generation, safeguarded and [then] lost, along with the Jews of Bursztyn, was recorded the first arrival of the Jews, whom Prince Jablonowski brought to Bursztyn. Along with the ungenerous [or stingy] words that remain in my memory, the objectiveness and honesty of our grandfathers, the simple Jews of Bursztyn, remain etched in my memory. Although they understood the factors that swayed the prince to bring the Jews and build special houses for them, they could still not forget the act itself, and observantly underscored this; the refined humaneness, which the Poles so seldom showed us in all the later generations, up until the final destruction.

At R. Zelik Hammer's [home] there was a registry book, which was already hundreds of years old. In this registry, all the important events in Jewish life in Bursztyn were recorded. Many generations recorded the events of their [own] time, there.

In that registry was also recorded that the first Jews had been brought to Bursztyn by Prince Jablonowski, who hailed from the Polish royal family, Skarbek.

The prince built

[pp. 157-158]

special houses for the Jews. Some of them stood until our [own] time, and we [still] recall them. 1) The inn/tavern, which bordered on the prince's palace. More recently, Chaim David Glaser Z"L and his family, as well as the children of Wolf the Great [or Big Wolf] Z"L, lived there. 2) Opposite the inn/tavern was the house of Yehoshua Hammer Z"L, where until the Second World War lived his son, Itshe Hammer Z"L and his family. 3) Opposite the house, from the other side of the street, was the property of Moshe Leib Tobias Z"L (opposite the pharmacy). On that property there also once stood such a house. The house burnt down in 1901, or 1902. 4) There, where the profanation, a tavern in which sharp [alcoholic] drinks were sold, once stood – the profanation was the property of the prince – up until the First World War. Jews would lease this from him.

R. Wolf Krochmal Z"L

For many years he was the buyer and seller of the prince's mill.

If I am not mistaken, the last lessee was R. Berish Gelernter Z"L. As a seller, I recall R. Itshe Gutstein Z"L, there. Until more recent times, the children of Berl Haber Z"L lived in the house. From Meir Gutstein Z"L there were also a few stores in the house.

The houses that were mentioned were big, massive, all built in one style.

In these houses, the prince settled "his Jews." The prince brought the Jews, so that they would develop commerce in the town and in the surrounding area.

The large mill that belonged to Prince Jablonowski, was likewise, up until the First World War, in Jewish hands. It was leased for many years by the Friedlander brothers.

The mill stood beyond the village of Ludwikowka. It worked by steam and by water. At the time, it was the largest mill in the area; the Bursztyn mill was known throughout all of eastern Galicia.

Above the gate of the mill was written: "Pray and work."

This is what the prince demanded of his workers, who were all Christians. The administration was, however, entirely Jewish.

Direct and indirectly, the Jews earned their livelihood through the prince's mill.

The courtyard itself at the time, was nearly entirely sealed off to Jews. The palace, as it was called in Bursztyn, stood in the center of the Jewish neighborhood/area. A Jew, however, did not dare to venture there.

They would sometimes call in a Jewish artisan when he was needed. A Jewish physician, then, when there was no Christian one.

Jewish merchants would not be permitted into the palace.

Opposite the courtyard, in the equerry, where the stalls were housed, was also housed the administration, the office. There, one would settle matters with the Jewish merchants.

Following the death of the old prince (he committed suicide), in 1910, approximately, the "younger prince,"

[pp. 159-160]

as he was called in Bursztyn, took over the inheritance. He did not take over a terribly big inheritance, for the elder [prince] had already squandered a large portion of his estate.

Several tens of villages surrounding Bursztyn were at one time the property of Prince Jablonowski.

Following the First World War, the younger prince apportioned the majority of the remaining fields and lived well. From the great estate remained the palace with 700 acres surrounding the mill. The younger prince indeed, died young. There remained the princess and four daughters. The princess, who hailed from Greece, ran the small enterprise by herself. She was a very likeable and liberal-minded woman.

Over time, Jewish merchants, artisans, and so on and so forth, began to enter the courtyard. The writer of these lines would frequently arrive before the princess and her daughters, so as to cut their hair and give them permanent waves. The eldest daughter married a baron, Heydel was his name. Following the princess' death, Baron Heydel was the landowner. He transformed all of the terrain into rivers and raised fish. Bursztyn's Jews partook of this fish on the Sabbath. Part of it went to livelihood. Jewish merchants from Lemberg, Drohobicz, and even from Warsaw, would come to purchase the fish.

The Jablonowski courtyard does not exist any longer, exactly like there are no existing Jews in Bursztyn.

The Russians sacked the palace. All that remained was a small house in a corner, a chamber. In the ruins lives the only surviving Jew of Bursztyn, Fishl, the tailor's son-in-law, Ulke the shoemaker.

[pp. 161-162]

The School Named for Baron Hirsch
[or The Baron Hirsch School]

Yosef Schwartz, New York

Yosef Schwartz, New York

A legend from the olden days tells of our wise men, that they lay covered by the snow, so as to learn Torah. The urge for knowledge thrived in various forms among Jews at all times. In the hungriest homes of our impoverished town, fathers and mothers dreamt of giving their children knowledge, Torah, and Gemara. Over the course of time, this thirst also included secular knowledge.

How much dedication and endurance, devotion and intelligence was demanded, in order to establish in those up-to-the belt sinking-in-muck Jewish towns in Galicia; schools, which should inwardly, in [terms of] content, be Jewish, and should give their children modern mastery [or knowledge] and secular knowledge!

The school named for Baron Hirsch in Bursztyn was the source from which the most dedicated and active of our town drew spiritual [or intellectual] resources at that time, for the holy matter of education.

The Jews of Bursztyn did not agree so quickly to send their children to a school in which "Goyish" was taught and one sat without a cap [i.e., a yarmulke or kippah]. It did not take long, however, and the poor Jewish populace was persuaded by this serious aid, which the school was offering. Already in the beginning of the school year 1898/9, 135 children registered, among whom 28 were from the surrounding villages, where Jews dwelled.

The school consisted of two first grades. In the kitchen, which was organized by the school, sat 80 children; one hundred benefited from aid and clothing and schoolbooks with writing utensils. With time, the aid included even more children. The school arranged various excursions, in which children who were also from outside of the school, participated.

That same year, the school administration arranged evening courses for adults, in

[pp. 163-164]

which 58 fully illiterates participated. The same teachers taught them in the evenings reading and writing. 42 of them sat through exams, which they did well on.

The second year, many new students arrived, and two more classes were added. They added another teacher for general studies, Miss Solomka Reichmann, and a new teacher for Hebrew, Peretz Gross.

In 1902/3, the school received an official permit. At that time, it consisted of four grades, and still belonged to the lower category. The number of students climbed to 219.

The school was once visited by the district inspector from Stanislawow, and twice by the national inspector, Baranowski.

The crowdedness was felt and disturbed the school's development. A decision was made to build a special school building. A place was already even purchased, but apparently, the board of trustees was lacking funds to proceed with the building.

The same year, the school administration sent several students to artisans, to teach them trades. One as a tailor, two as tinsmen, and two as carpenters.

The school expenses for that year, not counting the pensions of the teachers, came to 10,394 kronen. To this, the city municipality contributed 1,000 kronen, and the cultural municipality, 400 kronen.

The small yeshiva in Bursztyn

The number of children that attended the school was, according to age:

Under 6 years	3 boys
6-7 years	15 "
7-8 "	26 "
8-9 "	21 "
9-10 "	26 "
10-11 "	18 "
11-12 "	13 "
12-13 "	16 "
13-14 "	7 "
Over 14 years	1 "
	145 children

In the first grade there were – 46 children, second – 50 children, third class – 68 children, and the fourth grade, 32 children. In total, there were 145 school children, with an increase that same year, 1902/3, in the evening courses, in which learned:

From 14-17 years	8 students
" 17-20 "	16 "
" 20-24 "	8 "
" 30 and above	4 "

Just as soon as the boys completed the fourth grade, the school administration saw to it that the child should study further, or they saw to it that two years later, the child was handed over [i.e., admitted] to learn a trade.

At the end of 1904, when the school was already in

[pp. 165-166]

its own building, in the so-called narrower street, or, as it was referred to: Asher Deichsler Street (under table/chart no. 628, which cost 24,560 kronen and 25 heller), the school administration gave [the building] over to the schooling of artisans, bakers 1, tailors 1, shoemakers 1, tinsmiths 5, carpenters 1, boys. The school administration would itself also pay the costs of sending poor children to study in higher schools [schools of higher education], gymnasia and government schools, and would take care of them in their dormitories in Lemberg, Stanislawow, and also Krakow, insofar as room and board.

The elementary school in Bursztyn, hundreds of Jewish children received elementary knowledge here

In 1906, at the Baron Hirsch representation, a fund was founded for vocational schools for girls. Also, in Bursztyn, under the leadership of the director, Antshl Fogel's wife, such a school was founded in the building – following three years of study, the girl, who completed the sewing school with excellence, received a Singer [sewing] machine for free. The majority of the girls who received these machines were sewers, as they were called by us, "needlewomen" of undergarments. There were, however, also cases (truthfully, not too many) when those who completed the Baron Hirsch Vocational School went to the bigger cities, so as to progress further in their trade.

I began attending the Baron Hirsch School. It was at Asher Deichsler's home, where we school children would ourselves work the garden. Already for the children of the third, fourth grade, small wallets were distributed by the leadership of the schoolteachers. Under the personal inspection of Fogel, every boy, following the teacher's example/demonstration, buried his own wallet with a diskal. They passed out various seeds: carrots, beets, beans. The school child, the owner of the wallet, after attending to his wallet, recorded his name on a writing tablet, and placed it in the front of his wallet. Twice a week, beginning in the fall, the teachers went out to attend to [matters] (repairing, cleaning out the muck, and in this manner, pick up the pieces of earth that would crumble/break down during a beating rain) with the children. Everyone with his [own] wallet.

Every boy was so bound with love to the agricultural work, that even when one was out of school, he would go to see the fruits of his labor. The children were enchanted by this work, such that if

[pp. 167-168]

one [of them] found a piece of free land next to his parents' house, about which one was scarcely bothered insofar as a garden [was concerned] (it was sooner a place in which to pour out the slops) these very children from the Baron Hirsch School would clean it up and plant it with something, at least with flowers – and the parents, overworked, worried about where it [i.e., money] would come from – after all, it was already Thursday – for the Sabbath, would reap joy from their Yossele, Shloymele, or Chaim'l. Although most [of them] conceded that God must help, and that he would soon help [them] out with their livelihood, he was already viewed as a companion/an assistant by some of the artisans.

The Great Virtue of Attractive Handwriting

The school instruction, as generally in the government schools, was in Polish. The teachers would also speak Polish amongst themselves; only the Hebrew teacher, Peretz Gross, would speak to us in Yiddish, even when he taught something from another subject matter. Discipline was strict. The teacher was never without his rod, although it was seldom used for beating. The first grade would learn all the time, all the subjects, aside from Hebrew. That was taught by Miss Segal. The second, third, and fourth grades were taught by Fishl Rottenstreich and Fogel. Also, Gross would assist with the general subjects. And when he would have the Hebrew one in the first grade, Miss Segal would help out with other classes with something from the general subject matter. Religion was taught in the Polish language. There were chapters from the prayer book that were specially translated for the Baron Hirsch School into Polish. In the third and fourth grades, religion was taught by Director Fogel. From the very beginning, we had to translate "Ma tovu ohalecha" up until "Aleinu le-shabeach." If one of the children became an orphan, he would be taught extra to understand the Kaddish. All the children would receive ready-made notebooks for writing in calligraphy. Just as soon as he [the child] completed one notebook, he received another. I recall my friend, Yitzchak Schneiweiss-Cohen (today in Israel), whom I always envied for his beautiful and quick penmanship. Until I had completed one notebook, he had already completed two. Excelling in beautiful penmanship were Nachman Kutner and a carpenter's son, Duntzi, who became a home schoolteacher, after completing the Baron Hirsch School. He would instruct children, and in this manner, aided his poor parents.

In every classroom hung four pictures. The Kaiser Franz-Joseph 1 and his wife, Elizabeth, and the Baron Moshe and his wife, Clara Hirsch. At the beginning, before the study hour began, we would always say a prayer in the Polish language for the life and well-being of the Kaiser. If I am not in error, we would also sometimes say the same prayer in the German language.

From 8 to 10 we learned. Then, there was a break of approximately fifteen minutes. We would go out to play in the yard, where there were swings prepared for gymnastics. There was also a broad, splendid bar, where we would do "squats." There was also a special hour for physical culture. Our teachers, each one with his class, would spend this hour outside. Even at the coldest times, we would have to be outside.

In the lowest level of the building were: an administrative office for the teachers, where they would hold their conferences, an apartment for the school caretaker (this was a tall Gentile, whom we called "speedy"), and the bathrooms.

She [the caretaker] would have [more than] enough trouble from us. Given that we small urchins were not always disciplined, we would occasionally write on the walls in the corridor, and not one of us was severely reprimanded for doing this, if caught. Particularly, by Director Fogel.

During the winter, in a special, prepared room, lunches would be distributed to the poor children. These were cooked by an experienced cook, Mennie Mindeles, whose boys went to school together with us. One of her sons, Itzik Hersh, studied very hard. The school administration sent him, after he completed school, to a tailor, to learn; and indeed, up until the Second World War, he was a good men's tailor in Bursztyn, where he was gassed [to death], just like all of the Jews of Bursztyn, by the Hitlerists and their accomplices, may their names be obliterated.

Every year, on the occasion of Franz Joseph's birthday (the 18th of August), would be a holiday for us children. We would arrive, festively dressed-up. The "tluzmizshlekh" or boots were shined or smeared with trona (which we would purchase for a greitzer [i.e., a 'kreuzer'] from Itzele Schapira, or Koppel Henech). At the synagogue, we would cover the Torah ark with the festive curtain [used for covering the Torah ark]. All the important proprietors, along with Zelig Hammer, would already wait at the synagogue. The rabbi, as well as the adjudicator of Jewish law, would hold a talk for the Kaiser, and at the end, we would sing – not in Polish, but in German – "God Save." Once, I recall, the mayor, Bodni, an old Ukrainian, who by profession was a bricklayer, also came to the school.

At the school would also gather the Jewish intelligentsia, lawyers, doctors, and also their children, who came for vacation from the gymnasia in the large cities, such as Lemberg and Stanislawow.

The Jewish pharmacist, Tierhaus, would come with his wife and two sons. After finishing the birthday of the Kaiser, we began preparing once again for the school year (the 1st of September). Already two weeks before the beginning of the school's instruction, the teachers would sit for a few hours of the day in the school's administrative office and record the small 5-6-year-olds, who had begun to attend the school.

"Better" and "Lesser" and the Big Scuffle

An entire year during which we learned, it was not too bad for the schoolboy, but a few weeks before the end of the school year (the end of July), most [of us?] attempted to reconstruct/retrace that which had come earlier, which had perhaps been frivolously/rashly lost. With fear in our hearts, we awaited the certificates [i.e., report cards]. Not one [person] was yearning to be [simply] a "passing" [student], just so that he could enter the next grade. He who schmoozed the best, those who knew for certain that they would pass, waited with fear in their hearts for the "award" of a little red book with lovely stories for their best certificate/report card. In every grade there were 2-3 such boys.

The worst was for the boy who was not a bad student, but whose single shortcoming was his conduct. There was a special category on the certificate, which in the case of a negative comment, would impede one from going on to a higher class. It happened to me, myself, during the first half of the year when I was in the second grade, that I received such a "reprehensible" [mark or comment], but I tried (with the help of my mother Z"L, who explained to me the entire half-a-year, what came of disobedience) to repair this. And with "manners/mores," it was not at all an easy matter. Children would divide themselves up according to the "better" and "lesser" [ones]. Arguments with name-calling would occur, and this would often lead to scuffles in the yard, during the "break" [i.e., recess].

And I recall such an instance. By us there was a boy who was a big slugger. We would refer to him as Shmuel Reczki (Wolf the horseman's boy. Naturally, he had friends who were strong horsemen). There was an instance when he picked a quarrel with Sumer Kleinfeld, one of Ezriel Kleinfeld's strong lads from Korostowice. It was precisely at the pump (where one had hung a chain inside of a small cup [with the message]: pumped water for drinking). Shmuel and his

[pp. 171-172]

friends had already long since prepared the strong lad (who was, in spite of his 12-13 years, a student in the fourth grade), [and] picked a fight with him; however, Sumer, a sturdily built, hardworking village boy, who would help in the village, along with his brothers, attend to the fields on their property, did not want to suffer from this little Shmuelikl. And when he [Shmuelikl], under the pretension of his friends, wanted to tear out the cup of water from Sumer['s hands], Sumer did not spend much time thinking, and split open Shmuel's forehead with the cup.

In a minute, all of the teachers were [standing] around. They brought a doctor. He bandaged up Shmuel's head. But with lightning speed, Shmuel's father, Wolf the small one, as well as other boys, big ones from among the horsemen, came to get a hold of the village boy. But Sumer was already on the other side of the fence, and through Prince Jablonowski's garden, he ran to his home in Korostowice. It was long months that Sumer did not appear in the town. Over a year later, in the summer, he left for America. People schmoozed that it was on account of the horsemen that he had fled.

Such a lot of scuffles in smaller numbers would often be played out among us little "urchins." So it is no surprise that every year, there would at least not be any large percent, but indeed, [there were a] few with "reprehensible actions."

In general, though, the Baron Hirsch School was a blessing and a help for the children and for our parents in the town. Even the most religious Jews in the town, who were initially not satisfied with the Baron Hirsch School (out of fear of a bad Jewish path) to send their children to [the] school, would indeed with respect, bring to our teachers their children to register them. It is a shame, they would say, that there is no Baron Hirsch School for girls.

Speaking about the Baron Hirsch School, we will also recall the so-called Baron Hirsch Banks. In the town there were two official private banks. One was Avrahamele Bobar's bank, and the other one, if I am not in error, Neiberger's. Aside from this, there were the so-called "chashters," [i.e., money lenders] who would take very large percentages. A poor artisan or a petty merchant could never come borrow there. Firstly, one needed to have good co-signers, and secondly, as much as was possible to pay up such high percentages, these "IKO" Baron Hirsch banks became a salvation for the poor artisans and petty merchants. One could borrow there up to 200 kronen for a year with a very minimal percent [i.e., fee]. This percentage was taken so as to cover the administrative expenses, and at the time of the co-signing, they did not scrutinize so carefully. It used to be that the borrower could be both the husband and the wife. It could reach up to 400 kronen within the [same] family, and every week they would bring in partial payments. Director Fogel and one of the teachers oversaw the banks. Mostly, it was our teacher, Fishl Rottenstreich. The school as well as the bank were [both] active until the outbreak of the First World War in 1914. After the war, when Austria broke up, the building of the Baron Hirsch School served the Jewish community. The Peretz Library was there until 1939, approximately 20 years, since 1919.

[pp. 173-174]

Our Teachers

These were people whose desire and activity was driven by a deep feeling of responsibility and by much love for the Jewish child. They possessed within themselves the synthesis of old Judaism and new scholarship, lofty humane ideals and moral beauty. They dreamt and believed that the loftiest and most beautiful ideals of humanity would be fulfilled, and that the Jewish people would have its national establishment. Therefore, they and their teachers are so deeply etched within our memory.

Anshel Fogel

Anshel Fogel was the soul of the Baron Hirsch School. Always serious, even strict. One seldom saw a smile on his face, even in the company of the other teachers. Not only the school children, but the entire city had a great deal of respect for him. When teaching the students every class period, he would make it so clear, that the children would leave [at the end of] the hour of learning with him like newborns. He would place the most weight on that which he had taught, so as to plant love for physical work in the children. He hated idlers. It would occasionally happen that the poor people would come to the town with their wagons; right away they would take the children on their hands, letting them loose through the doors. But if a single wagon were to come into the school, Fogel would become terribly upset. Even then, if it was an older person, he would give him a donation with such anger; one time he said to us children: You will turn into such parasites if you do not learn a trade. He held highly of farming peasants. He would also persuade children who wanted to learn something to go to the IKO school in Slobodka-Lesna, next to Kolomyja. But in our town, there were few who participated. If they were already going to learn a trade, then they would learn to be carpenters; tinsmiths, plumbers, and watchmakers. Fogel was not strictly religious. He would only go pray with a Minyan on Jewish festivals and holidays. But when his father died, he only first shaved after thirty days, and for an entire year, went three times daily to the synagogue to say Kaddish.

Devorah Fogel

His wife was a book peddler's daughter. His name was Yaakov Ehrenpreis. He had three daughters and a son, Dr. Mordechai Ehrenpreis; the chief rabbi of Sofia [Bulgaria] and then of Stockholm. Three of Yaakov Ehrenpreis' daughters lived in Bursztyn. These were Fogel's wife, Dr. David Maltz's wife, and one that was not married, [who] represented the lawyers' administrative office of her brother-in-law, David Maltz, the well-known Zionist leader, who twice ran as a candidate for the Austrian Parliament. Mrs. Fogel ran the girls' vocational school. They had two daughters. One, the younger one, died young. The other one, although raised by Polish

[pp. 175-176]

-speaking parents, later became the well-known Yiddish writer, Devorah Fogel. Anshel Fogel, right after the First World War, left for Lemberg, where he worked as the secretary of the Jewish community. He died in the 1930s.

I visited Devorah Fogel in 1937. She was married to an engineer. They had a two-year-old child, Anshl. Also, her elderly mother lived with them. They had their own house. I visited her a second time in 1940, when the Soviets were already there. She was bitter about the order [of things]; as a devoted Zionist, she saw to what sort of sense this would [all] lead. As a well-known writer, she had the privilege, like other Yiddish writers, to belong to the Ukrainian Writers' Union. She did not want this. She, her husband, and children were murdered like all Lemberg Jews by the Hitler murderers and their accomplices, may their names be obliterated.

Fishl Rottenstreich

His refined face was framed by a lovely coal-black beard. In my memory, he remains [standing] with his fiddle in hand. Just as soon as he appeared before the lectern, even the rowdiest children grew silent. With a shining face he played "God Save, God Protect Our King, Our Land." We also sang after him with much reverence.

Fishl Rottenstreich was a cousin of the well-known Zionist activist and senator in Poland with the same name. Fishl and his wife hailed from Kolomyja. Aside from singing with us, he also taught us to speak Polish and German. With his students he spoke only Polish. With the adults during the evening courses, he spoke Polish and German.

Following the First World War he returned, following a short hiatus, along with his family, to Bursztyn, where they had their sole house, and he was a teacher in the government [state] school.

He died in the beginning of the thirties. His two daughters were teachers somewhere in a small town in Wolyn.

Peretz Gross

The most well-natured teacher, whom I recall. He would speak a juicy Yiddish with us, and would have long talks with us, in which he attempted to plant nice manners in us and tendencies toward proper actions. Also, during the excursions, which he would attend with us in the hills and forests, he would make declarations for all of us in Yiddish.

He was a fiery Zionist and at the same time, a religious person. Every day he went to pray in his Tallit and Tefillin. On the Sabbaths and Jewish festivals, he prayed with Neiberger's Minyan.

Pertaining to his most beloved subjects during his talks with the students, were the stories regarding Israel, regarding the beauty of the land, and the vastness of the Jewish heroes.

To the town once came a messenger from Israel. He carried with him a red cap like that of the Turks and spoke only Hebrew. He came to collect money and also sold soil from Israel. Religious Jews purchased it in small sacks and hid it to place under their heads, following their death, in the grave.

Our director, Fogel, looked askance at everything that he considered deception.

[pp. 177-178]

Gross, however, became so carried away by this Jew's lovely Hebrew, that he invited him nearly every day to his home for lunch and would carry on lengthy discussions with him about the Holy Land.

In my memory remains such a picture: in class there is a tumult, which reaches the point of a scuffle between two children. Then the teacher approaches, calls the two excited children over to the table and asks them good-naturedly why they were beating each other up. Chaim, excited, related how he had lost all of his buttons to Moshe yesterday, and so prior to leaving, he had torn off the buttons from his [Moshe's] pants and jacket. Now, he was once again bothering him.

The teacher turned to the children: "Is this nice?" All those in the choir responded: "No!" Later on, all the children listened to his lecture regarding morals and ethics among children and adults.

This took place in the third grade of the Baron Hirsch School. The name of the teacher was Peretz Gross.

During the excursions that we would take beyond the town, the teachers would provide information in Polish. Peretz Gross would always provide his information in Yiddish.

Peretz Gross taught at the Baron Hirsch School from 1900 until 1914, when the First World War broke out. His specialization was Hebrew and Mathematics. If one of the teachers became ill, he would also fill in for other subjects.

When the Russians approached our town, he left for Vienna, along with his entire family.

In 1936, in Lemberg, I visited the Yiddish writer Devorah Fogel, the daughter of our school director. There, I also met our former teacher, Perl Segal, who was already quite advanced in years, around 80-ish. From her I received the address of Peretz Gross. I wrote him a letter in Yiddish, but his reply arrived in German. He was living in an old people's home. He wrote me that his son, Henry, was living in America.

Yaakov Bigel

For Yaakov Bigel it was characteristic that from his very earliest years he had strived to learn and to teach others. He had very early-on begun to dream about his studies. Until the last day of his life, he clung to the Zionist ideal of liberating the Jewish people from its two thousand-year-long diaspora. In the words of the prophets, he read out [extrapolated] the ideas of social equality; by obtaining higher education he wanted to become more useful and valuable in the struggle for the solution to and existence of the Jewish nation.

He attained higher education but did not live to see with his own eyes the actualization of the Zionist idea.

Yaakov Bigel

[pp. 179-180] [pp. 67-70 - Hebrew]

Zionist Organizations in Bursztyn

Y. Fenster

In our town the Zionist idea began to develop among the masses with the relocation of Dr. David Maltz. [It was] approximately 1900. At that time, that is, before the First World War, the Zionist association

"Chovevei Tzion" was founded. Already then, the association attracted the progressive strata of Jews in the town.

The active proponents and co-fighters for the Zionist idea at that time were: Bunem Schapira, the accountant for Friedlander's mill, A. Tauber, Zalmen Stern, Meir Redisch, Moshe Schumer, Vove Wolf David Frankl, Yisroel Jampol, and Minne[1] Tobias.

A group of members of the "State of Israel" Association
Hertz Weinert, Yona Krochmal, Yosef Schwartz, Isaac Walpitin, Sala Bernstein, Tuvia
and Krancia Schwartz, Koppel Bernstein, Bomech Zager and more

It is worth recalling the characteristic episode (conveyed by Yitzchak Roher, [who today] resides in America), which demonstrates how courageous, determined, and militant the first Zionists in Bursztyn were.

In 1908, approximately, the elections for the Austrian Parliament were held. The Zionist movement already at that time took an active part in the election campaign when the well-known Zionist activist, Adolph Stand Z"L came to Bursztyn to speak at an election meeting. The trustees at the time, who were purveyors of liquor (which they sold to the nobleman), did not want to let him into the synagogue, where the people's gathering was supposed to take place.

The young group opened the synagogue and the crowd, for which A. Stand held a fiery speech, entered.

At a second election gathering, which took place at the Polish People's House, spoke the then-current mayor of Bursztyn –Mayor Diltz. He was very angry at the Zionists, who had the chutzpah to send Jewish candidates to the Austrian Parliament, and menacingly called out: "Do not call out the Wolf from the forest!" – To which Dr. Maltz responded: "We are not afraid, do not frighten us."

Right after the First World War, a Zionist association was once again founded under the same name – "Chovevei Tzion." The association was active under the leadership of Dr. Wolf Schmarak Z"L.

This was a period when the Jewish youth in Bursztyn spiritually [or intellectually] blossomed, and along with that you had all the different Zionist hues.

A "Poalei Tzion" group was founded, which for many years had an impact on the Jewish cultural and political life of Bursztyn.

Almost at the same time, the Zionist Socialist Party – "Hitachdut," was founded, which later on had a great influence on a portion of the youth and was one of the strongest organizations in the town.

The leaders of the "Hitachdut" were very active and oversaw broad information work [i.e., the dispersal of information, knowledge] among the youth. They established courses for those who were preparing to make Aliyah to Israel. They created Hachsharah spots, they taught the Hebrew language, and so forth.

I would like to mention two of the leaders:

    1.   Dr. David Besen was for a period of time a lawyer in Bursztyn, [he was] a dear and beloved person, did a lot of work for the "Hitachdut," [and] as a maven of Hebrew literature, he held

[pp. 181-182]
literary lectures and was always concerned about the cultural level of the party.

    2.   Shlomo Handschuh-Segal Z"L, a lovely figure. Aside from the cheder, it seems that he did not possess any systematic education, which is why he possessed a strong desire to know and understand. He learned on his own – read a lot, he knew Hebrew well, was versed in the Yiddish and Hebrew literature, [and] was a good speaker. He believed fanatically in Zionistic Socialism and was proficient in all the ruminations and folds [i.e., all the detailed ins-and-outs] of the Torah.

A distinguished place was taken up by Beitar, which carried out a two-fold [form of] work. In the final years [prior to World War II], a portion of members went over to the Grossmanists, parting ways from them – [but] nonetheless, Beitar remained one of the strongest parties in the town.

In our town there was no dearth of followers of all the existing Zionist parties in pre-war Poland: "Mizrachi," "Hapoal Hamizrachi," "Noar Oved," and so on and so forth.

All of them, all of them, lived with the hope of being absolved of the diaspora and of someday living a free Jewish and humane life in their own land -------

It, however, turned out differently ----

How horribly different.

Members of the "Hitachdut" in Bursztyn

Among other members: Yaakov Nachwalger, Leib Hersh Kimmel, Gedaliah Kitner, Shlomo Handschuh, Shlomo Mandelberg

Translator's Footnote:

1.   This is a male name, although similar in sound to the female name, "Minna" or "Mina."

[pp. 183-184]

Hebrew Schools

Yisrael Fenster

Those who are mentioned here have, through their dedicated work, earned for themselves much more than these limited words; in this same manner, many others who haven't been written about here, only because we know such few details regarding their life and activity, have likewise earned this.

The several individuals who are mentioned here are a model of the Jewish national consciousness and unrequited thirst for Hebrew culture, with which these very Jews from our town led their stubborn struggle for the education [or upbringing] of the younger generation.

I do not recall anything precise about learning Hebrew in Bursztyn prior to the First World War, however, there were certainly efforts toward establishing Hebrew courses and bringing in modern Hebrew teachers; [and] aside from that, Gross, the teacher, taught religion, [and] Hebrew in Hebrew at the Baron Hirsch School.

Just after the First World War, in 1919, approximately, Dr. Glazer began to teach Hebrew. He later married a zeman[1] and became a teacher at the Hebrew gymnasia in Stanislawow.

Following him came Michal Schwartz. During his time, the study of Hebrew became very popular.

He became an able organizer, a good speaker. He founded the Hitachdut, nearly all of whose members learned Hebrew.

M. Schwartz was in Bursztyn for a few years. He was also culturally active.

When M. Schwartz left Bursztyn, and transplanted himself as a lawyer in Lemberg, Miss Sobel, a very capable and energetic [individual] arrived. Aside from Hebrew courses, she also ran, for the first time in Bursztyn, a kindergarten.

Later on, Haliczer arrived. He moved with his family to one of the rooms in the Baron Hirsch School. Haliczer was a religious person with much education and intelligence; we, a group of already grown-up individuals, learned Tanach from him. From all of this, he received no livelihood; [and] as is the custom, when there is no livelihood, one argues with one's wife. [So] he used to say: I speak to my wife and children only in Hebrew, but when I argue with her, "I shift over to Yiddish," [as] it has another flavor.

Translator's Footnote:

1. It is unclear what "zeman" means in this context. It may refer to a surname, a geographic name, or even a profession. For example, if we consider the possibility of it pertaining to a profession, there is a word in Polish that may be a cognate: "ziemianka," meaning a "landowner."

[pp. 185-186]

The Library in the Name of Y"L Peretz
[or The I. L. Peretz Library]

Yisrael Fenster

There are no more fermenting youths, the rebels against authority, who dared to bring the first shelf of books into the religious town, and called it a library. From these books, there are not even any remaining names [titles]. At that time, when death – with all of its horrors in every which way pursued everyone – the names of the library books fluttered in the wind, like naked shadows from a far-off world; they were desecrated and crushed beneath the enemy's boot.

Up until the First World War, the cheder and the religious study house were nearly the only source from which Jewish children and youth drew their intellectual nourishment in the town. Up until that time, there also existed the 4-grade Baron Hirsch School for boys. Individuals would read a Yiddish book, and a very small number, from [among] those who were perceived as the "intelligentsia," read German.

Following the First World War, during the time when Petlyura-ists and Polish bands staged pogroms against Jews in our area, from which Bursztyn also greatly suffered, the Jewish youth was very embittered. Many of them emigrated at that time to America and Germany, but not everybody had the means and not everybody was able to emigrate.

Following the pogroms, when the Polish powers in eastern Galicia became poisoned with a more-or-less liberal course for the Jews, the social and political life of the Jews also began to take shape. In our town of Bursztyn, the parties of "Poalei Tzion" and "Hitachdut" were then created. The founders of Poalei Tzion were Fishl Schneider and Yosef Schwartz; of Hitachdut – Michal Schwartz (the Hebrew teacher).

The Poalei Tzion represented the proletariat [faction] of the town. In the Hitachdut congregated the proprietary elements.

Theater groups were created. The first theater director was Isaac Breiter. He was a sign painter. The first "actors" were artisans. With the incoming funds, Yiddish books were purchased.

The first Yiddish books were purchased and brought to the town by Yosef Schwartz. On an old, small shelf they were placed, in the house of Nachman Geller. That is where the Poalei Tzion Association under the disguised Yiddish name: "Professional Association of Non-Professional Workers in Bursztyn" was found. The strange name was concocted, because the Poalei Tzion was

[pp. 187-188]

outlawed by the Polish authorities at that time.

The youth read with a rare and exceptional curiosity and fervor. They read Yiddish literature and translations. They "gulped down" these [types of] books: belletristic, political, and scientific/scholarly literature. In 1923, approximately, under the leadership of Minne Tobias, a dramatic circle was created, which stood on a serious level. Plays with a literary value were performed: "Tevye der milchiker" by Sholem Aleichem, "Der dorfs-yung" and the "Iberiker mentsh" by Peretz Hirschbein. "Der Vilner balabesl" by Mark Arnstein, and so on and so forth.

Thanks to the intelligence and good taste of our teacher and friend Minne Tobias, each performance was a cultural event in the town, and for the participants, a serious school, and a spiritual [or intellectual] pleasure. For the funds that streamed in from the performances, books, Yiddish books were purchased. Their count increased from one month to the next. The books were carried over to the Baron Hirsch School building. Also, the Hitachdut Association, which owned a certain number of books, disposed of these.

The idea of creating a non-partisan institution, in which all of the Jewish youth would gather, regardless of their party affiliations, was realized. The "Library in the Name of Y. L. Peretz" was founded in Bursztyn. The founders were: from the leftist groups: Fishl Schneider, Yitzchak Landner, Yehoshua Jampol, the writer of these lines, and others. From the Hitachdut: Shlomo Handschuh, Shlomo Mandelberg, Yaakov Nachwalger, and others. From Beitar: Munye Cohen; Velvl Ostrower and others from the General Zionists: Minne Tobias, Eliyah Fischmann, and others.

Leaders of the Y. L. Peretz Association and a group of youth activists in Bursztyn

At the library, a reading room was created. Intensive cultural activity was carried out. Lectures and readings were organized; youths who lagged behind were taught to write and read in Yiddish. Literary evenings were arranged. The eminent "box evenings," which took place often, drew in hundreds of participants. They were called "box evening" on account of the fact that they would present questions that had been written down, to the assembled crowd. The slips [of paper] would be placed inside of a box. One of those from the council would read over every slip [of paper]. They would usually have interesting questions regarding literature, science/scholarship, [and] politics. For each question, one person from those assembled could respond. Often, interesting

[pp. 189-190]

discussions developed, which were instructive and educational for the youth.

The number of members of the library grew permanently. With them, so did the number of books. They made big new shelves with a surrounding barrier. New tables. [They] painted the walls nicely. The Peretz Library became a tidy cultural corner. The professional intelligentsia in the town, which for the most part, was far-removed from Yiddish and Yiddish literature, began to look respectfully at the work of the Peretz Library. They became members and began to help with various events that the library would arrange. For a long period of time, the pharmacist, Grinhoyt, was active as the chairman of the Peretz Library.

Further drawing in the intelligentsia was the strong anti-Semitic course in Poland, which impeded every approach/drawing nearness of the Jews insofar as social life, in general. The young Jewish intelligentsia, which managed, following the torments and persecutions, to complete a Polish high school, could not, on account of hatred for Jews, receive any work. In the final years before the Second World War, nearly all of these young [members of the] intelligentsia remained sitting at their fathers' and mothers' [homes], in the town. They all gathered together around the Peretz Library.

Many endeavored together, held lectures, helped to organize literary evenings, performances: the Hertz Brothers and Syule Weinert, Lobcia Landner, Hersh Breiter, Goldwert [Goldworth], and others. Everything, it is understood, in the Yiddish language. Participating in the Yiddish performances were people who at home, never spoke a word of Yiddish. Hela Landau, in "Polish af der keyt" by Y. L. Peretz, Goldwert in the recitations of Peretz, which were presented in a rich program during a special evening, dedicated to the great Yiddish writer, and which the writer of these lines, directed.

The overseers of the library were always interested in better Yiddish theater. They brought the Warsaw Yiddish Art Theater to Bursztyn, with the artist, Ida

[pp. 191-192]

Kaminski [i.e., Kaminska], at the helm. Invited were Jonas Turkow and Diana Blumenfeld, as well as the Kleynkunst theater, "Ararat."

The Peretz Association remained in contact with the well-known dramatics clubs, "Goldfaden," in Stanislawow, which carried out its best works in Bursztyn: "Baynakht afn altn mark"[1] by Peretz, directed by the famous David Herman of the Vilner Trupe, the "Goylem" by Leivick, "200 Thousand" by Sholem Aleichem, and so on and so forth.

The Peretz Association had a name throughout the entire area. The number of books climbed into the thousands, everything [being] of the best and most refined. The library was careful/cautious about every [type of] literary trash and hollow novel writings. Many young Bursztyn people grew up/were educated there, learned to understand better and more serious literature.

The Library in the Name of Y. L. Peretz in Bursztyn taught us to believe in the world and human being, in fairness, equality, and in truth. In the final days prior to the Second World War, when many of the founders and overseers of the library left Bursztyn, some far away across seas, some in other places in Poland, those who remained in Bursztyn – although they grew older and were taken up with livelihood worries – they did not neglect the Peretz Library. For the Peretz Library, one always found time.

Dolek Wahl

Dolek Wahl came from Stanislawow. For a long period, he worked as a dentist in Bursztyn. He was an active Zionist. He was a co-worker in the Peretz Association. He stood out with his fiddle playing and would take part in many (social) events.

The 18th of September 1939, the Red Army marched into Bursztyn. Two to three weeks later, they called me in to the Commissar of Culture, a young Ukrainian, who was also the leader of the Komsomol (youth organization) in Bursztyn. The young Gentile was named Krivonos and hailed from Berdichev. He wanted to see the library's catalogs and also the condition of the cash box. He was happy with the book materials. They were kosher. Only, he demanded that I give him the keys to the library. That was the end of the Peretz Association in Bursztyn. Later on, the same fellow told me that they were taking the books over, in the meantime, to the Ukrainian "Proshvito";[2] that they were creating a big library in three languages: Ukrainian, Polish, and Yiddish. He threw down the books onto the top of the "Proshvito," but they no longer picked them up from there. They were eaten up and rotted.

The Polish authorities strongly persecuted the Peretz Library during the final days of its existence. During the years 1937-38, the library was shut down twice by the Polish police, under suspicion of

Communist activity. The last time, it was locked for three months. Following many interventions, the library was opened – but Dr. Avraham

[pp. 193-194]

Ziering and I had to sign a record in which we confirmed that there were no Communist books in the library.

On the 24th of June, 1940, the N.K.V.D. arrested me. I am a Trotsky-ite and a Zionist! – They told me. They had a "document" that I had been in the service of the Polish authorities. They did not show me the "document"; they meant, I believe, the aforementioned declaration that Dr. Ziering and I had signed. They asked me a lot of questions about

A group of Bursztyn girls at an evening of parting for their girlfriend Zelde Pomerantz on [the occasion] of her departure for Argentina

Dr. Ziering. Right away, he left Bursztyn, when the Russians entered. (He knew them well, having spent many years under the Soviet Regime). They sent me administratively (without a trial) for 8 years to an "improvement camp" in Siberia for this major transgression.

May the members who, for many years worked together, actively, in the Peretz Association and were murdered sanctifying the name of God and sanctifying the [Jewish] people, be remembered here.

Minne Tobias

Our rabbi and leader; he taught a group of us youths to comprehend a Yiddish book. He possessed a rare love for the Yiddish classical literature. For Mendele, Sholem-Aleichem, and Peretz. He would read to us from their works, as well as from Ch. N. Bialik, with great enthusiasm. He was a marvelous oral reader, and with his deep understanding, he would interpret in an interesting manner. Himself a Zionist with far-right views, but as a common man, the Yiddish language and literature was close to him, and his students were nearly all precisely from the leftist groups.

Minne Tobias saw in the appearance of the Peretz Library an important cultural and national factor for the Jewish youth at that time in Bursztyn. He was happy with every new book that was purchased. In the early years he was the heart and the brain of the Peretz Association.

Itshe Landner

[He] was among the first founders of the library. The most devoted and hard-working co-worker. For many years, he was the librarian. He initiated the first modern catalogs and introduced order and cleanliness into the Peretz Association. He co-performed in the dramatics circle. [He] was a trustworthy and most feeling friend.

Dr. Avraham Ziering

Right after moving to Bursztyn he became involved with the

[pp. 195-196]

Peretz Association and for a long time, stood at its helm. A proud, nationalistic Jew and a Talmud scholar, he would frequently hold lectures. He ran the box evenings. He participated in literary evenings. He was very much beloved by the youth for his voice of the people and accessibility to people.

Hersh Kaufman

Up until its destruction, he was the librarian, its last librarian. He dedicated a lot of time to the library. With genuineness and devotion [he] worked toward its development.

Koppel Bernstein

In the final years before the Holocaust, he actively co-worked at the library, namely, on the annual reports. As a capable illustrator, he would make tables and diagrams, which provided an idea of the activity and growth of the library.

Translator's Footnotes:

    1.   I have transliterated this title according to the orthographic rules of YIVO, since this is how many (or most) library catalogs appear to have transliterated it.

    2.   "Proshvito" refers to a Ukrainian cultural organization established in the 19th century, which was a proponent of the Ukrainian "folk" and enlightenment. It also served as a cooperative to support the Ukrainians against the Polish nobility and Jewish merchants.

[pp. 197-198]

Chasidism and Rabbis

[pp. 199-200]

Chasidism in Bursztyn

Rav R' Zeidele Eichenstein, New York

Bursztyn was a main type of Chasidic town, from which [Chasidism] streamed outwardly with light to the surrounding towns. "The Rabbi's courtyard" was not merely a physical concept but was also a Jew's path to carrying out the work of the Creator. A Jew should serve the Almighty out of love. More breadth of space also means more light. By doing good, one uproots that which is bad. The more good one does, the more full one will be of joy, with the exaltation of life's beauty.

The Bursztyn Rabbi's Courtyard

Rav R' Zeidele Eichenstein
Grandson of the Bursztyn Rabbi,
R' Nachumtshe ZT"L

.

In 5630 (1870), Rav R' Nachumtshe ZT"L, who came from Stratyn, settled in Bursztyn. In Bursztyn, Rabbi Nachumtshe was a notably good Jew and had Chasidim [or followers] in the thousands, who would come to him from all the surrounding cities and towns all the way to Stanislawow. So as to mention the Jewish communities for eternity, I am including here these cities, in which R' Nachumtshe had his Chasidim: Rohatyn, Bukaczowce, Bolszowce, Halicz, Jezupol, Mariampol, Uscie Zielone, Tysmienica, Nizniow, Nadworna, Tysmyczan, Łysiec, Chodorow, Kolomyja, Stanislawow, and Podhajce. There were many others, however, which I cannot recall. Hundreds of Chasidim also lived in the towns, which once belonged to Hungary.

The Rabbi's courtyard was the center of our town. All the happy occasions that took place there were also a happy occasion for the entire town. The hundreds of Chasidim who would come together here for the Jewish holidays, created an exalted mood in the town. They would also bring in nice business for the shops; and furthermore, they were invested and beloved guests.

In general, the Rabbi's courtyard was the honor of our town of Bursztyn. And in this manner, the Rabbi ZT"L remained in Bursztyn for 44 years. Until 5674 – 1914, when the courtyard was burnt down in the great conflagration, in which three-fourths of the town was burnt down, the Rabbi was compelled to relocate to Stanislawow, since there was no large house in the city, so that the Rabbi and his large family might move back

[pp. 201-202]

to Bursztyn. Were it not for the First World War, which broke out right away that same year, the Rabbi ZT"L would certainly have erected his courtyard in Bursztyn.

The Rabbi was a big Tzaddik [i.e., righteous man] and a big Kabbalist. He left behind 4 compositions. 1) Imrei Tov; 2) Imrei Chaim; 3) Imrei Bracha; 4) Imrei Ratzon – all of them, pertaining to the Kabbalah. The Rabbi had 1 son and 4 daughters. His son, Rabbi Eliezer'l, filled his position following his father, in Stanislawow. The sons-in-law were Rabbi R' Aizikl ZT"L of Podhajce, the Ishtsier Rabbi, R' Ephraim Horowitz. The Bilker Rabbi, R' Leibush. The Shotzer Rabbi, R' Moshe Leib. The Chasidism of Bursztyn split into two [parts], among Rabbi R' Eliezer'l, and the Podhajce Rabbi, R' Aizikl ZT"L. And so it proceeded until the Second World War. However, our city of Bursztyn was blessed with a Rabbi, R' Moyshele ZT"L, the son of Rabbi R' Eliezer'l [and] a grandson of Rabbi R' Nachumtshe ZT"L. He restored his great grandfather's courtyard. And he attracted thousands of Chasidim from nearly all East Galicia, who came daily from near and far. For he was a great wise man and everyone was happy with his advice, which were very often considered to be miracles. Rabbi R' Moyshele ZT"L of Bursztyn was quite famous throughout all of Poland. He led his courtyard in Bursztyn for approximately 15 years. During the extermination of

[Title page of the rabbinic tome: *Sefer Imre Hayim
al Taryag Mitsvot ha-Torah ve-Mitsvot d'Rabanan*
Lemberg, [5]653
Imrei Chaim
Publishing House N. Brandwein
Printed by U.W. Salat
Lemberg, 1893]

[pp. 203-204]

Galicianer Jewry, he and his 3 sons and Rebbetzin were murdered, may God avenge their blood, may their memories be blessed.

Rabbi R' Moyshele ZT"L was beloved throughout the city. [His] was a house where everyone found consolation according to one's wishes/desires. Thanks to the rabbis of Bursztyn, our city of Bursztyn was known throughout the world, and it should remain that way as an eternal memory, among all the people of Bursztyn at all times, wherever they should find themselves.

Unfortunately, from the large holy family there only remained a small remnant. By [sheer] miracle, the Podhajcer Rabbi's R' Aizikl's son, Rabbi The Tzaddik R' Zeidele Shlit"a was rescued and brought to America. He is called the Bursztyner Rabbi in New York. He was born in Bursztyn. And he was raised in the spirit of his great holy father, Rabbi R' Aizikl ZT"L. He carries on the holy chain of the Bursztyn rabbis and of his great father. The Bursztyner Rabbi in New York has a great following. He is famous for being a great activist, wise man, and sage, and in general, a man of Chasidism [or piety].

Kinsmen from Bursztyn and Podhajce are his strong supporters.

The Yahrtzeit of the first Bursztyner Rabbi, R' Nachumtshe ZT"L is the 15th of Elul – he died in 5675; the Yahrtzeit of the Podhajcer Rabbi. R' Aizikl ZT"L died on the 13th of Adar I – in Podhajce, in 1943.

The Environment Surrounding the Rabbi's Home

**R' Leizerl, the Rabbi of Stanislawow,
son of the Rabbi of Bursztyn,
Rabbi Nachumtshe**

Even prior to the First World War, Bursztyn was already a Jewish town. Most of the Jews were involved in trade. There were larger and smaller merchants of manufacture, leather, grain, eggs, cattle, horses, and other [things, goods]. There were also artisans of various types of vocations: tailors, carpenters, tinsmen, shoemakers, [and] capmakers. There were no majorly wealthy people in the town. Of the ninety percent of merchants, not all of them had an abundant livelihood. To the ten [percent] of better-off families belonged the Hammers, Breiters, Gelernters, Horniks, [and] Schumers. The Jewish community's institutions were not large. The only serious cultural institution was the Baron Hirsch School, where the poor children received a second breakfast every day, and twice a year, clothing. The Baron Hirsch School was indeed maintained by the Baron's funds, with a certain subsidy from the Austrian government. The studies were the same as in all the elementary schools, only with the addition of religion. The teachers at the school were Jewish. Their names: Fogel, Rottenstreich, Gross, and also a woman, a female teacher.

In the town were three or four Jewish lawyers, at one time, two Jewish doctors,

[pp. 205-206]

a pharmacist, and individual officials with government positions.

There was a small Zionist group to which Dr. David Maltz, a lawyer who once ran as a candidate on the list for the Austrian Parliament in Vienna, also belonged.

Aside from the school and the small synagogue, there was also a small religious study house, a Czortkower synagogue, a Stratyner, Haliczer, and a Chevra Tehillim. There were also individual Minyanim at the city rabbi's home, at Neiberger's, where one prayed only on the Sabbaths and on Jewish holidays. There was also a prayer house at the Rabbi's home in the town.

In general, it was a Chasidic town. 95 percent of the populace led a Chasidic [lifestyle], prayed and dressed in the Chasidic [mode] both on the Sabbath, and during the week.

[Photograph of newspaper clipping depicting the late
Rabbi Yitzchak Aizik Menachem Eichenstein, ztz"l,
the Admor of Podhajce]

The Rabbi's house played a ruling role. During the Sabbaths and on holidays, it was completely packed at the Rabbi's place. Whoever speaks about whether joyous occasions took place in the courtyard, [remarks] that this was simultaneously a happy occasion for the entire town. Aside from his being a moral authority, he also brought in livelihood to the town, on account of his hundreds of Chasidim who came here from the surrounding towns.

The Rabbi The Holy Tzaddik R' Nachumtshe Z"L was among the eldest rabbis of his time. He took over the leadership from his grandfather, the first Stratyner Rabbi, R' Yuda Hersh Z"L; from his father, R. Leizerl ZT"L of Stratyn, who was the son of Rabbi R. Yehudah Hersh. The Bursztyner Rabbi R. Nachumtshe became rabbi very young, at eighteen years of age. In the year 5625 [1865] he filled the position of his father in Stratyn. Following several years of living in Stratyn, he established his residence in Bursztyn. He was the Rabbi [there] for a full fifty years. Aside from being a big scholar and Kabbalist, he even published four books pertaining to Kabbalah, and so he was also considered a great wise man.

He led the rabbinate with broad involvement, was one of the greatest prayers, naturally, also in the style of Stratyn. In his house of study there were always inhabitants who were provided for by him. His home was open to every Jew. With food, drink, and [a place to] sleep. At his home there was always a movement of Chasidim, who came from near and far for salvation/help and advice. He loved Jews and helped everyone in whatever way that he could. All the children spent many years on Kest/rooming and boarding at his home [i.e., the institution of Kest, whereby sons-in-law were supported by their in-laws, as they learned in a yeshiva or some similar type of institution]. His married grandchildren also lived on Kest at his home. His Chasidim were devoted in heart and soul. His influence on them was quite great. And this influence was felt in all the cities and towns in which his Chasidim resided. Among his loveliest traits were joy, joyful melodies, and dancing. His Chasidim came from various strata: rabbis, ritual slaughterers, melameds [i.e., teachers of children in a cheder or cheder-like setting], rich men, merchants, and artisans.

[pp. 207-208]

Bursztyn prayer houses were in various towns.

Every summer, the Rabbi and his entire household would leave for the mountains, taking with them some of the trustees and his ritual slaughterer. He would spend time in the mountains from just after Shavuos until halfway through Elul. Even there, in the village of Dora next to Dytiatyn, Chasidim from near and far would come for the Sabbath.

This is how the Rabbi's courtyard was run until a fire broke out in the town. That was in the month of Tammuz, in the year 1914. Three-fourths of the town went up in smoke, and the Rabbi's courtyard, as well. The Rabbi was not in the town at the time, but in the village, as [he was] every year. In this manner, the kingdom/royalty of Bursztyn that had existed for a full fifty years was destroyed.

ספר

אמרי ברכה

לעמבערג

תרנ״ח

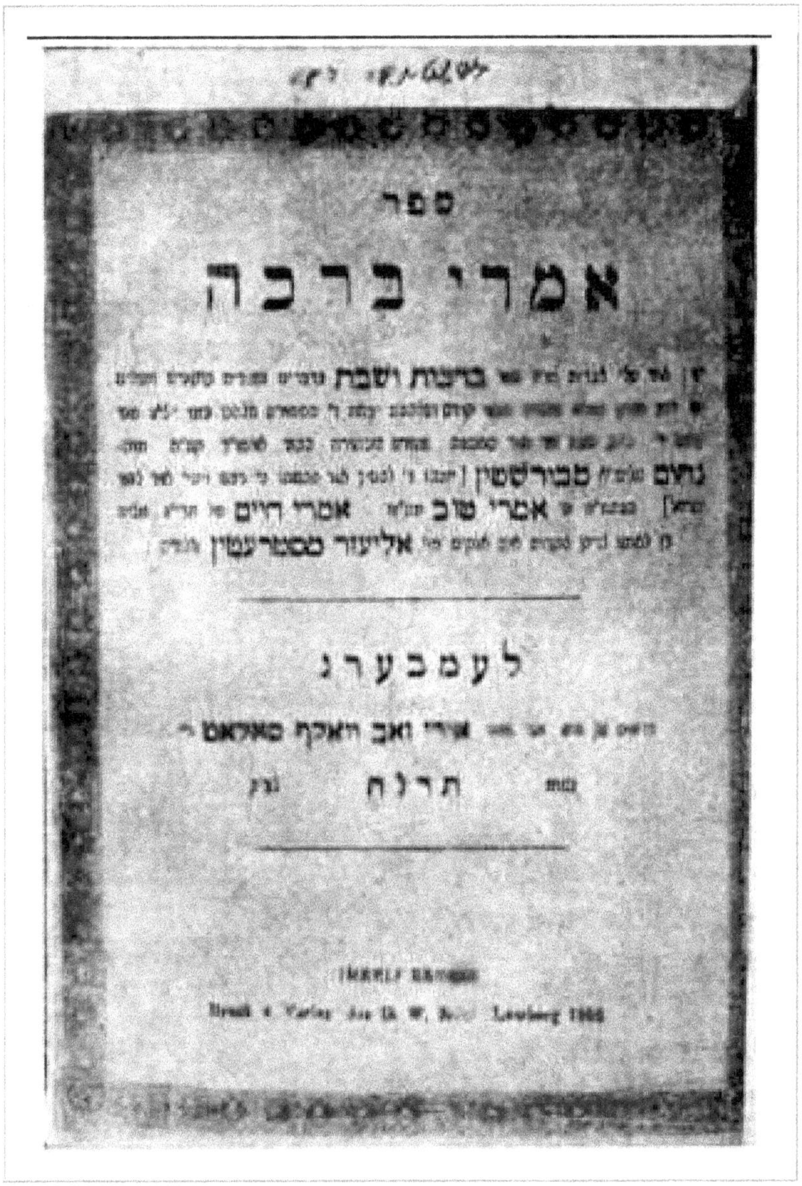

[Title page of the rabbinic tome: Sefer Imre Bracha

Lemberg, [5]658
Imreij Bruchu
Printed by U.W. Salat
Lemberg, 1898]

[pp. 209-210]

Rabbis and Ritual Slaughterers

Rav R' Zeidele Eichenstein, New York

There were many more of them, the beautiful and great Jews, whose memory kindles our hearts. These lines are dedicated only to one passage/segment of time that I lived through. The time, just like the people, remained awake in my frame of mind and does not give me any peace. These people elicited relationships and warmth from everyone who knew them well.

R' Vove the ritual slaughterer,
of blessed memory

Bursztyn possessed rabbis who were famous for their brilliance far beyond the boundaries of the town. From those that I recall, was the Gaon R' Meir Segal-Landau Z"L. After him, his son, R' Moshe David Segal-Landau Z"L took over. Both of them were huge Gaons [i.e., brilliant men, geniuses] and stood out for their energetic conduct in conjunction with the town. When it came to religious matters, there was nobody whom they did not take good care of; they made no distinction between poor and rich. They were thus beloved among all the strata of the Jewish populace.

The ritual slaughterers were Chasidim, religious, [religiously] cautious Jews. There were three ritual slaughterers: R' Sholom, who was the special ritual slaughterer for the Rabbi's courtyard, and who, in either case, became one of the 3 city-wide ritual slaughterers. Each of the ritual slaughterers had his [own] watch, during which he would slaughter chickens and cows/cattle. R' Sholom the ritual slaughterer was a big/major

Jew and was also a good Torah reader, naturally, also one of the Rabbi's fiery Chasidim. His home was open to all guests who passed through the town.

There were also lovely figures: R' Vove the ritual slaughterer, a Chasidic Jew, with huge, humane virtues; R' Yankl the ritual slaughterer, a huge scholar and a huge maven in his field. They were [considered] distinguished and loved by all the Jews in the town.

[pp. 211-212]

Rav R' Yoel Ginzburg

Shmuel Schapira, New York

Shmuel Schapira and his wife

He came to Bursztyn around the year 1910.

It was following the passing of R' Leibele Jupiter, who left behind 3 sons and 2 daughters. The youngest was Yeshaya. They used to call him "Shaye, the adjudicator's [son]." He sat day and night, learning in the religious house of study. The younger fellows would approach him with difficult questions, for which they could not find an answer. Yeshaya gladly responded to them and clarified [matters for them]. No single question or query was too difficult for him.

Indeed, the Jews in Bursztyn sought a big rabbi for themselves, and invited R' Yoel Ginzburg, who was then the head of a yeshiva in Brzezhany. The yeshiva was established by the Gaon Sholom Mordechai Hakohen Schwadron, and R' Yoel Ginzburg received this position while he was still very young. He exemplified himself with his tremendous breadth [of knowledge] and ability to convey [all of this to others].

I was then one of his students and saw the respect and love for him from all of the students. I was also the one who invited him to the office of the religious adjudicator in our town and to come and give his first sermon.

The Sabbath when Rav Yoel Ginzburg held his first sermon will remain unforgettable for me, as well as for everyone else. It contained within it some sort of exaltation, which inspired; all the learners from the town expressed their amazement at R' Yoel's sharp-mindedness and incredible breadth [of knowledge].

He remained in this position, serving the town honestly and devotedly until the day of the major destruction [i.e., the Holocaust]. This great spirit persevered through all the trouble and wrath, which was unleashed upon our people, and perished cruelly, just like everyone [else].

In the beginning of the 1920s, that is, just after the First World War, the youth of our town, just as in all of Poland, embraced every new idea, every new solution. The socialist and socialist-Zionist parties had the strongest effect and influence on the youth. Right after the war, a revolution of ideas took place among the young people; and just as with every revolution, they sometimes overstepped their boundaries, overtook the masses.

Some of the Bursztyn youth were sympathetic to the Communists, Left Poalei Zion, and the Bund, [and] fought, it is understood, against the fanaticism of the "unreasonably conservative" [i.e., the rigidly religious elements]. They openly violated

[pp. 213-214]

the Sabbath, and so forth. Their behavior elicited wrath and embitterment from the religious.

In this instance, the religious law adjudicator R' Yoel Z"L found himself in a particularly difficult situation. Incidentally, the 3 children of R' Yoel – in the eyes of some of the religious – were also not clean of sin.

The children, having received a strict religious upbringing, all turned outwardly; they threw themselves in with fire and learning, so as to attain a secular education. They attended university and specialized in various areas.

All 3 had an effect on Jewish national life, 2 were teachers in Hebrew gymnasias. But according to the thinking of some of the religious people, the children of the adjudicator had "left the straight/upright path."

As [previously] mentioned, as a religious judge, R' Yoel had to come out with the greatest severity against the heresy of the youth, then. It would often happen, though, that when he spoke in the religious house of study about this matter, Jews would rebuke him that his [own] children were likewise Goyim [Gentiles].

R' Yoel knew [full] well that his children were not Goyim. His greatest pride was in his children. Himself a deep believer in Zionism, he was happy about their activity within Jewish social life. His daughter, Zisele and older son, Chaim Z"L were active in the "Hitachdut Poalei Tzion."

The youngest son, Gershon Z"L [was] in the Beitar. It is understood that although they were educated people, they nonetheless kept Judaism and were religious.

The adjudicator of Jewish law would indeed ask, demand, and request from the youth that they not stray too far.

[Even] with his strong religiosity and duties as an adjudicator of religious law, he nevertheless had much understanding for the younger generation. It was particularly evident during the last years before the Second World War, when the youth had already quit declaring their free-thinking ways, which to a great degree stemmed from ignorance.

It is interesting that R' Yoel used to love schmoozing with Minne Tobias, the rabbi of the awoken youth. These two figures shined through out of the terrible darkness, loneliness, fear, and human decline, which ruled during the time of destruction and extermination in our beloved town.

Minne Tobias, the first chairman of the Judenrat in Bursztyn, when he received a command from the Germans to hand over the first Jews to be murdered, officially resigned from his position.

Our adjudicator, R' Yoel Ginzburg ZT"L, appeared his entire life not to be very energetic, not to have high tolerance for that which befell him. This human being, during the downfall of the town, demonstrated super-human power and exaltation.

R' Yoel Ginzburg comforted and encouraged the exhausted, tormented Jews of Bursztyn. Proud and fearless he went to his death.

It was in Bukaczowce, on the day when a large number of the Bursztyn Jews were taken to Belzec, when the adjudicator went around among the Jews of Bursztyn and said Viddui [i.e., the confessional prayer uttered when one is near death] with them. It was then that the bullet of a German murderer shot through his heart.

He merited being buried in accordance with Jewish ritual in Bukaczowce's Jewish cemetery.

Among us remnants of Bursztyn Jewry, his holy figure will remain eternally etched within our hearts.

[p. 215-216]

R' Yankl the Ritual Slaughterer

Buntche Pomerantz, Moisés Ville (Argentina)

How much moral greatness this Jew possessed insofar as humility and fear of Heaven. At that same time, he was inflamed with rebellion against everyone who wanted to disturb his notions regarding the may not's and may's, which were forced upon us from Mount Sinai, but so stemming from his own Jewish-humane disposition, from his vigilant love for God and from his no less vigilant love for [God's] creations, as he understood it, he wanted to prevent people from [committing] a sin.

Buntche Pomerantz

This happened in Bursztyn during the years 1912/13. Being a ten-year-old boy at the time, I did not absorb what was happening very close to me, but later on, finding myself [living] for a couple of years in the home of my uncle Yankl, I heard a great deal about the investigation, which held all of East Galicia in suspense.

Because of the major rains that fell during those years, the pasture fields became flooded and the cows [or cattle] went about day and night in the deep mud, and this led to a new illness among the cows/cattle, which was crowned with the sonorous name, "Red Spots."[1] Red dots appeared on their tongues. And as it turned out, there was no reference in the books to this illness. And this presented the ritual slaughterers with a difficult question, kosher or traif [i.e., not kosher]? As usual, they went to the Rabbi, examined the lungs, felt them, [and] squeezed them. Unfortunately, this type of illness was not mentioned. So, what was one to do? The ritual slaughterers, my uncle Vove, and R' Sholom the ritual slaughterer looked at the Rabbi, and everyone together, at Yankl the ritual slaughterer. If somebody recalls those days, life in Bursztyn then, then he will be able to appreciate the role that Yankl the ritual slaughterer played. Aside from his inborn intelligence, he was considered one of the leading ritual slaughterers. And in this realm, he was an authority. His opinion was counted on not only by us in the town. People came to him with questions regarding the laws of ritual slaughter from far, far-off places; and if a young man wanted to be a first-class ritual slaughterer, he strove to receive an approval or a notification/proclamation from Yankl the ritual slaughterer.

Yankl the ritual slaughterer was also a wise Jewish man. People would come to him for advice and even for remedies during times of illness. For one should

[pp. 217-218]

not forget that at that time it was not so customary to call upon a doctor, [and so] one would count on the opinion of Yankl the ritual slaughterer. He would come to the sick person at home, examine him, feel his forehead, listen to his pulse, and if he said that it was not necessary, then they did not call upon the doctor.

And so, one stood and considered what to do; [for] this problem [i.e., the illness affecting the cows/cattle] was very sharp. At that time in the Jewish towns of Galicia, one had to live within an environment of ritual slaughterers and butchers, all of them poor people, particularly the latter, whose entire livelihood stemmed from the calf, which they would bring from the village, often times, driving [or chasing] it on foot, in the rains and mud; and if God helped, it was slaughtered and came out kosher, then the meat was sold at the butcher shop, and one had a beautiful Sabbath. It was bitter, very bitter, when the ritual slaughterer uttered the word traif, and unfortunately, in most cases this terrible word was uttered by Yankl the ritual slaughterer.

According to the order [of things] in such a situation, the butcher would be asked to leave, and a discussion would ensue. One ritual slaughterer would say such and such, the second one would say otherwise, the rabbi would wrinkle his brow, and in the end, Yankl the ritual slaughterer would prevail [with his] ruling … Not kosher!

And from that point began a series of traif cows/cattle with "Red Spots." The Bursztyn butchers went about miserably with downturned heads, and empty pockets. That year they became the poorest of the poor.

Questions poured in from the surrounding towns, because the "Red Spots" also appeared there on the lungs, and it became a general misfortune in the entire area.

A story transpired with Moshe the butcher traveling one lovely day to Lemberg, and as was customary for a butcher, he went to the butcher shops, and how he trembled when he saw hanging lungs and livers with the sadly familiar "Red Spots." Speaking to the butchers, he asked them whether the cows/cattle with the "Red Spots" on the lungs garnered high prices, since in Bursztyn, most of the cows/cattle that had been slaughtered that year had had the "Red Spots," and the butchers had become the poorest of the poor. They raised their shoulders and asked him why it mattered to him if the meat had red spots. And so, he opened up widely a pair of eyes to them and said: What do you mean, where shall we place so much non-kosher meat? [And so] they laughed heartily at him, [remarking] that among us, they say that this is kosher, like all kosher cows/cattle. Go home and porge [i.e., remove the forbidden fat and veins from meat to make it kosher] them [the meat] through your butchers, together with the rabbi. And he, Moshe the butcher, stood there and his blood was running from his heart; so much of his hard work had been wasted on account of the culpability of the ritual slaughterers; and before his eyes stood the figure of Yankl the ritual slaughterer, the most culpable of all.

Returning home, Moshe the butcher mobilized the entire family of butchers; and in the evening, one felt that the air smelled of gun powder. Right away they went after Yankl the ritual slaughterer. The shouts were exceptional, so far[-reaching], that it nearly came to blows.

Uncle Yankl did not even eat any dinner that evening. Seeing as he was standing and walking with a lung and liver under his arm, he took the train following that same evening to Lemberg, where he immediately went to the rabbi with the question, [and] the rabbi examined the lung. "I do not see anything on the lung" – was the rabbi's response – the lung is kosher. Yankl the ritual slaughterer remained standing, stunned, for one ought not to forget that this was the Lemberger Rabbi. "Well, and you don't see the 'Red Spots?'" inquired Yankl the ritual slaughterer, upset. "Yes, I see them. It's nothing. It's kosher." They began to argue. The rabbi held fast to his [opinion] and said kosher, and Yankl the ritual slaughterer was not frightened, and shouted traif. The rabbi saw that he was dealing with a ritual slaughterer [who was] not of the usual ritual slaughterers, with an opponent who was bold and not frightened,

[pp. 219-220]

and above all, a big maven, [and so] the other ritual slaughterers were called in. But notwithstanding all the opinions, all the arguments, which Yankl the ritual slaughterer brought, that the "Red Spots" are traif, the Lemberger Rabbi and the ritual slaughterers held their ground that it was kosher. And following an entire day of discussions, they did not reach an agreement; Yankl the ritual slaughterer remained with his opinion, and the Lemberger Rabbi and the ritual slaughterers with their opinion.

The noteworthy [one] in that episode, did not end with this. At that time, a religious periodical appeared in Lemberg with the title "Machzikei Hadas" [i.e., Strengtheners of the Religion] and began to air the question in the columns of the newspaper. Rabbis and ritual slaughterers polemicized about this matter and two sides were created; each side zealously defended its standpoint, and it is understood that the leading position was taken up by the figure of Yankl the ritual slaughterer. And given that the two sides could not come together, since each side passionately defended its standpoint, a project was enacted to call together a congress of rabbis and ritual slaughterers from all of Galicia that would issue the decisive ruling.

They threw themselves intensively into preparing for this congress. Yankl, the ritual slaughterer, greatly prepared himself. He assembled a cluster of materials, which were supposed to show the world his correctness.

It never came to the congress. The First World War broke out, which at the same time, put an end to the entire dispute.

Translator's Footnote:

1.   The name used in the vernacular – Hebrew, in this case – was "Nekudot Adumot."

R' Sholom the Ritual Slaughterer

R' Z. Eichenstein

R' Sholom was the special ritual slaughterer of Rabbi Nachumtshe. He was brought up to Bursztyn during a major dispute, on account of ritual slaughterers. The Rabbi's fiery Chasidim supported him and he remained the most distinguished ritual slaughterer in Bursztyn, and the butchers thought very highly of him.

Rosh Hashanah and Yom Kippur, he prayed in the religious house of study before the lectern. His two sons, Yidl and Meir, were the choirboys. His "Kol Nidrei" stirred hearts. People came to hear his "Unetaneh Tokef" even from the synagogue.

R' Sholom the ritual slaughterer owned [i.e., he saw to, was responsible for] the Musaf prayers and Neilah service. Shacharit [the morning prayer service], R' Yitzchak Yidl Moyshe's Lasberg. R' David Breiter received the rights to Mincha, [the afternoon prayer service].

Cantors and Melameds

R'Z. Eichenstein

R' Dovidl was a melamed the entire week, and on the Sabbaths and holidays he was a cantor in the synagogue; he prayed with great sweetness.

R' Itzik David was the cantor of the religious house of study, a clever man of a Jew. It was a pleasure to hear him pray. The words, sung out with much simplicity, poured themselves into people's hearts.

The Melamed, R' Hershl Strelisker, was a Belzer Chasid, and learned Gemara with boys. R' Hershl Azipolier was also a Gemara Melamed. Naftali Lysicer, Yisroel and Vovele were teachers of the youngest children.

In the Rabbi's courtyard there were special Melameds for the Rabbi's children and grandchildren.

R' Yidl, the Rabbi's trustee, was a big music player [musician]. In addition, he was very smart and a major writer. He was a beloved figure among the thousands of Chasidim, who

[pp. 221-222]

came to the Rabbi's tish [i.e., table]. Hearing R' the trustee's singing was one of the greatest pleasures. Ephraim Schneider – the letter-carrier. For many years he was an official of the then Austrian government. [He was] a Chasid, a learner, with a long beard and sidelocks. During the weekdays, when he distributed the mail in the town, he wore the royal cap. But on the Sabbath, he did not carry any mail, due to it being a desecration of the Sabbath, and he wore a beautiful fur-edged hat [commonly worn by Chasidim] and a silk long jacket [also worn by Chasidim]. He was a fiery Chasid [or follower] of the Rabbi. All the years, he was a prayer leader and Torah reader in Neiberger's Minyan. This is how he conducted himself until the outbreak of the First World War.

Aside from him, the 3 town policemen wore uniforms. I recall their names: Karl, the policeman and Antony, the policeman. The third one I do not recall. All of them spoke Yiddish. And they would come to Jewish happy occasions as in-laws.

This is how the town conducted itself for several generations, until the First World War. One can say about the town of Bursztyn what Rashi said about our Forefather Yaakov, when he left Be'er Sheva, "While the righteous is in the city – he is magnificent, he is glory, he is splendor. When he leaves there – the magnificence, the glory, the splendor departs [with him]."

Following the major conflagration, when the Rabbi ZT"L left the town, the idiosyncrasies of the Chasidic way of life fell to the wayside. The war changed the entire appearance of the town. New customs developed. New ideas, parties, right and left.

Indeed, the memory of the former town remains within every person his entire life.

Berish Meller, the son
of Vove the ritual slaughterer
Died 22 August 1958

The Lysicer Melamed and His Cheder

Y. Schwartz

Mechl the Lysicer was perhaps called such, because he hailed from the town of Lysica. But in Bursztyn, he was the eldest Melamed of young children. Most of the town's children went through his cheder. Just as soon as they turned three years old, their fathers took them to the Lysicer, and at that, they were reminded of their own childhood years, when they, too, were brought to the very same cheder.

The cheder was located inside of a large house, of which Hershele Trud, by trade a tailor, was a partner. It was a large house [or room] with an alcove in which the windowpanes were always broken, covered up with rags. Along with Mechl and his wife, Chaya-Sarah, their sons Zalmen-Ber, Chaskel, and their daughter, Zelda, also lived there. The eldest daughter, Sheindel-Rivka, and her husband, Asher Blecher, lived separately on another street.

Shaye, the Melamed's assistant, would carry the three-year-old students to cheder upon his back. In the large room stood two long tables; at the head of one of the tables sat R' Mechl and learned with the older children how to pray from the prayer book. At the second table, Zalmen Ber taught the smaller children the Hebrew alphabet and the vowel signs. Shaye the Melamed's assistant saw to the youngest group, the three-year-olds.

[pp. 223-224]

In his hand he held a twig, which had come from a broom. R' Mechl and Zalmen-Ber already held leather whips in their hands, the same sort used to beat the Rabbi Malkus [i.e., symbolic lashes used as a sign of atonement] on Yom Kippur.[1]

He is standing before my eyes as with fifty years ago, when I learned by him [at his cheder]. He was a Jew of stately appearance with a long, grey beard. Notwithstanding the large number of students, he frequently did not have [anything to eat] for the Sabbath. More than once, the Rabbi's sickly wife returned [home] from the shop on a Thursday evening with empty bags. The shopkeeper, Itshele Schapira, did not wish to give [her] anything more on loan.

She died in [a state of] much want. R' Mechl continued to learn with the children, but his eldest daughter, Sheindel-Rivka already came to his aid. Her husband, Asher Deichsler, did a bit better and they helped her father, married-off the younger sister, Zelda, to Velvele the Melamed's assistant. Chaskel was sent off by the director of the Baron Hirsch School, Anshel Fogel, to Krakow, to study tinsmithing. Zalmen-Ber left for America and would from time to time assist his father, who grew weaker with every year.

The street on which the cheder was located was situated in a valley. Notwithstanding the fact that there was a "vat" through which the filthy water passed, the valley was full of all sorts of filth. On rainy days the children could not leave the cheder to play in the street. Thus, however, during the summer, when the rabbi would doze off, tired, [and] hungry, the boys would run off into the street, touch and roll about in the garbage. It would so happen that a boy would occasionally "unintentionally" receive a slap, and blood would start running from his head, from his nose, and at the same moment his mother, or a grandmother, who right away came running, ranting at the rabbi, and grabbed up the child for home. But the following morning, Shaye the Melamed's assistant brought him back [to cheder].

Translator's Footnote:

1.   Generally, this expression appears in Yiddish in conjunction with "Erev" [the eve of] Yom Kippur, although here, there is no reference to the "Erev."

R' Hershele Strelisker

Shmuel Schapira

They called him "The Strelisker Melamed." All of the parents who wanted their son to grow up to be a learner, sent their child to learn with R' Hershele. The [act of] learning was a profession for him, to which he devoted his utmost devotion. Permeated with the strong desire to convey to the children as much as possible of the fundamentals of Torah knowledge.

At that, he was a fanatical Belzer Chasid, strongly loved the rabbi, and believed in his greatness. He would travel there once a year, and would return, steadfast in his belief.

In the evenings, after having worked hard with the children, he would only just begin to sit back and learn by himself until half of the night. At that time, a passerby could hear a quiet, muffled cry tear through the closed shutters. That was Hershl Strelisker sobbing about the destruction of the Temple. Marking the event until the middle of the night.

He was the Torah reader in the small Ziditshoyber synagogue, which was located next to the religious house of study. They

R' Hershele the Strelisker Z"L
The father of Shmuel Schapira

[pp. 225-226]

would ask him to pray before the lectern, however, he avoided doing this, unless he had a Yahrtzeit, or when the worshippers already strongly insisted [that he do this]. That occurred in rare instances.

Rabbi Moshe David Landau would sometimes call him over, so as to consult him regarding various important questions of religious life in the town.

The weeks of baking matzoh for Passover have become inscribed within my memory. He would go around following the evening prayers to [all] the bakeries and halt the baking of matzohs in the ovens, because the workers were tired, and could thereby lead to [the creation of] chametz [i.e., leavened dough or bread, which is not kosher during Passover]. He did this with the consensus and complete authority of Rav R' Moshe David.

Returning from this work, we all felt his devotion to this holy work, and we became infected by his enthusiasm.

Esther, the Strelisker Female Melamed

The children would call her the Rabbi's wife. The adults – the Strelisker female Melamed. Only those people who were close [to her] called her simply by her name: Esther.

She was a learned woman; she recalled the laws from the Shulchan Aruch [i.e., the Code of Jewish Law] by heart. And pages of Gemara. Sitting in the distance, doing her work for her job responsibilities, she would overhear how the rabbi would teach the class of Gemara to the students. In the middle, the feathers would be plucked, or perhaps she had overheard some other work whereby a cheder boy was making a mistake or had not understood something correctly in the Gemara. She would then draw closer and correct, or quietly prompt [the cheder boy], so the "rabbi" would not hear.

She was always busy doing good for everybody [i.e., she was a do-gooder]. Here she collected donations for poor widows and orphans. Another time, for a poor bride. Friday, she spent part of the day collecting challahs for poor people. During the winter days, she would distribute wood to heat the cold homes of needy people.

Once, while carrying some wood to a poor widow, who did not have [anything with which] to heat her home, she caught a cold, until the highest temperature forced her into bed. The fever devoured her, she contracted consumption, and did not leave her bed for two years, until her soul expired.

[pp. 227-230][1]

Way of Life

[pp. 231-232]

The Tailors' Little Synagogue

Yisrael Fenster

Our town was too young to find the romance of historical olden days in it. Bursztyn does not have any glorified letters of pedigree of the old Jewish communities in Poland; it just began to grow larger during the last decades of the 19th century; it vegetated during the interwar years and went under, along with the destruction of all of Polish Jewry. However, the simply built synagogue and religious houses of study with their drooping walls, so natural in their oldness, so self-evident in their poorness, have remained precious and forever dear to the hearts [of its former inhabitants].

Such was also true of the Tailors' Little Synagogue, where there were no eastern walls, no head [of table]/place of honor, simple and plain, like the worshippers, without any aristocratic pedigree and without bitterness, without pathetic outcries and Chasidic religious ecstasy, yet authentic and soulful, as the verses in the Psalms, which they would murmur quietly, stubbornly devoted in their belief.

At the passageway of the anteroom of the Great Synagogue there also stood a little synagogue. It was called: the Tailor's Little Synagogue. Factually, other artisans also prayed there, such as shoemakers, carpenters, butchers, and simply poor people, who, just as in the Great Synagogue, only came to pray here Friday nights and on Sabbath days.

Actually, there was also enough room in the Great Synagogue for the three types of Jews. What then, was the reason that swayed people to join a separate little synagogue?

The primary reason was that the proprietors of the synagogue looked down upon the artisans; they sat down in the lovely spots at the "eastern wall." For the poor people there remained seats at the door. They were also not honored with any lovely Aliyahs [i.e., being called up to read from the Torah in the synagogue] to the Torah, which resulted in the people rebelling, and as they said: making Sabbath for themselves.

**Aharon Nute Glasthal, trustee of the Tailors'
Little Synagogue, the president for many years of
the Artisans' Union, "Yad Charutzim," [and] later
chairman of the Bursztyner Society in America**

[pp. 233-234]

Here, in the Tailors' Little Synagogue there was no higher-up. That is to say, there were no lovelier and worse spots. Here, there were no rights to titles. [These were] tired [people, worshippers] from a whole week of hard work, not having eaten, with pale faces, but well-washed, well-scrubbed/shampooed in honor of the Sabbath. They looked with suspicion upon every "unfamiliar person," who entered the little synagogue – should that person laugh at their Hebrew. Because they were not any sort of big scholars. They did not comprehend any of the words. And their Hebrew also limped along. But therefore, they were dear, genuine Jews. They did not lie to anyone, they did not rob anyone. There was always an embitterment in their faces, not only because of their difficult and poor life; it was embitterment, hatred, and scorn toward the beautiful proprietor and the "fine Jew." This could be seen the most during the High Holidays, when they did not pray at the Tailors' Little Synagogue, [and] the worshippers would come to the Great Synagogue. For them, they would place tables and benches near the door.

There was a large number of synagogue proprietors, who were not any greater scholars than those of the Tailors' Synagogue. These were, however, Jews with money or who had beaten their way with their fists to the "lovely positions" in the synagogue.

And so, the poor, good-hearted, naïve Jews would, during the Days of Awe, stand with downturned heads before the Almighty God – but deep in their hearts, they had complaints against him.

They did not have their own Torah reader – aside from Fishele Schneider, who would pray on Friday night and during the Sabbath morning prayers. He very much liked to pray before the lectern. Even during a weekday at the religious study house, he would go over to the lectern, and with his heavy Hebrew, he would very loudly pray aloud. The scholars would good-naturedly smile and overlook his mistakes.

The Torah reader at the Little Synagogue was Davidzshele the cantor. And he was also the leader of the Musaf prayer. The final years, once Davidzshele had already left Bursztyn, Davidek Gutstein did the reading. He was a Melamed and would learn attentively with children at the Tailors' Little Synagogue.

Translator's Footnote:

> 1.   There appears to be an error in the pagination at this point in the book, since there should technically be one more double-sided, double-numbered page between the cover page and the opening, double-sided, double-numbered essay page: pp. 231-232.

[pp. 235-236]

Jewish Livelihoods

Yisrael Fenster

One's heart sobs for the tortured [and] lost [Jews of Bursztyn], but their illustrious memory demands of us a strong and emboldened heart, so that there will be an atonement for their death, in our ensuing, bright superstructure [or universe]. Retelling about these figures and types, our hearts are permeated with love and longing for all of them, who once were, and are no longer. Speaking about them, we indeed also see the faces of our brothers and sisters, among all of them, who are a part of our body and soul.

Those of us who merited surviving the great conflagration, always have before our eyes, the ancient commandment, which remains etched with[in] the letters of fire and blood: "Remember that which Amalek did to you" – the Amalek of the twentieth century.

This is actually the role and designation of this book; not merely memories of the distant and closer past, not merely a memorial candle for the pure and holy souls, who met their ends through all sorts of terrible deaths. In recording our memories, we fulfilled the need to elicit the special illustriousness of the Jewish common folk in our town. May this grant the coming generations a deep understanding of this destroyed beauty.

The majority of the Jews in Bursztyn lived in great poverty. Difficult, very difficult were the worries concerning livelihood.

80 percent of them were involved in trade. Everything was referred to as "trade." Firstly, the stores in and around the marketplace, from which approximately 10 percent of the Jewish population earned an honorable living. This included: grocery stores, fabric dealers, metalwork, haberdasheries, grain [dealers], and restaurants. The customers in the stores were Ukrainians and Poles from Bursztyn and the surrounding area, as well as Jews, who had other livelihoods.

Following that, there were merchants: "travelers." They would go around to all the fairs. Jews would ride around with fabrics, ready-made clothing, with leather, with dishes, [and] with furs. Every day, they went to another place in another town, where the weekly market was taking place.

[pp. 237-238]

Perl Klirsfeld and her daughter standing in front of their shop in the marketplace

In addition: village travelers; Jews who went about among the villages, peddling [their wares]. They would buy some grain, a calf. Sometimes they would trade it for merchandise, which they brought with them, and which were needed by the peasants.

A significant number of Jews was employed in the cattle trade, as well as with the breeding of cattle/livestock, or fattening, as they referred to it by us. Some of them would purchase the cattle already fattened and would send them to the large cities in Poland.

Summertime, some Jews would pasture the cattle in meadows, until they grew fat.

Some dealt in horses. They dealt with the peasants, as well as with wealthy men and well-possessing [people] – from the area, and also, from far away from Bursztyn.

There were a few active bakeries, which sold baked goods in the city, and also took these to the villages.

Jewish butchers sold kosher meat to Jews and traif meat to the non-Jews.

In the town, resided Jewish artisans: tailors, shoemakers, tinsmen, capmakers, and others.

Among the tailors, some were good professionals, men's, as well as women's tailors. During the final period [before the Holocaust], those who practiced as women's tailors were nearly exclusively women. There were also Gentile tailors; that is how one referred to those who sewed for the peasants. Some of them would go around in the villages and serve their clients on-site. The old-style tailor who could sew up a Jewish article of clothing, a long jacket [commonly worn by Chasidim], a jacket, totally disappeared during those final days.

The shoemakers mostly worked for the peasants, or they repaired old shoes.

The holy articles that were assembled by those who had religious needs: the rabbi, the religious judge, the ritual slaughterers, the cantor, the trustees, and others were sustained by that small upkeep, which such a poor Jewish community was able to give it.

During the old Austrian times there were Jewish officials in various government positions: In the court mail[room], even in the police. Prior to Polish times, there only remained the old/former ones [in these positions]. Not a single Jew was allowed into any of these places.

Miss Kimmel with a group of Bursztyn residents at the marketplace

In contrast, the number of Jewish lawyers rose, in comparison to prior the First World War. Nearly every lawyer also employed a Jewish employee; it is understood that the officials and lawyers lived much better-off than other Jews in the town.

[pp. 239-240]

The Jews in the Villages Surrounding Bursztyn

Yisrael Fenster

They were initially the lessees of goods [property] or lessees, as they were called.[1] They leased the farm/ranch estates of the Polish property owner, in closest villages surrounding Bursztyn: Kuropatniki – the Fischers, Nastaszczyn – Breitbart, and Kaniuszki – Laufer, and Swistelnik – the Klarreichs.

The property lessee of Nastaszczyn. For many years he leased the estate, following the death of his father, the property [came from] Count Bielski. During the period of destruction, he hid in the woods of Bursztyn. A short time before liberation, he was murdered by the local peasants.

Dziuno Breitbart

I no longer recall the times when there were Jewish lessees and tavern keepers in the villages of the old style, and who were the nobleman's property. Following the war [of] 1914-18, this type of Jew entirely disappeared. There were no longer any taverns in the villages. There were no more inns; from many villages, these Jews completely vanished. Eighty percent of the remaining Jews in the villages surrounding Bursztyn took up agricultural work/farming and feeding animals.

The Klarreichs in Kurow, the Scharfs and Mandelberg[s] in Sernik, the Kimmels in Korostowice; in Tenetniki there was the Nutes family, and many others.

I must say a few words about the noteworthy Nutes family. The elder R' Hersh Z"L (I believe, a brother of the longtime secretary of the Bursztyner Society in America) was a first-class agronomist [or farmer]; the peasants in the village would come to consult him and to learn from him.

It was a wonder and a pleasure to see how the whole family would stand in the field and cut the grain or dig up potatoes. One could see the old man – next to him his daughter and son-in-law with their children, who were already at that time, assiduous tillers.

It is understood that all these Jews, in addition to this work, traded [on the side] and earned a respectable livelihood.

The village Jews belonged to the Bursztyn Jewish community.

These dear, hard-working Jews were the first victims [or martyrs] of the Hitlerist murderers. Many of them were murdered during the initial part of the Nazi occupation.

Translator's Footnote:

    1.   The terms used here, respectively, in Yiddish, are: Gutspechter and Posesorn.

[pp. 241-242]

Fires and Epidemics

Yisrael Fenster

In a sense, it is difficult to place a boundary for the Jewish occurrences in our town. Want, worry, and fear were always an organic part of the existence of Jewish life. Indeed, there were such stormy, worrisome days, which, with their fatefulness, left behind deep marks in the life of the town and in the soul of every individual. The epidemics and fires pertain to these occurrences, which would take on menacing forms and would endanger the lives of the entire population.

Just as in all small towns, it also burned very often [i.e., there were frequently fires]. There were small fires and huge conflagrations. The reason was simple: rooftops made of shingles and even of straw. A tiny spark would immediately burn, [and] there was nothing with which to extinguish. It depended on the weather. If it was calm, no wind – 2-3 houses would catch fire, and the fire would subside. However, when it burned during a period of wind, at that time, the fire would persist freely; then, entire streets would burn.

Before our time, there was a major fire in the year 1914, just before the outbreak of the First World War. In the conflagration the Great Synagogue and the religious study house burnt down. All the nearby little streets, a large part of the marketplace, as well as the house of the Rabbi R' Nachumtshe ZT"L were then burnt down.

Just as soon as the war broke out, once the Russians had invaded, they burnt down a large portion of the Jewish homes, the remaining marketplace, and the streets, all the way to the "Gnila Lipa."

In 1921, approximately, once again on a beautiful morning, a great fire broke out, which once again destroyed the poor Jewish homes.

It was a frequent event, when the Jews would ring at the church; that would happen whenever a fire broke out, the Jews would run into the Polish church, which was surrounded from all sides by Jewish homes, and ring the alarm, also while ringing; in the "small garden" there was a bell for this purpose.

During the years 1915/16 – the years of the First World War, the most terrible of all epidemics raged. The cholera, which created destruction among the town's Jewish populace. There was almost no house in which there was no death. In some families, two or three victims succumbed.

I believe that in 1916 a [wedding] canopy was staged at the Jewish cemetery. That was supposed to be a remedy and hope that the epidemic would subside. The groom was: Motkele, the son of Zalmen Yossel Yonah's; the bride, the daughter of the elderly cantor; they hailed from Bukaczowce.

Yitzchak Kurtasz, the son-in-law of David Schneider Z"L, brought the gramophone with the large trumpet/horn; the procession toward the canopy was accompanied by music,

[pp. 243-244]

[and] people drank L'Chaim! And God indeed helped...

After the cholera, however, came the stomach and spotted typhus; the epidemic saw short intermissions – until the year 1921, approximately. From the typhus epidemic, a few hundred Jews in Bursztyn died.

Yes, there was no shortage of pain, misfortune, and sadness in the Jewish life of the town. But the largest fire came upon the Jews of Bursztyn when the most major igniter of all times, Hitler, with his collaborators, exhausted, starved, and annihilated all the Jews of Bursztyn through burning and other violent forms of death.

A Story That Happened in Demianow

Buntche Pomerantz

If one of us Bursztyners occasionally recalls, during moments of longing for one's childhood years, which we spent in our small Jewish town prior to the First World War, he must also recall Demianow, because Bursztyn without Demianow is, for example, is like a house without an alcove. Even the train station is called by the name Bursztyn-Demianow, and the conductor would call out in a single breath: BursztynDemianow.

I recall how we, small lads, would during the summer Sabbath days when our parents would go to sleep, run barefoot to Demianow. The road is straight; on both sides [there are] fields with grain that is ready for cutting, but here and there one could see male and female peasants cutting with sickles and binding in sheaves. The scent of the cut grain filled air, it was quiet all around, and we, small lads, galloped barefoot uphill, and then downhill, until close before the village. Not far from the village the road splits [in two], one going to the right, which leads to Martynow, and the other, to the left, cuts into the village. Before the road splits stood the tavern, in which resided the elderly Naftali Demianower and his wife Breina (children, I do not recall). In the center of the village lived our cheder colleague, Berl, who spent a whole week living at his grandfather, Itshe Gutstein, and learned together with us from Hershl Strelisker, and for the Sabbath he would return home to Demianow. We, young children would be drawn to go to Berl on the Sabbath, following lunch. Unfortunately, we did not always succeed at this, because before reaching his home we had to run through an entire series of peasant streets. And as much as we tried not to wake up the village dogs, we were not always successful, and many times we had to turn around from the middle of the village, so as not to barge into their canine snouts, because just as soon as the dogs began to bark, impudent Gentile fellows would appear; and right away they would become provoked against us, and in unison, begin to pursue us. And we, not [being] dead, nor alive, ran back; and more than one of us returned home with torn pants and occasionally, even worse... And the Sabbath day escapades very often ended with... beatings, which we received from our fathers.

Later on, Demianow had another provocation for us. We, already boys of 10-11 years of age, would chase after the couples in love, who would stroll in the summer evenings up to Naftali Demianower's place, and there, behind his house, in the orchard, where there stood simple, unfinished tables and benches, they passed around cold sour milk and black bread and butter. And we, young lads, stood at the other side of the fence, swallowed our saliva, and were envious.

For the children who prayed at the

[pp. 245-246]

Stratyner synagogue, Naftali Demianow was quite valuable in conjunction with the [Jewish] festival of "Shemini Atzerert." An early-on precedent was established, whereby Naftali Demianower would invite the whole Stratyner congregation to his home, Shemini Atzeret during the day. He and his wife Breina prepared broiled duck and mead, the tasty Bursztyn mead.

Entering Naftali's home, one could already smell the broiled duck, which Naftali and his wife placed with shining faces upon the tables. The crowd did not wait to be called. We, small ones, also did not turn down [the opportunity], and chewed with both cheeks. And in the evening, [once it was] already a bit dark, we went to synagogue, singing, to the Hakafot [i.e., the ceremony during which there is dancing around in a circular motion with the Torah on Shemini Atzeret, Simchat Torah, and other occasions]. And so, there was an account involving our dear Naftali Demianower, which became inscribed within my memory.

The chametz, on Passover Eve, Naftali would sell, already for many years, to his nearest neighbor, an old peasant, Ivan. Until one lovely day, Ivan died. Before Passover, he called over Ivan's son, Stefan, and told him that for many years already he was conducting this business concerning the chametz with his late father and taking into consideration the long-term acquaintance that bound the two of them [together], he now wanted to conduct this business with him; that is, with Stefan. And he charted out all the conditions for him: he must sit for eight days in the tavern and be the full-standing proprietor of the business. All of this would be indicated on paper; and then, that is, following the eight days, the business would be transferred over to the previous proprietor, that is, to Naftali.

The business was completed. Naftali served Stefan a glass of 96 [i.e., some type of alcohol dating back to 1896]. Stefan ended off with another glass and went home. On the way [home], being under the influence of the second glass, a bright idea occurred to him, and he thought to himself, if I am indeed the proprietor of the tavern, why should I not serve my chums a glass of pure liquor? He thought about and did this. He stopped off at his chums, and just as with good brothers, invited them over for the following morning to the tavern for a glass of liquor.

The following day was the morning of the first day of Passover. Naftali comported himself as usual; he rose and went with Breina to the town to go and pray. Having finished praying, they went home. Coming close to the tavern, the exceptional for a usual weekday movement around the tavern attracted their attention. But not sensing anything bad, they went home in peace. But just as soon as they opened the door, everything grew bad [i.e., literally, "it grew dark in their eyes"]. Around the tables sat half a village of spread-out peasants, and Stefan was handing out with his generous hand whatever somebody requested. Liquor and accompanying food as with a king. Poor Naftali called Stefan over to a side, and between the two, the following dialogue ensued:

Naftali: Stefan, as far as I know, you have no holiday today.

Stefan: No, today is a usual weekday for us.

Naftali: Then why are they sitting here stretched out and drinking?

Stefan: That's because I invited them to come and drink a toast in honor of my becoming the proprietor of the tavern.

Naftali: What are you talking about, Stefan, proprietor of the tavern? Don't you know that this business is a joke and that you haven't invested even 5 greitzer in it?

Stefan: You are making a mistake. I in fact purchased the tavern, and we didn't speak at all about money, such that you must now leave me alone, because I need to take care of my chums.

The elderly Naftali Demianower remained

[pp. 247-248]

standing with his head downcast, with a pained heart, as he watched his labor being poured freely down the Gentile throats. For a long time thereafter, people would schmooze and relate the story that had taken place in Demianow.

He Knew it in Advance...

Yisrael Fenster

R' Zelig Hammer and Reuven Schuster

In the "rynek" [i.e., Polish for market square] in the extreme corner of the left side stood the house of Zelig Hammer. On one side it bordered on the house of Leizer Landner, and from the other side, on the house of Chaim Hochberg. Toward the street was a saloon, and behind it, a residence.

Zelig Hammer did not get involved in the saloon; his wife Baila oversaw the business, and with much success; a woman of valor on whom one could depend.

R' Zelig Hammer, a stately appearance, a lovely, tall figure – a tended-to beard, always clean and elegantly dressed.

An intelligent, energetic Jew. For many years he was the dominant [force] in the Jewish social life of the town; he was the head of the Jewish community, the overseer of birth certificates in city hall, the head of the Jewish councilors, and for a long time, the factual mayor of the city.

His leading admirers were the simple common folk, the artisans, cattle merchants, and horse dealers. Without R' Zelig, they would not initiate anything. They would confer with him, and he would give them advice.

The episode that I am bringing down here, I once heard told by R' Zelig Hammer himself. This episode shows us what sort of naïve, innocent, genuine Jew Reuven Schuster was. R' Zelig told it as so: one time Reuven came over to me, worried and scared, "R' Zelig – he says – I received a slip from the court. What do they want from me? I was never in my life in court, says to me R' Zelig; what shall I do?"

R' Zelig looks at the slip and says: "Yes, they are summoning you to court, Reuven. They are summoning you as a witness. Your two Gentile neighbors got into a brawl and gave [your name] as a witness."

**Reuven the shoemaker, the long-term trade
union leader of the artisans in Bursztyn**

But R' Zelig, what shall I do? I am already over fifty, and never before tread across the threshold of the court. What shall I do and what shall I say? – asked Reuven.

Don't get scared – R' Zelig said to him – go to the court at 8 o'clock in the morning; when you come to the floor/landing, you should go to the right side,

[pp. 249-250]

you should count 3 doors, and you should enter the third one. There, you will see the judge sitting on a high chair. You should not say anything, only when the judge asks you your name, you should say – Reuven Drucker. Afterward, he will ask you, Did you see the neighbors engaged in a brawl? You should respond – No, I did not see anything. Then the judge will say to you: Go home.

On the designated day Reuven went to court. He went with fear. But he was surer of himself, on account of the instructions from R' Zelik… He counted 3 doors on the right side. He entered the third door, saw the judge on the high chair in the black robe, and a fear fell upon him, but remembering R' Zelik's talk, it became easier for him.

What is your name? – the judge asked him.

My name is Reuven Drucker.

Did you see your neighbors Ivan and Peter having a brawl?

I did not see this.

You didn't see this at all?

No.

You may go home.

Reuven the shoemaker ran straight to Zelik Hammer. Gaping [and] full of delight, he asked: "R' Zelig. It was exactly as you said, but precisely according to every shred. How did you know this? I counted up 3 doors on the right side. I opened the door, and the judge was sitting in a black robe on a high chair – and asked me, What is your name? So, I said, Reuven Drucker, [and] so he asked further – Did you see Ivan fighting with Peter? So, I said, No, I didn't see anything… So, he showed me the door and said: Go home! But from where and how did you, R' Zelik, know how all of this would take place, in advance?"

He Cannot Sit His Head upon Him

In our town there were Bursztyn Jews who traded in horses, broad-chested Jews, with healthy red faces, scorched by the sun and wind.

Wolf the Big and Wolf the Small. Eli Moshe the Big and Eli Moshe the Small, Shmuel Hreczka – Matye Shed [i.e., this is likely a descriptive and not true surname, meaning "devil/demon"] – and others; they were mighty, strong like oaks. Entire fairs of Gentiles would tremble before them. They were utterly good-hearted. If they only had one groschen in their pocket, they would often share it with a poor person.

I would like to relate here about Eli Moshe the Big. He was a completely nice fellow, but he was no great scholar. Eli Moshe the Big had 5 sons: Aizik, Shmuel, Luzer, Nachman, and Leizertshe; they were 5 strong men, but with the teacher in school they had no peace. The cheder also did not entice them; they were more drawn to the pasture, to cracking with their whip and to kicking on their horse.

From the youngest one, from Leizertshe, Eli Moshe the Big wanted to make a human-being, and so with force, he kept him in school; he did not spare any tuition money the Melamed, Yidl Purim. However, it did not help any.

He completely ran away from the school and from the cheder. Eli Moshe would complain to everyone and justify himself: You see, good people, I do everything that I can. I want the youngest should at least know [something], that he should become a human-being. But what can I do; he only wants horses. Well, tell me yourselves, can I then sit my head upon him…[1]

[pp. 251-252]

The Bursztyner Bontshe Shvayg[2]

Moshe Leibele was a newcomer to Bursztyn, but I recall him from my earlier childhood in Bursztyn. His wife, Libe, or Libkale, as people called her, was the sister of Yankl, the Gentile tailor. The couple, in fact, lived together with Yankele in one house.

Moshe Leibele, a small little Jew with a beard and sidelocks, belted in thick rope, although he seldom used it, because his primary work was to carry water to the houses. The rope he would occasionally use to carry a half a tenth of wood from Aryeh Shayeche to a poor homeowner.

It was difficult, very difficult for Moshe Leibele to piece things together for the Sabbath. However, he never complained, he did not ask anything of anyone.

Friday evening he would throw off the dirty, patched-up clothes and put on the long jacket and fur-edged hat [traditionally worn by Chasidim on the Sabbath and on Jewish festivals], so as to go pray at the Tailors' Synagogue. Here, too, he did not have any designated spot; he would sit down next to the door.

One would not hear him speaking loudly; he never wrangled about the wage that he received for his work. It goes without saying that he did not raise his voice or curse, which was a frequent occurrence among other porters. During the week, he would stop in at the religious study house and recite a chapter of Psalms.

It was related how, standing once in the yard at Zelig Hammer's place, and dragging water from the well – he looked in through the window and saw how R' Zelig was eating noodles and broth. He snatched away his head; it apparently "passed over" his heart; he once again took a look and averted his eyes.

He murmured to himself: What does it matter to you, Moshe Leibele, if Zelig Hammer is eating noodles and broth?

Once he received 50 dollars from a relative in America; he was afraid to keep it at home.

He came to Yankl Rudy, who at that time had a bank, and told him: R' Yankl, I received 50 dollars; I ask you to accept these at your bank, and for a percent, I will carry water for you.

A Match on the Sabbath...

It was the Bursztyn of those days, when the children obeyed their father and mother, and as good, religious people say, young people did not smoke any cigarettes on the Sabbath, girls did not wear any clothes with open backs. Just the opposite – with a collar up to the neck, long sleeves, and high lace-up shoes. They observed the Sabbath and the Jewish festivals, as God commanded.

It was during that time when Devorahtshe Banner sent her son, Moshe, to Lemberg, to be an assistant in a haberdashery store.

This young fellow spent a year in the big city – he longed for home, for Bursztyn; [and so] he visited "for the Sabbath."

Sabbath day, after the food, he went out to the street. His friends did not recognize him, fancy as he was, in long trousers and yellow/amber shoes, a collar and a tie; a complete German [i.e., in the German or Western mode], he went for a walk with his gang toward the court, far, far away, en route to Nastaszczyn. He related all the wonders of the big city of Lemberg to them. Of the big walls, of the tramway that ran along the streets. Of the big stores, of the wealth, [and] of the wonderful people. He told them how progressive he had become. He went to the theater; and namely, he no longer prayed,

[pp. 253-254]

he no longer recited the Shema. His friends heard him out with open mouths, gaping from all the wonderment.

Suddenly, Moshe stood in place. He had taken out a match stub from his pocket and lit it, --- calling out with a trumpeting voice (a bit nasally): So, this is what Moshe can do!...

His friends all together cried out in fear: "On the Sabbath!" And they ran away.

One Waits at the Post Office

Do you remember how one would go to the post office? Standing there and waiting for the letter carrier?

At the post office old and young would wait. The intelligentsia, the fancy proprietors; youths would wait for the newspapers, which arrived at their party headquarters, but did not have any patience to wait until they would be brought there.

Stable waiters were: the leaders of the "Hitachdut," who would wait for party literature and newspapers.

The leaders of the Peretz Association – for the "Literarishe Bleter," which one would learn as a page of Gemara; [and] the representatives of "Beitar" would wait for their mail.

One would nearly always see Mrs. Wattenberg and Shlomo Geller.

While waiting, one would often debate about various current events.

One liked going to the post office during the week, and particularly, on the Sabbath. One person would be reading a correspondence from America; another one, a certificate to go to Israel, and so forth.

It is understood that the only ones waiting were Jews; and while waiting, one would begin schmoozing about this and that. More than once, the clerk, Bogochwalski, would be shouting through the window that there should be quiet. For a few minutes it would grow quiet, until people once again became fired-up and noisy. – But then suddenly, the door would open, it would grow pitch quiet, [and] the letter carrier would appear with various mail packages in both of his hands. And in the blink of an eye, he would be surrounded by tens of individuals. The mail carrier would loudly and indifferently call out the names of the addressees. There would be outstretched trembling and greedy hands. When he finished, there would be many blotted eyes. Everyone slowly dispersed.

Did Not Read the Megillah

When Davidzshe Breiter Z"L built his large house in the middle of the marketplace with a story/landing, the significant people flocked there: judges, lawyers, teachers, and so forth. Just opposite of the residence, where he, Davidzshe himself lived with his family, moved a judge who had, not long before, come to Bursztyn; he was a Christian.

On Purim, proprietors would send the synagogue beadle to their homes, so that he would read the Megillah for their wives.

This is also what Davidzshe Breiter did that time; being himself at the synagogue, he sent Avraham Itzik the synagogue trustee, so that he would read the Megillah for his wife.

Abraham Itzik, already then, was a bit deaf. Coming up to the big wall, he got confused, and instead of going to Davidzshe Breiter's wife, he went in where the judge's wife was. Upon entering, he broadly conveyed a "good holiday." He retrieved the Megillah from its long, metal canister, placed it down on the table, and… began to read.

[pp. 255-256]

The wealthy woman, who did not know what was happening here, began to ask, it is understood, in Polish, what he wanted here. A Jew does not reside here. Avraham Itzik did not hear and did not respond – he continued reading the Megillah… You, Jew, what do you want here? Leave my home – shouted the wife of the judge.

Avraham Itzik began to notice that something was not in order, so he shouted:

Well, there, at once, at once, woman!

You get out of my house, you, vile Jew – she ran up to him.

Avraham Itzik, the synagogue trustee, apparently did not finish reading the Megillah, because the judge came in and threw him out of the house.

Began to Speak…

There was once a Jew in Bursztyn named Zalmen Ber Laufer. He was a big scholar and very smart. A person with principles. It was said of him that he had once overseen a trial involving a Bursztyn Jew, and he took it all the way to Kaiser Franz Joseph, who granted it an audience…

The older Bursztyn Jews ought to remember him. He was steeped in fine pedigree, that Zalmen Ber. He hailed from generations upon generations of rabbis and good Jews. He himself, though, was a Mitnagid. That is, he did not abide by any Chasidim.

And so R' Zalmen used to love relating: After my wedding, my father ZT"L, the Nadworner Rabbi, saw that I was taken by the matter, and that I was already considering something different, and not rabbinics. So, he once called me into his room and said to me as so:

I want to ask you something, Zalmen Ber, and want you to answer me. You know that your great, great grandfather, the Apter, the great master of miracles – [that it was] with him that our rabbinic dynasty began?

I remained silent.

Do you hear [me]?

I hear [you], father.

And your great grandfather, R' Meirtshe, you hear?

I hear, father.

And your grandfather, the Gaon, you hear?

Why are you silent?

And I, your father, should the rabbinate of our family, heaven forbid, end with me?

Speak! Why do you remain silent?

I remained silent.

I command you to speak.

If father will forgive my words, then I will speak.

Speak!!

If so, I will tell my father that it never began…

Belief in Justice

The Landner Family

Rivka and Leizer Landner had 5 sons, a walled house, and a food shop. Whoever came up with the notion that a Jewish merchant must be a swindler, deceitful, should have been taken to Leizer Landner's store. The second [son] of the eldest son, Nunue, worked with the father [Leizer] in his food shop.

Both of them, the father and the son, were exemplars of honesty and decency.

R' Leizer, a religious Jew of the old style, was innocent as a small child. His 5 sons, just as innocently and honestly, believed in their ideas of rights, from the right to the extreme left. All the Jewish parties, which at that time

[pp. 257-258]

were active in the town, were represented in Leizer Landner's home; R' Leizer would listen to the fiery debates of his sons. He did not believe in their doctrines, but he was tolerant.

His eldest, Itshe, said that it is not sufficient to speak nicely; one must live like a proletarian-born person. One must work, [so] he went to Stanislawow and studied locksmithery. His brother, Lobtshe, who studied law at university, simultaneously studied tailoring.

Leizer Landner's sons believed with a complete faith in the world, the human being, and in its justice.

It was this very world, this very human being, this very justice that so bloodily fooled us.

One son, the youngest, survived; her [i.e., Rivka Landner's] Landner studied in Paris. He fought in Spain; he was captured by the Germans. He lives in France. A daughter of my dear friend-from-youth, Itshe, who lives in Israel, also survived.

He Carried Through

Koppel Henech's narrow, single-story house stood at the edge of the marketplace. Tightly sealed, to the left, stood Aryeh Shayech's small house. Next door lived R' Sholom Baumrind, a God-fearer and fiery Chasid. In addition, he was also a big scholar. Notwithstanding the fact that he was a poor, bitter man, he never lost his confidence. He had grown-up and overgrown sons and daughters. An entire week, one seldom saw a bit of cooked food at R' Shlomo's home, but on the Sabbath, a piece of meat [or] fish, had to enter his home; it is understood, not, for heaven's sake, to gorge oneself; rather, in honor of the Sabbath…

One Friday night, when R' Sholom returned [home] from praying and enthusiastically said the Shalom Aleichem, said the Kiddush, and sat down at the table, his wife right away passed him the broth with noodles. R' Sholom asked, strongly wondering, What happened? Where is the fish?

His wife quietly told him something; apparently, that there was nowhere to purchase it – or, perhaps, she had no reason to buy it…

R' Sholom remained seated, deep in thought. He had not touched the broth with noodles; it did not help any talking or coaxing. "There must be fish on the Sabbath – he said – and there will be."

Where shall I now find fish, Sholom? – his wife asked. You are a Jewish woman! You don't understand. There will be fish – Sholom's eyes glazed over, he roared/hummed to himself, again and again: "There must be fish, there must be fish on the Sabbath, in honor of the Sabbath."

The broth grew cold. The Sabbath candles went out. The residents were already asleep – R' Sholom sat in the dark and still murmured with confidence, There must be fish in honor of the Sabbath… He woke up once it was already [the next] day. He had slept through the night, sitting, with his hands clenched upon the table, waiting for the fish.

He used to relate, following this, that he had carried through: he ate fish…

The Carousel

She arrived on occasion, like something that had fallen from the heavens. We, children, had left the school. On the way home, we noticed that in the middle of the marketplace something exceptional was taking place. There were long and thick banisters thrown about, wooden planks and many-colored canvases. Next to this

[pp. 259-260]

stood a large, wooden wagon, and from a small window a girl with strongly colored cheeks looked out. The children said that she would walk on a rope…

It did not take long, and there already stood individual divisions: a "circus," where one could see various clowns, a booth where one threw tin cans at a table with numbers. There, one won important things.

The primary thing, though, was the carousel – with moving carriages and horses, as though they could gallop the greatest gallop…

The carousel attracted all the children from the town. The poor ones spun the wealthy ones, as follows: up above stood ten children, who, with their little hands, pushed the big wheel in one direction; the wheel upon which the horses hung. With their strength, the carousel was spun. For spinning it ten times, a poor child went on a horse once.

Even grown-ups looked at the spinning and took pride in their children's feats.

I stood with my mother after I had already sacrificed/relinquished that which was mine. Next to my mother stood another Jewish woman, Chaya-Faige, they called her. She was Yankl Rudy's wife and always had a pale face.

They both observed how the children were climbing into the moving carriages and jumping up onto the horses, and it looked like the children's radiance was bouncing off their tired faces. The owner of the carousel gave the long-awaited chime, and the horses began to run in pursuit, growing faster over time. It dizzied the eyes, and the children shouted, shrieked, and laughed. Following several minutes, a chime could once again be heard. This was a signal that the carousel was coming to a halt. The galloping had ended, the "people" crawled down, for soon there would be another group with other people taking their places.

You see, Malka – Chaya-Faige called to my mother – this is the countenance/appearance of a person's entire life. He is seated in a wagon, and someone turns him around in a mind-dizzying gallop. It stops and lets off steam. But before he looks around, he is told to get out of the wagon. His spot is already taken up by another person…

My mother nodded her head [in agreement] and with a thoughtful voice, said: Yeah, yeah, that's how human life looks.

Bygone Girls…

It would often happen that our dear teacher, Minne Tobias, would invite his students over to his home; he would read us Sholem Aleichem or Bialik – his most beloved writers. We had tryouts for a play, which we were preparing to stage for some type of holiday.

Aside from reading to us or directing, Minne did not have any great interest in spending time with us. He did not dance or participate in any of the young gang's fun.

Following the reading we would schmooze with the girls or dance, organize a collective game, and so forth.

Minne had relatives in the village of Luka. Once, his cousin came for a visit. Her name was Roize; [she was] a young girl.

We were there for the Sabbath. Minne read for the gang, and afterwards went out into the street. The gang remained [behind] and had a joyful time. We played "Zakonnik" [Polish for "Monk"]. The game consisted of making a corner partition of the room;

[pp. 261-262]

a boy would go under and then invite over a girl; then the fellow would leave, and the girl would again invite another fellow, according to her wishes. We, the "modern" and "revolutionary" youth, conducted ourselves very well.

Under the partition, it would often happen that the fellow and the girl would merely look at each other bashfully, and with this, everything ended. Olya Fischmann invited the guest, Roize from Luka, under the partition. It happened – he hugged her and gave her a kiss.

The girl emerged from behind the curtain with a cry, and shouted ---- What will I do now? What will I do now?...

Translator's Footnotes:

1.   This expression is supposed to connote that the father, Eli Moshe the Big, would like to be able to take pride in – be built up by – his youngest son, but his wishes seem to have been for naught.
2.   "Bontshe Shvayg" or "Bontshe the Silent" is a literary allusion to a story by I. L. Peretz.

[pp. 263-264]

Types and Figures

Yosef Schwartz, New York

Faige the Grandmother

The doctors who lived in Bursztyn at the beginning of the twentieth century, Mondschein and Mach, definitely needed to break their heads insofar as earning a livelihood. For who used a doctor, then? Both the Christian and Jewish residents had their own male and female curse removers. In our town there were several such grandmothers. But the most popular of them was Faige the grandmother [i.e., in this context, a midwife].

She was tall, thin, and dried-out, with long, dangling arms, but on her face she always bore a smile, and always greeted everyone with a nice word. She delivered 7 of my mother's children, from which four died soon [thereafter]. By my grandmother, Rochel, at the birth of her son, Naftali, they called upon Faige the grandmother. She had her remedies for all sorts of illnesses. Honey dough for swollenness, hot wax if the child was rickety; one had to bathe it in milk and honey.

To take care of a poor pregnant woman, moreover, with a small yoke, there were in the town Rochele Hammer, Leahtshe, Meir Tepper's [wife]. They already knew that it was necessary to take care of the pregnant woman at a particular time.

Faige the grandmother helped approximately fifteen hundred children come into the world. From many pregnant women she did not take any money, because at home there was simply nothing for a piece of bread. In her older years, Faige's stars as a grandmother began to become extinguished. Schooled midwives began to appear, [there was] Mrs. Nadler; and in the last years, Asher Blecher's daughter, Mrs. Sarah Zommer. Bursztyn was already more enlightened, and if it was very necessary, they would already call upon Dr. Zusmann , or upon Dr. Schumer.

Faige passed away in the 1930s. Her final days were spent at [the home of] her son, Petachiah the doctor.

Female Candle Makers

Fifty years ago, a great deal of effort was invested, so that the Yom Kippur candles should be made of pure beeswax, and that at the point of putting on the wicks, the names of deceased family members should be mentioned. This was expensive enough, and not everyone could afford it. Leahtshe, Meir's [wife] and Malka Berkes were involved in this [line of work]. Their candles cost a lot of money. Only the elderly Rochele Hammer did this without [asking for] money, for the sake of the good deed, but only for select individuals.

Her livelihood Rochele Hammer earned from a small shop, which she had next to a Polish church. On account of this and several good deeds, she neglected the shop.

Aunt Libtze and the Korban Mincha Prayer Book

She hailed from Podorozhnie, a village next to Rohatyn. [She was] a good-hearted [woman], always smiling,

[pp. 265-266]

a master of honesty, innocence, and religiosity. Living in poverty, she always gave away from her little bit, to those who were even poorer than she.

Aunt Libtze was a friend of Y. Fenster's mother O"BM [i.e., Of Blessed Memory], and of his mother's sister, Shifra, who hailed from Rohatyn.

The surviving Jews from Rohatyn relate: When the local Jews were driven out behind the city (to the brickyard) to murder them, Aunt Shifra went with hundreds of kosher Jewish women and children, and from the open "Korban Mincha" recited Psalms aloud.

Eli the butcher and his wife, Liftze

Chevra Tehillim[1]

On the Sabbath of the Torah portion of Genesis, the Chevra Tehillim had the precedent of running the proceedings at the religious study house. The trustee of the Chevra Tehillim circle, Sane Yidele the Butcher's [son?], stood by, reading from the Torah, and saw to it that his people be called up for good "Aliyahs." There was almost no Sabbath Genesis when a brawl did not ensue. The trustee of the religious house of study, Avrahamtshe Breiter, wanted to give his people the "third [Aliyah]," or the "sixth [Aliyah]." The butchers stood on the side of Sane and the Chevra Tehillim.

Sabbath Genesis had scarcely ended, [and so] the disputes also disappeared. The town became submerged in monetary concerns, in the difficult toil of daily [life].

Merchants

Every Tuesday there was a fair in Bursztyn. From the furthest-away villages, male and female peasants came to attend. From the closer villages, such as Nastaszczyn, Kuropatniki, Demianow, Korostowice, Martynow, Czahrow, and others, the female peasants would come on foot. They would sell chickens, butter, and sour cream, all sorts of grain, and cattle/cows. There were merchants who immediately grabbed everything from them. There was even a Jew who dealt in pigs.

Bursztyn Jews conducted business with Vienna and Prague. Entire transports of slaughtered calves and various foods would arrive in these cities. Among the sponsors there were also lessees of estates and such, who themselves worked the soil. Among them were: Ezriel Kleinfeld from Korostowice, Eli Treiber, Leibush-Eli Kimmel, and his father, Shlomo, Moshe Haber, and yet other Jews. To these ox-merchants belonged: Aizik Breiter, Velvele Yonah-Leib's, Yitzchak Kortasz, Yitzchak Berkes, Leib Moshe Ziskind's, and my father. The primary expediter of eggs to Germany was Berish Hornik, who employed approximately ten Jews.

Around the merchants at the marketplace there moved about various types of poor brokers who sought a way to earn a piece of bread. They would stand next to the peasant customer and give the appearance that they were giving more [than they were, in actuality]. From Bursztyn, one also went to fairs in other cities.

[pp. 267-268]

Carriage Drivers

Simple, good-hearted people, always ready to give away their last groschen as a donation.

Avraham Moshe Daniel's [or possibly Daniels] allowed his son, Yekele, to study at the University of Vienna. Yekele was a fiery Zionist and took an active part in social life.

Avraham's brother, Meir, was also a carriage driver. His children were also active in the social life of Bursztyn.

Avrahamtshi "Spitz," a carriage driver, a sweet person, with a great deal of inborn genteelness/politeness.

Wolf Faige's Chatshulik [i.e., possibly a horse breeder or dealer] always had, during the most difficult times, a ready joke, a good word to say. Once, standing next to R' Nachman Breiter's shop, he consulted him:

R' Nachman, do you have today's newspaper?

Why do you need the newspaper – Nachman Breiter asked him – are you able to read?

For heaven's sake. I can't read, but seeing as I don't have any oats, any hay to give to my horses, I would like to collect the newspaper, so that they should at least have what to read.

All those who were present laughed. But many of them knew that not only the horses did not have what to eat, but also at home, Wolf's wife did not have a piece of bread for the children. This was just before the outbreak of the First World War.

Wolf had the loveliest harness. The children, Itzik Hirsh, Moshe Godele, and Berl helped out day and night with two drunkards, guarding the Demianow station, but they always ended up in dire straits/impoverished.

During the first year of the war, not far from his house, stood a division of the Austrian military, which carried with it, in a wagon, a large money chest. Wolf knew about this from the soldiers who were quartered at his home. At some point, the Russians began to shoot at the division. Two soldiers were killed on the spot. The others fled. Wolf and his son went outside and dragged in the chest of money to their home, and later buried it in the yard.

With this money, Wolf began to carry out major transactions. [But even] with that, he remained the same good-hearted person. In the town, one knew about many people who would have died of hunger, were it not for Wolf's help. During the nights, he would deliver whole sacks of flour to these people with his horses. Aside from that, he helped with money, and all of this [he did] with the greatest modesty and concern, that the people not be embarrassed, not become dejected/downhearted.

The Friedlanders

My memory does not recall Avraham Hersh Friedlander. I only recall the two brothers, Shmuel Mordechai and Yossel Friedlander. They ran the big mill, which operated day and night.

Next to the large mill was a small water mill where the peasants would come to grind for their home usage. Town cattle/cow merchants would also grind grain there for their cattle/cows.

In the year 1914, the entire Friedlander family fled from the town. The Russians plundered the mill. The peasants from the surrounding villages divided up the plundered flour, and the mill went up in the fire.

The Legend about the New Jewish Cemetery

Approximately one hundred years ago, cholera broke out in the town. People fell like flies. There began to be a dearth of space in the Jewish cemetery, when a major righteous man ordered that they designate a new Jewish cemetery.

[pp. 269-270]

The Jewish Burial Society at the Bursztyn Jewish Cemetery

Then, God would help them, and the epidemic would subside. And that is how it was. Following the first four deaths, [the bodies of which] were buried in the new Jewish cemetery, the epidemic subsided.

The Spring

Next to the new Jewish cemetery stood a spring, which for many years was surrounded by a fence. People called it: the Water Elder Spring.

The entire surrounding population believed that bathing in this spring would heal all sorts of eye infirmities. In many homes they had water from this spring in sealed jars, ready as a remedy for some sort of trouble. When a boy cut open my head with a stone, a Jewish woman washed off the wound with that water.

Sh. An-ski in Bursztyn

Once, during a winter's night in the beginning of 1915, a Russian officer, a tall and sturdily built man, with silver armbands and a Cossack cap, perched to the side, and a nicely trimmed, grey, pointed beard, entered the religious house of study.

1.   The crowd at the religious study house became frightened and stood up from their places, but the officer immediately began to speak with them… in Yiddish. He extended his hand to everyone, looked inside of the Gemaras, which lay open on the lecterns. Later on, he took out a notebook and went over to R' Leibush Kletter with questions. R' Leibush responded to him about everything, and we, boys, stood around them with open mouths.

The Rohatyner Klezmer players: Moyshele Poist and his sons: David, Itzik-Hersh, Mordechai-Shmuel, and Yankl, and others.
Over the course of two generations, the Rohatyner Klezmer players led grooms and brides to the wedding canopy in Bursztyn.
The four sons were murdered by the Hitlerist murderers.

[pp. 271-272]

The officer asked him how many Jews had left the town and how many had remained, [and] how they earned a living.

When leaving, he said that if any Russian should try to do something bad, they should come to him. He lived in the courtyard of Prince Jablonowski. His name was Shloyme [Shlomo] Rapoport. That was Sh. Anski.

The Jews in the town once again waited for the officer, the following day. But he no longer came. For that very night, his unit transferred to another city.

Translator's Footnote:

    1.   An organization oriented around the recitation of Psalms.

[pp. 273-274]

<u>Jewish Intelligentsia</u>

[pp. 275-276]

Jewish Intelligentsia

Yisrael Fenster

Our town, with such a small Jewish community; nonetheless, during the final decades of its existence, managed to take in and absorb within it, social, cultural, and political streams, and aspirations of the major creative Jewish collectivity in Poland. Little Bursztyn also had a number of Jewish intelligentsia [members] and serious social leaders. The notions of national and social freedom struck deep roots here. With Chasidic fervor and devotion, the youth threw itself into the struggle for the realization of the thousand-year-long dreams of the Jew and human-being.

This was mostly people who had leapt over the fence of our town, into the broader world, and felt the crowdedness there; for in their hearts, they carried with them the soulful breadth of the town and returned to serve it and to be the tenth man to make up the Minyan, with the goodness and joy of Jewish stubbornness, unrest, and desire for creativity.

Dr. David Maltz

I recall Dr. David Maltz as if in a dream. He was a lawyer, a man of average height, with a pointy little beard. A distinguished personality in the Zionist movement of East Galicia. If I am not mistaken, he was among the delegates at the First Zionist Congress. He was a first-class speaker. He was very popular and beloved far beyond Bursztyn by Jews and non-Jews.

They would relate in the town: before Austrian times, while he was running as a candidate for Parliament as a Zionist representative, who was also supported by the Ukrainians against a Polish candidate, Dr. Maltz once held an election speech, at which the Ukrainians even hoisted him up in their arms.

Dr. David Maltz was an able journalist; his articles were mostly about Zionism, [and] would be printed in the Yiddish newspaper, which appeared in Lemberg, "Dos Tag[e]blatt," as well as in the Polish liberal press.

His children he raised in the Jewish and Zionist spirit. His son, Edik, he sent to the Baron Hirsch School, along with the children of the simple common people.

His daughter made Aliyah in the beginning of the 1920s to Israel. She worked hard at building roads and houses; she became ill and died.

The brother-in-law of Dr. Maltz was Dr. Mordechai Ehrenpreis, Chief Rabbi of Stockholm, and a well-known Zionist activist. The wife of the director of the Baron Hirsch School, Anshel Fogel, the wife of Dr. Maltz, and Mordechai Ehrenpreis, were sisters and brothers. Their father was a bookseller in Lemberg.

[pp. 277-278]

Following the First World War, Dr. Maltz did not return to Bursztyn; he settled in Lemberg.

He did not take any part in Bursztyn's political life of Polish Jewry during the two world wars. This was likely because of his poor state of health.

Dr. Maltz died before the Second World War.

Wilhelm Rohrth (Valya Rapoport)[1]

Before the First World War, there lived in Bursztyn a family named Rapoport. There were 2 adult sons and a daughter in the family. The older son was named Valya. He was a teacher at the Polish school. This Valya possessed the rare ability to observe and describe people. When he was still a youngster, he wrote essays [that appeared] in the Polish newspapers.

Following the First World War, he was once again a teacher in Bursztyn. He kept himself far-removed from Jews and from Judaism. He was a member of the Polish Socialist Party (P. P. S.).

During the course of time his first work, "Before Caesar's Times," "Za czasów Cesarza," appeared. After that, [there was] a comedy, "Manageria," which was a satire on the social life of the intelligentsia in Bursztyn.

These two books right away made a name for him in Poland.

The comedy was played in all the largest Polish theaters.

In 1922, he fell ill with tuberculosis. (His younger brother, Maciej, also died from the same illness).

He lay in critical condition, receiving one blood transfusion after the next. The doctors saw in advance a quick end.

I would often visit him at that time, devoting myself greatly to him. Around him walked a Christian girl who was working during her post.

Once, when he felt very weak, he called me over to him and asked: I should go to the religious house of study, see a few Jews there – they should recite Psalms and beg God that he become well. I fulfilled his request. The Jews begged God – and he became well. That is why he married the Christian girl… He left Bursztyn. He became one of the greatest humorists in Poland, under the well-known name, Wilhelm Rohrth. It was said that he had totally left Judaism. He would frequently come to Bursztyn to refresh the graves of his father and brother. Primarily, he would always leave behind money so that candles be burned in the synagogue and that poor Jews recite Psalms.

Dr. Wolf Schmarak

Dr. Wolf Schmarak moved to Bursztyn during the First World War. He took over the house of the director, Anshel Fogel. He hailed from a well-known Zionist family in the vicinity of Stryj; he was tall, slim, with an original Jewish face. He right away became socially active in the town.

Following the First World War, when a large part of the Bursztyn youth was leftward-inclined, Dr. Schmarak was the leading champion of the Zionist idea.

We, young ones, who believed with

[pp. 279-280]

complete faith, that Socialism would bring equality and salvation for the Jews in the diaspora, strongly opposed Dr. Schmarak.

I recall the following episode: It was in the beginning of the 1920s. Dr. Schmarak Z"L spoke at the religious house of study, which was packed full of Jews. He said the

President of the Bursztyner Credit Treasury
Sitting from the left: Dr. Wolf Schmarak, Yisroel Lasberg, and Shmuel Muttermilch

following words: "For the Jews there are two ways: to emigrate to Israel and build a new life there, or... for everyone to become apostates. A huge tumult developed in the religious study house, from the left-winged side, which saw in this "black reactionism." From the other side – the religious, who were struck/hit by this heretical presentation.

Unfortunately, the prophecy was fulfilled in an utterly terrifying form.

Despite the opposing outlooks, he would meet with us, discuss. Regarding the Poalei-Tzion he would say: You are Zionists in quotation marks. The Galicianer Poalei-Tzion was, as is known, much more radical in its Socialism, than the Poalei-Tzion in other parts of Poland. It called itself: Jewish Socialist Workers' Party ("Poalei Tzion"), and this is what he referred to as Zionists in quotation marks.

Dr. Schmarak was a contributor to the Zionist daily newspaper, "Chwila," which appeared in Lemberg. He was one of the most distinguished Zionists in the area. A sharp polemicist, but always in an elegant form, not personally offensive.

He was one of the most popular lawyers in Bursztyn and was a long-term councilor at the Bursztyn Magistrate.

I had the honor of sitting with him for two years in the Magistrate's Jewish sector. His every move made an impression on all his listeners. Jews and Christians. He always fought for Jewish rights and honor. The final years he was ill and had much pain in his legs. One would frequently encounter him on the street clasping his wife's arm.

[pp. 281-282]

Dr. Lipa Schumer

A Bursztyn-born, learned in cheder, and at the religious study house. He studied medicine in Vienna. Right after the First World War, he came and settled in the town.

At that time, a terrible typhus epidemic raged in the area, and Dr. Schumer right away had his hands full of work. I recall him running around from house to house. He climbed down from one wagon and up onto another one, until he himself grew ill with spotted typhus. His young, healthy body overcame the illness; he became well [again].

He was the most popular physician in Bursztyn and the surrounding area.

The Jews of Bursztyn were proud of him, one of their own people. When he would come to the religious study house to speak about Zionism, or about civil matters, Jews would beam from pleasure. He would interweave a verse or Midrash with his sermon.

Unfortunately, Dr. Schumer never had any time to devote himself to social, cultural life in the town. He was always racing, always running.

Until … until the Second World War broke out. The Russians entered the town. Living in fear. Not being able to sleep calmly through the night, should someone come to "take you [away]," the ache from the plunder of that which was hard-earned – [and so] Dr. Schumer aged early. I remember very well those days. The truth is that compared to what happened afterwards, during the time of Hitler, this was heaven.

Dr. Schumer and his family had the fortune of rescuing themselves from Hitlerist hands and being among the small remnant of surviving Bursztyn Jews.

Dr. Schumer did not live to see our "memorial book." He died on 10.11.1959, 18 Cheshvan 5720 [1960]. May his memory be for a blessing.

Minne Tobias

When the First World War broke out, Minne Tobias, the son of Avraham Eli Tobias, was studying at the University of Lemberg. He was called up to the Austrian military, served as an artillery officer, took part in the battles, and was wounded.

Following the war, he returned to the town. It is worth mentioning two facts that had a major effect on Tobias – formed his world outlook and path in life as a Jew and human-being.

During the war, he became acquainted with a Russian Jew who was taken prisoner by the Austrians. This Jew, who was very enlightened [or, an adherent of the Jewish Enlightenment] and proficient in the new Hebrew and Yiddish literature, became the attendant of the Austrian officer, M. Tobias. That very attendant, the simple Russian soldier, began to read and recite with his master Yiddish and Hebrew literature, Bialik and Peretz, Mendele, and Sholem Aleichem. The Russian Jew had a tremendous influence on Tobias as a Zionist and Jewish man of the people.

Following a characteristic episode, which demonstrates the relations that existed between an officer and his attendant. Minne related it himself:

Once, in the evening, my attendant read Peretz, as usual, with heart and fervor, and I swallowed up each of his words. That day, I grew very tired, and I do not know how it happened. My eyes closed

[pp. 283-284]

and I fell asleep… I was awakened by the book closing loudly with a bang. My attendant stood up red with anger and shouted: You are indeed nothing more than an "egg-man" (Minne's father was an egg dealer)… Tobias forgave him, and the Russian Jew continued to learn to love his people and his spiritual treasures.

During the years 1918-1920, when the Ukrainian-Polish and Russian-Polish battles took place in our area, when our town of Bursztyn was transferred, hand-to-hand, and Jewish possessions, Jewish honor was for naught, Tobias once saw how a Polish officer was making fun of a Jew and wanted to shave off his beard. Minne defended the Jew and said to the hooligan: I am also an officer in the reserves… The response from the Polish officer was a slap in Tobias' face.

When the Polish forces were mobilized, Minne informed the military forces about this situation, and at the same time withdrew his rights as a Polish officer. The Polish military forces won/made a hit with this [information]. M. Tobias received a message that he was being freed, entirely, from his military service.

After the war, Minne did not continue his studies. He opened a bakery, and together with his brother, Mendel, worked hard and supported his mother and sister. He married the daughter of Moshe Strickendreier.

Minne was an original personality. Intelligent and sharp-witted. He had a major influence on the youth, particularly on the left-wing [ones]; they impressed upon his relationship with work. One could see him carrying loads, carrying water, and in general, carrying out the hardest physical labor. He was an anti-clericalist and an absolutist opponent of Socialism. The solution to the Jewish question he saw in Zionism.

The major reason for his energetic attraction was his great knowledge of modern Yiddish literature. He was the instructor of a whole group of youths. He learned the Yiddish classics with them.

Who from among us does not recall his readings on literary themes? His enthusiasm while reading Peretz, Sholem Aleichem, and Bialik. His theatrical productions, he would bring, together with Binem Lev, to Lemberg, while the Vilne Trupe was strolling [through]. He would observe their performances and later on, their direction and performances of the best plays of their repertoire in Bursztyn.

Minne Tobias did not want to conduct any political discussions with us. Regarding Socialism he spoke with disregard, saying: "You want to make all people equal? Impossible. They are born unequal. Look at me and my wife Hinda! And look at Daniel Krantz and Peya!"

The distinction was not only a physical one, but also a moral one; nobody could deny it.

Minne worked for many years in his bakery. A few years before the war, he purchased a farm in the region of Lemberg. He settled there and lived in a village.

September 1939, when the Red Army conquered East Galicia, they took away his farm, and drove him out of the village.

He arrived in Bursztyn, broken. He once came into my place, holding onto a cane. The wounds of the previous war pained him. He raised the cane and with his deep voice said: "I should whack you over the head with this cane, but you already have enough trouble."

A few weeks later, the N. K. V. D. arrested me as a "contra-revolutionary" and sent me to Siberia.

[pp. 285-286]

The surviving Jews of Bursztyn relate that Minne Tobias right away recognized the devilish Nazi plans against the Jews; he refused to work with them – he was sent to the Rohatyn ghetto and died there.

A group of the intelligentsia in Bursztyn

Sitting from the left: Dr. Schmarak, Mrs. Rurberg, Dr. Klugmann, Mrs. Dr. Schmarak, and Dr. Hacker
In the middle: The veterinarian Adolph Wattenberg (he was murdered in the woods of Katyn)

Translator's Footnote:

    1.   I have searched several sources, including the Polish National Library's online catalogue, but have been unable to locate any information about this Polish-Jewish writer. I am also uncertain precisely how to spell his nom de plume in Latin characters.

[pp. 287-288]

Types of Religious Scholars

S. Schapira, New York

R' Feivel Frankl

He was a Czortkower Chasid. The entire day he was busy in his glass shop, and in the evenings, he would sit until late at night in the religious study house, and learn together with all the young men, among whom he was distinguished with his learnedness and breadth [of knowledge] in Tanach. He was known as a smart Jew; he had a ready joke for everyone.

R' Feivel Frankl and his wife, Chaya

He raised fine children. One of them, David, left in the 1930s for Israel. But he, too, is no longer living. He died in 1954.

One of the highest virtues for which R' Feivel Frankl stood out, was his uncompromising way of holding himself to the truth [i.e., stating the truth]. At every opportunity, he told even those people who were closest [to him] the truth to their faces. This is also what he taught his own children.

R' David Frankl

The son of R' Feivel. While learning in the religious house of study, he joined the First Zionists in the town. He made Aliyah to Israel, was active in "Mizrachi," and was a trustee of the Great Synagogue of Haifa, being all the while a laborer. He died in September 1954.

R' Leibush Kletter

He belonged to those well-off Jews for whom money did not mess with their heads, who did not become conceited. Leibush Kletter became friendly with all the fellows [learning] at the religious study house, learned a page of Gemara with them. On the Sabbath, following the meal, he would learn Pirkei Avot [Ethics of the Fathers] with the commentaries, together with them.

He possessed a sharp head and loved to steep himself in the Rambam's [Maimonides'] philosophical method/system.

[pp. 289-290]

He helped us to understand in an accessible form the logical conclusions of the Rambam.

Every morning one would see him sitting in the religious study house over the Gemara. At that time, he would learn alone; and at that, he smoked a great deal.

R' Leibush Kletter was known as a wise man in every area/field. Just as in the Gemara, so too in politics, he also possessed the ability to explain and demonstrate.

His learning, alone and with students, interested him more than his flour shop, where the main burden lay upon his wife and children. Among his students were also: Yankl Vove, the ritual slaughterer's son, Yisroel Schneeweiss, and I.

R' Berish Gelernter

He was wealthy, had an aristocratic demeanor, but at the same time, learned a lot. Nearly every day after praying, he would sit in the religious house of study over the Gemara. The fellows in the religious study house had in him a human-being, to whom one could turn with a question concerning a difficult spot in the Gemara. He possessed the strength to clarify in an understandable manner. The same was true of secular matters.

R' Itzik-David the Cantor

A learned man of a Jew; there was not a day in the week that he was not among the first at the religious study house, where he sat and learned until the final Minyan, which ended around eleven o'clock. Monday and Thursday, as well as Rosh Chodesh [i.e., the beginning of the Jewish month], he would read from the Torah at every Minyan.

R' Itzik the cantor was concerned that at the religious study house there should always be prepared cake and liquor, with which everyone who had a Yahrtzeit could serve the worshippers.

Aside from the six hours in the morning, he would also learn during the evening hours until late into the night.

R' Uri Kleinfeld

I still remember him as a gentle young man, how in the middle of a beautiful day he would interrupt his business and go into the religious house of learning to learn a page of Gemara. On the Sabbath, following lunch, he would come to my home and call upon me to learn until the time of the Mincha [prayers]. He did not like to learn alone and did not consider that someone might think that it was beneath his honor to call upon a boy, that he should learn with him. I felt exalted by this very honor. In my memory remains his great love for learning.

Binem Schapira

A noteworthy type who represented within him a harmony of enlightenment and Chasidism. He was a Stratyner Chasid, and at the same time, an adherent of secular education.

His only day of rest was the Sabbath. Right after the Sabbath day meal he would already be sitting over the Tanach. He read modern Hebrew literature and was enthralled by the poems of Bialik and Tchernichovsky. The young fellows who took up Hebrew literature were his frequent guests on Sabbath afternoons.

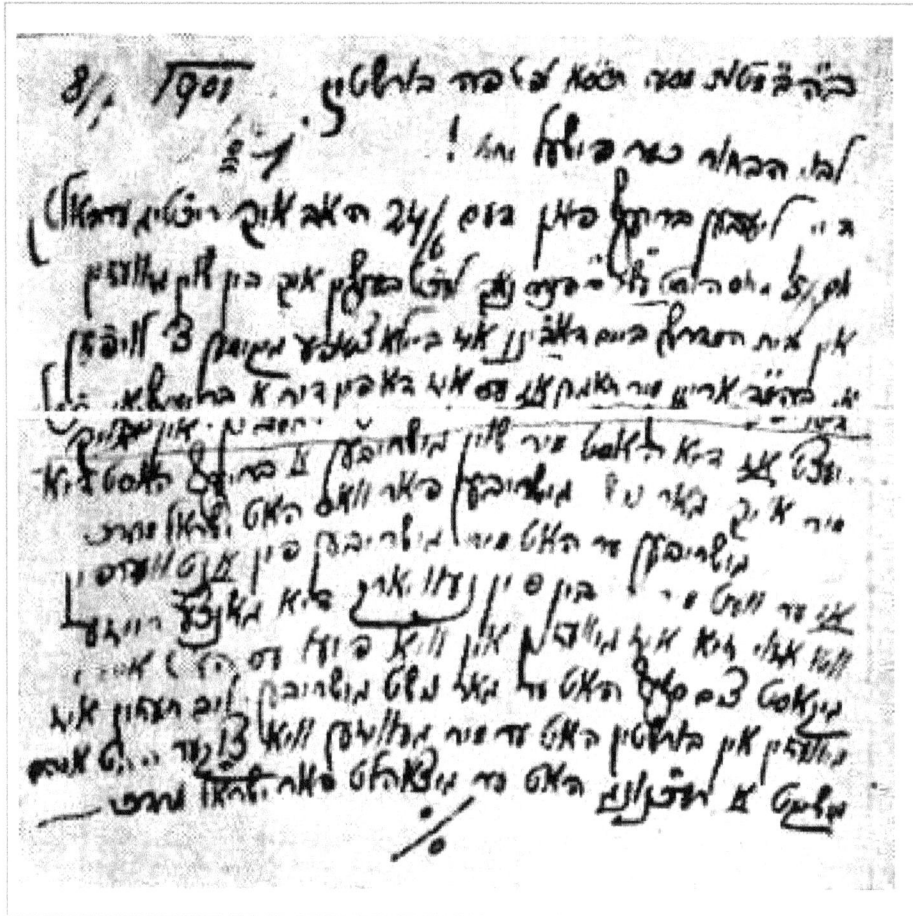

The handwriting of R' Itzik-David the cantor

[pp. 291-292]

He read Hebrew poetry together with them and the Hebrew weekly, "Hamitzpah," to which he subscribed at that time. We, Yankl, Vove the ritual slaughterer's [son], and I, gave donations toward the costs of subscribing to this weekly. He was permeated with the deep desire to help the youth receive an education. His ideal was: a religious Jew with a modern education.

R' Koppel Henich

Yosef Schwartz, New York

He hailed from Kolomyja, from a rabbinic dynasty, and was the son-in-law of Moshe Haber, who owned his own fields, a brickyard, and dealt in cattle. After getting married, Koppel did not want to be on Kest [i.e., provided room and board by his father-in-law] and began to trade. He learned at dawn and in the evenings.

The Henich family in America (sons and daughters of R' Koppel Henich)

First row (from the right): Wolf, the mother, Mattel, Ruchtche, Chaim
Second row (from the right): Meir, Ola, Bronia, Harry

Koppel did not get involved in Jewish communal matters. However, one knew that he devoted himself to charity for latently poor people. He gave much time to the education of his children, who were noted for their decency. Their father's word was holy to them.

In 1915, when the Russian Army marched into Galicia, they transported thousands of Austrian prisoners through our town. Coincidentally, at the time, Koppel was at his

[pp. 293-294]

father-in-law's [home], whose house stood near the main road, where the Cossacks accompanied the prisoners on their horses. Koppel noticed how one of the multitude of prisoners had stepped out of the line. The Cossack galloped over to him, gave him a whack with his rifle,[1] and the fellow collapsed, bloodied. Koppel, risking his life, ran out to him with a bowl of water and washed off the wounds. At some point he overheard the wounded man murmuring something in Yiddish. Koppel looked around and saw that the Cossack was busy with other prisoners, so he quickly dragged the wounded man to the fence of the neighboring Christian cemetery. The Cossacks noticed it later on, but they were certain that he was being dragged [away] to be buried and did not react.

Koppel hid that Jew somewhere, and only when the entire body [of soldiers] had left the town, did he take him out of this hiding place. It turned out that the fellow was from Kolomyja. Koppel hid him at his place during the entire period of the Russian occupation.

A year later, 1916, when cholera raged in the town, Koppel died. During the same period, his father-in-law, R' Moshe Haber also died.

His wife, Mattel, resides today in America, along with her children: Velvl, Hersh, Chaim, Meir, Pinye, Ephraim, Rochel, and Sarah.

Translator's Footnote:

1.   The word that appears here in the original Yiddish text is "rapnik," whose exact definition I was unable to find in any dictionaries. The closest related word that I have found to-date is "rapier," which is a type of sword that was used namely in the 16th-18th centuries, particularly in France. In the given 20th century context of World War II, it is possible that this was some type of sword, but perhaps more probable, that it was some form of rifle or revolver.

[pp. 295-296]

Dr. Zev (Wolf) Schmurek[1] [a]

Ilana Meschler-Schmurek

He was born in 1881 in the city of Bolechow, in eastern Galicia. His mother, Bertha, an enlightened woman, passed down education to her children, so that they should learn according to their talents. Zev studied in a gymnasium in Stryj, and at a young age, the merit of bravery and feelings of self-respect became recognized within him. While he was a student of the gymnasium, a strike was initiated by the entire class, on account of the insulting behavior of one of the teachers. The students were standing up and leaving the classroom every time that the teacher with the boorish behavior would enter. The administration of the gymnasium commented on the unprecedented disturbance with much severity but realized that the 17-year-old youths were standing their ground insofar as their wishes to remove the despised teacher, and that they were not frightened by any threats. The administration was forced to conduct business with the "rebels," and the event merited publicity among the public and in the newspapers. In the end, the teacher was removed from the classroom, and the administration of the gymnasium took revenge on the forces [behind] the strike and its organizers, who informed on them. Among the students who were sentenced for expulsion was Zev Schmurek and two of his friends. And the decision [was made] that they would complete the seventh grade in Stryj and then transfer to a gymnasium in another city. When he came to study in Lwow [i.e., Lemberg], the students of the gymnasium organized an enthusiastic welcome: a Jewish young man showed the Gentiles how one fights for human honor.

Zev Schmurek studied law in Vienna. Indeed, most of his time and energy he dedicated to Zionist movement activities. The movement was then at the beginning of its existence, and the path of its pioneers was very difficult and full of obstacles. They were met with apathy/indifference and suspicion, with mockery and loathing from among their [own] people, as well as from the environment in which they lived; however, their efforts bore fruit and their lines continued to grow.

Zev Schmurek worked in Vienna and in the provincial towns, particularly, in his city of Stryj, and was a speaker at assemblies and festivities, appeared at assemblies of opponents of Zionism, and let his words be heard, despite the attack on him by the crowd, the heckling, and raising of fists against him.

He and his friends founded a Hebrew school in Stryj, at which generations were educated in the Hebrew language and with love for the [Jewish] homeland. The Jewish students were a target for anti-Semitic teasing, and Zev Schmurek was a member of a combative academic Zionist corporation, and he learned to a great degree to protect the national honor that he possessed. A branch of the corporation was also established with his efforts in Stryj, and he merited celebrating the 25-year jubilee of its founding.

When he returned from Vienna to Galicia, he worked as a lawyer and continued in his Zionist activity. In the year 1911, he married Fannie Frisch, the daughter of Menashe Frisch, the communal activist whose brother was the writer, Ephraim Frisch. During the First World War, he was conscripted into the army, and returned home a sick man, and from then on, he did not return to us. After Poland became independent, he decided to put down roots in Lwow as a lawyer and prepared to make Aliyah to Israel with his family. As per the advice of his friend, Dr. David

The family of Dr. Schmurek

From the left: Fannie, the wife of Dr. Schmurek, his mother, Bertha, and Dr. Z. Schmurek. His daughters: Ilana and Milia Standing from the left: His brother, Dr. Eliezer Schmurek Z"L

Maltz, he settled temporarily in Bursztyn, a small town, so that he would be able to make a living there and also do something on behalf of Zionism.

[pp. 297-298]

In Bursztyn, he was greeted hospitably, and [so] he decided to settle in the town up until the time that he made Aliyah and did not imagine that it would last 24 years – up until his death at the hands of the Nazi murderers.

When he arrived in Bursztyn, [as] the first lawyer there, he quickly became famous throughout the region, as somebody possessing excellent professional talents; and his work did not prevent him from continuing his Zionist activity among adults and youths in the planning and preparations for their Aliyah to Israel. Aside from his work in Bursztyn, he was also a member of the Zionist Histadrut Council in Lwow; he was also involved with Zionist journalism and wrote articles in Polish and in Yiddish. During the elections for the Polish Sejm (House of Electors), he was selected to be a delegate, but the doctors warned him against strenuous work, which would involve trips to Warsaw, and thus he did not agree to be selected as a delegate. However,

The Zionist Youth [in Hebrew: "Noar Ha-Tzioni"] of Bursztyn

in all the institutes/establishments, and particularly in the courthouse, he would appear as a Jewish nationalist; and with his national pride, he received respect, even among the noteworthy Jew-haters. He would force Polish judges to permit Jews who did not know Polish to submit their testimonies in the "Mother Tongue," in Yiddish, which grated on the ears of the anti-Semites. With his sharp tongue and sense of humor that he displayed in his appearances, he became a [much] sought after defense attorney in criminal and political trials. While he was studying legal defense, he publicized the [situation faced by] Ukrainian nationalists and proved that the officers extorted confessions from the mouths of the suspects through beatings and cruel [forms of] torture; the accused were freed, and several officers were punished, and he acquired a name for being "enemy number one" of the Polish police.

Indeed, the police meted out revenge against him, after the passage of several years, when Sejm elections were organized within an environment of blatant terror. Nonetheless, they did not dare to forbid/prohibit Dr. Zev Schmurek; rather, they placed an armed officer at the gate of his home, whose job it was to prohibit him and his wife from leaving the house until the end of the elections. The intention was that Dr. Schmurek would respond sharply to the violation of his civil rights, and they would be able to prohibit him in accordance with the law. However, he did not say anything about the "guard of honor," but rather, secretly exited his home from the backdoor, accompanied by his wife; and by way of gardens and fields, they reached the ballot box station [i.e., voting station]… With great effort, while he was ill, he crossed the road that was full of barriers, and when he entered the ballot box station, it was understood from the facial expressions of the council members, that they had not at all expected his arrival. The news of his deed spread through the city and elicited laughter and joy among the Jews, and encouraged the vacillators and those who were frightened to go to the ballot box station and vote for the Zionist list.

The celebrations on the Jewish street in Bursztyn were small: the economic situation of most of the residents was very difficult, and the miniscule favored ones, peddlers, and merchants, suffered from a lack of cash flow. Dr. Schmurek exerted himself and established a branch of the "Cooperative Bank for Credit" and the enterprise succeeded and functioned until the outbreak of the Second World War. Dr. Schmurek stood at its head, and all the members of its administration worked as volunteers; from all of them, only one survived, H. Ruhr, who resides in the United States.

Dr. Schmurek hoped that he would succeed in realizing his dream

[pp. 299-300]

and make Aliyah to Israel with his family. His two daughters studied Hebrew. In the year 1928, their father was granted a travel ticket for Israel, with the desire of acquiring a house [there] and bringing over his family members. Two months before his designated departure, he took suddenly ill, and he was not able to go, due to his incurable illness, and he was forced to give up on the realization of his dream.

When the Second World War broke out, the Soviet army regiments invaded Bursztyn, and Dr. Schmurek suffered hardship and persecution: he was driven from his home and stood to be imprisoned, but managed to escape to Lwow, entered the hospital, and his health condition worsened once the Germans reached Lwow. He suffered, along with all his fellow Jews, much torture and oppression. With the Nazi takeover, he did not have any illusions insofar as the fate of the Jews under their rule and was troubled [by the fact] that his health condition prevented him from fleeing to the forest to the partisans, to live or to die there. The job of the members of the "Judenrat" also did not appeal to him; and when the respected members of the Jewish community advised him to lead the "Judenrat" – he refused to accept the position and explained that only a scoundrel would be able to collaborate with the Nazis.

In October 1942, he was deported, together with his wife and mother and their fellow Jews, to the town of Bukaczowce, and from there they were deported to the extermination camp, Belzec. The last time that Dr. Schmurek was seen, he was walking to the train of death, together with his beloved mother. The murderers whipped them and ordered them to separate, but they continued to walk arm-in-arm and with blood dripping, to the train. There, they were separated by force, and they each entered separate compartments. Bertha Schmurek died upon entering the compartment. They said about her that she merited a merciful death on account of the contributions of her heart and her good deeds; she worked a great deal for the sake of the poor, and also established an "Ezrat Nashim" for the infirm and for women giving birth, in the town.

The murderers did not want to open the compartment and to remove the deceased woman, and her corpse rode all the way to the extermination camp.

The wife of Dr. Schmurek was not at home when her husband was taken by the Nazis. When the horrible news reached her, she did not flee for her life; she did not want to live alone and attempted to rescue him with a high price. She walked to the train station and requested from the murderers to search for her husband and to take her in his stead.

As is understood, the murderers did not agree to free Dr. Schmurek, and also placed her inside the train of death.

Dr. Schmurek's youngest daughter, an attractive woman, an artist, resided in Bialystok. Her husband, Dr. Bernzweig, was a lawyer and Zionist activist, and he was among the first victims. Sometime thereafter, she too, perished in the Shoah. In addition, the brother of Dr. Schmurek, an enthusiastic Zionist, was murdered during the first weeks of the German conquest. May their memories be for a blessing!

From the entire family, only his eldest daughter and nephew survived. They were rescued and reside in Israel.

Translator's Footnote:

1.   This surname has been spelled alternatively in this text as "Schmarak." The fact that there is generally no punctuation in this memorial book makes transliterating surnames of unfamiliar individuals somewhat of a challenge and involves a certain amount of educated guesswork.

Original Footnote:

a.   This text was received separately, after the printing of the articles in Hebrew, [and] thus, appears in this section.

[pp. 301-305]

<u>Destruction and Holocaust</u>

[pp. 305-306]

A Surviving Account:

In the Valley of Lamentation and Horror

The Testimony of Yankl Feldman and His Wife, Dasza

Recorded by Y. Fenster, Haifa

I will not recount all the events that occurred in Bursztyn right after the Germans entered the town, and which were conveyed by Dr. Schumer and others. First, I would like to relate the truth about the Bursztyn Judenrat members, among whom the most notorious were Philip Tobias and Yehudah Hersh Fischmann.

I would also like to take note of a few events, which I believe are worth recording, and which took place during those terrible times in our town.

We would receive a distribution of bread from the Judenrat, a fourth of a loaf; this was given to those who worked hard. The other people's souls would expire while waiting at the Judenrat for a small piece of bread. Whomever they wanted, they gave, and whomever not, expired. They treated us like dogs. The overseer of the labor camp was Yehudah Hersh Fischmann. Whoever did not tend to the work in accordance with his wishes was so [severely] beaten, until he collapsed. And later on, he would be dragged, ill, to work. Seldom did anyone slip out of their hands; I myself felt this upon my [own] body.

The engineer, Baranowski, created a special Works Division, which had to build a road for military purposes. He selected a number of fit, strong Jews, and it is understood, those who had connections with him. All these Jews received legitimizations from the Gestapo, approximately 30 people; I was also among them. The Judenrat no longer had any right over the people – but once, returning from work, the Judenrat members detained us. We thought that they wanted to turn us over in the Germans' hands, so as to kill us. They took us to the militia and told us that they needed to turn over 40 young Jews, whom they had not been able to catch for a long time. I right away – anybody I was able to inform – told him that he should flee.

This was a terrible period for the tortured Jews of Bursztyn – many died of hunger; one had a few poor goods that remained, following all of the Germans' robberies, [which one] sold for a piece of bread, or a few

[pp. 307-308]

potatoes. One would go to the Bursztyn woods, [a distance of] 4-5 kilometers, to collect a few twigs in order to kindle them and warm oneself up a bit – usually, the Gentiles would grab the twigs along the way, and would further accompany this with good beatings. When everything ran out, the Jews of Bursztyn began to fall from hunger, they became swollen, and died. The dead would lie for a few days because there was nobody to bury them. Everyone was drained of energy.

Before Yom Kippur of 1942, roughly, there was an action in Rohatyn. There, they were lacking Jews, so they let it be known in Bursztyn that they needed to bring over 2 wagons of Jews to be killed.

I will never forget that Yom Kippur; the religious law adjudicator, R' Yoel Ginzburg ZT"L still wanted us to pray that holy day. A few Jews gathered together at Shmuel Mastel's home. The adjudicator prayed an entire day and cried; he comforted the Jews and told them that they must accept this verdict, they should not be afraid, they should accept the verdict, [and] they should go with an uplifted head in opposition to death. I do not know how those weak, starving people came by their superhuman strength and courage.

A day after Yom Kippur, the Germans entered the city and began to shoot Jews in the streets. Many of them they grabbed and sent to Rohatyn. My mother, Perl, was also taken away then. The members of the Judenrat knew about the action and hid their wives and children.

Almost at this same time, Bursztyn became Judenrein [i.e., clean/rid of Jews]; the Jews were taken away to Bukaczowce. From there, they were loaded into wagons and deported to Belzec for extermination. The Bursztyn adjudicator ZT"L was shot in Bukaczowce while he was going around among the Jews and comforting them, and saying Viddui with them. They buried him in the local Jewish cemetery. All the remnants of the Jews from the entire sector were driven together into the Rohatyn ghetto.

At the same time, Baranowski's works division still existed. These few Jews were kept together at Yusye Feffer's house. Once, Germans barged in on us – drove us out and began to shoot at us. I was lightly wounded and ran away. At that time, [the following individuals] were shot: Shimon Feffer and Shlomo Feffer from Sernik.

I got through that same night at Skolski's home; I had things that I had hidden by her. I was then in the Rohatyn ghetto, where my wife and child still lived. Right away, they assembled all the healthy young men and sent them away to the labor camps in Brzezhany and Tarnopol – from which nobody emerged alive. Many Bursztyn Jews were dragged away there, then, including Shlomo Mandelberg, who said farewell to me and said: I know that I am going to my death. How terrifying that is. I returned from Israel so as to fall here in the murderous hands.

The Jewish militia there advised me to join them; in this manner I would have a chance at remaining alive. I categorically refused this, just as I had also done this in Bursztyn, although they had thus beaten me murderously – and taken everything from my home.

Then they took me into the division, which fed the people. The Jewish militia in the Rohatyn ghetto was silently involved with selling meat; for this, there was a death penalty, but even here, one wanted to earn money, because one believed that with this, one would bribe one's way out. I worked with the meat; I helped a lot of Bursztyn Jews.

Once, a German Volksdeutscher [i.e., in this context, a Pole of ethnic German origin who collaborated with Germany's Third Reich], who was spying about, arrived, and wanted to learn where we had the meat. Once we had

[pp. 309-310]

discerned that we were sunk, we gripped him and lanced/pierced him, and buried him on the spot.

At the edge of the ghetto stood a house, [and] in that house resided Bursztyn Jews: Fitshe Schneeweiss, Feier's wife, Rivka Haber, and my present wife, Dosia. There were also other people living [there]. Across the way, on the other side, stood a house in which S. S. men resided. One of them would sit down with a weapon and aim it at the house across the way. When somebody would exit – he would immediately shoot down that person. I would, at night, drag in whatever I was able to, there.

One day, the murderers fooled hundreds of children, and shot them all. They let it be known that at a given time, they would be distributing bread to the children – that they should come. Receiving a piece of bread was indeed a question of living, [and so] hundreds of children came running. In such a bestial manner, the children were murdered.

Following the liquidation of the Rohatyn ghetto, I procured weapons for myself. I made a bunker for myself at the home of a Gentile, next to the Bursztyn woods. Jankiew was his name. Then, I went searching for my wife and child, who had left the ghetto during the time when it was being liquidated. They had gone to the fields; unfortunately, I did not find them. The murderers caught them and killed them.

Returning to the bunker, I met Dr. Schumer and his wife there. They were utterly broken. They wanted to commit suicide. It was difficult for me to prevent them from [doing] this. Together, we dug out a larger bunker; we sat there together for half a year's time. In mortal danger, I would go during the nights to Bursztyn to Losek and bring back something to eat. (Losek the photographer). Mail from Dr. Schumer's daughter, who was living under Aryan papers, would also arrive there.

After the murderers discovered the hiding places of the Jews who still remained following the extermination of the Bursztyn Jews, which included: Mundzia Fischmann, Velvl Ostrower, Lottie Bernstein, who died heroically; as well as Berele Landner. Following this, Jankiew threw us out.

We moved on to the Polish village of "Ludwikowka." The Pole, Kochman, took us into his home. We made a bunker in his home. This saved the Pole and his family from death. This happened in the following [manner]: It was in February of 1944, [and] the Ukrainian nationalists befell the village of Ludwikowka and burned it down. The people would not allow them to escape from the fire; whoever attempted [to do so], they caught and murdered. A small number survived the Mazoyrs[1] (as they called them in Bursztyn). We remained in the bunker, as did Dr. Schumer and his wife, and the Kochman family. The Germans arrived and collected all the surviving [Jews] and deported them. It was very cold; we all bound ourselves up in rags, and together with the surviving Poles, they drove us out of the village. Nobody recognized us.

It was evening; we threw ourselves into the snow [and] remained lying [there]. At night we went to Priest Moricki in Korostowice; he allowed us to stay [there] overnight. Following difficult experiences, I returned to Jankiew, not far from the Bursztyn woods. In the forest were other hidden Jews from Bursztyn with whom I was in contact.

We received a letter from Dosia Haber that we should come and rescue her; she was hidden under ruins, en route to Demianow. The clothing that she had on was rotten/decayed. She was in a terrible state. In addition, there were German soldiers surrounding the house; at that time, they were already beginning to retreat from Russia.

[pp. 311-312]

With great effort I got her out of there. She arrived at our good Gentile, Jankiew's place.

The terrible life [of living in] fields and woods, in various Gentiles' attics, lairs, bunkers, and cellars had begun for us. The searching at night for food, the threat of being captured every time by the Gentiles and turned over to the German's hands; the desire, however, to live, overcame everything.

My wife Dosia, the daughter of Rivka and Pinye, the grandchild of Avrahamtze Yossel Yonah's, remained [alive] following the deportation of the Bursztyn Jews from Bukaczowce to be burned, there, hiding in Bukaczowce. Her parents, who were then taken to the Rohatyn ghetto, gave her money and also gold. She left for Lemberg and had Aryan papers made for herself there. In Lemberg at that time, they would seize Christian women and send them to Germany to do [forced] labor. On a lovely day, she was also seized. However, there was right away a suspicion that she was a Jewess. She was led in for an interrogation. She succeeded in jumping out of a streetcar. She entered the Lemberg ghetto, where her uncle Itzik Feldbau still lived, at the time. At the same time, her father died in the Rohatyn ghetto. Her mother sent a peasant from Martynow to her, to bring her to her in the Rohatyn ghetto. She was there until the liquidation of the ghetto. That was June 1943 – she hid in a bunker, she left and returned to Bursztyn, was hidden at Glowinski's place, at Jankiew's place, and at other Christians' places. I helped her a great deal. Only God helped both of us and saved us from the murderous hands. And thanks to him, we now reside in Israel. We have 3 children, may they be well, and we live nicely.

As I said, I would still like to relate a few [more] accounts.

The Valiant Death of Mundzia Fischmann, Velvl Ostrower, and Lottie Bernstein

During the period when Bursztyn was already "Judenrein," there still lived a few Jews around the city, hidden by Gentiles or in the woods. Mundzia Fischmann, Velvl Ostrower, and Lottie Bernstein dug out a bunker in the "equerry" (the stalls that were across the way from the count's palace). They had a revolver with them and a number of bullets. The lame shoemaker, Rafal, who was a guard in the courtyard, aided them. He would take care of getting them food. That was the summer of 1943.

I would frequently meet with Mundzia and Velvl; Mundzia told me that Velvl had a lot of money on him.

On a Saturday the equerry was attacked by Ukrainian police and a German who was their commandant. The bunker was good, but it was a denunciation from the equerry keeper's son, Fed Buben, as he was called. The police began to call out that they should come out of the bunker, which they had surrounded. When Mundzia sensed that they were lost, he came out first, with the revolver in his hand. He critically wounded the Ukrainian commandant. Also, the one who was shooting with a machine gun, he critically wounded. Mundzia and Lottie fell. Velvl grabbed the revolver, returned to the bunker, and exited it through another opening, which led to Asher Deichsler's garden. The murderers pursued him; Velvl Ostrower fought valiantly. Not far from the house in which Dr. Schmarak lived, he wounded another Ukrainian

[pp. 313-314]

policeman. Already wounded, [with] blood running from him, he shot everything at the murderers who were still pursuing him. He fell outside of the city; Fed's son shot him.

Honor their memories! Their valiant death is a ray of light and honor in the darkness of destruction and the mass death of our entire town.

We Take Revenge

The chimneysweep, Fed Buben, bloodily participated in exterminating the Jews of Bursztyn. His son collaborated with the Germans. Many Jews who were hidden in the Bursztyn woods, or among Gentiles, were turned in by them – often times, murdered by themselves. Included among those [murdered were]: Shmuel Mastel and his son, and Shaike Granwitter.

We, a group of Jews in the forest, decided to take revenge. We dressed up as peasants. At night we entered the city, seized the night watchman, a Gentile whom we found on the street, [and] forced him to go with us. We approached Fed's house. We ordered the Gentile to knock at the window and call Fed to come outside. He did this, [and] when Fed came outside – we seized him and slaughtered him on the spot. When his wife came outside, she also got what was coming to her. The son, the murderer, we did not find. Later on, we learned that he lay hidden in the oven – that was a huge shame. Those who participated in this were: also Kalmen, Sarah the baker's [wife?], and Bukaczowce Jews.

Fed's son left Bursztyn. The Gentiles in Bursztyn learned a great deal from this. Our situation in the woods improved; the Gentiles would not bother us after this incident.

Kalmen, Sarah the Baker's [Wife?]

During the period that the Rohatyn ghetto still existed, Kalmen fought with weapons against the Germans. He and a group of Jews attacked Germans along the road, near Kaniuszki. Some of the Germans were killed. They, however, were [only a portion] of a larger number. Kalmen and 3 other Jews were seized and brought to the Rohatyn ghetto. There, they shot all 4 of them. They turned them over to the Jews to be buried. The Jews noticed that Kalmen was alive. He was, though, critically wounded in the head, but he was alive. They hid him. In his place they brought another body; there was no shortage of dead. Every day there were tens of dead who had died of typhus.

Kalmen grew well and fled to the woods, where he lived for a period of time. Already shortly before the liberation, the woods were overtaken by Kalmuks. These were Russian prisoners who had gone over to the Germans from Vlasav's band. The Germans had sent them to wipe out the last remaining few Jews who lived in the woods.

At that time, the Jews had weapons and staged a bitter uprising. The Germans did not want to risk their [own] necks, so they sent the Kalmuks. In such a fight with the Kalmuks, Kalmen valiantly perished; with weapons in hand, he died with honor.

With honor and esteem, we will recount his name.

[pp. 315-316]

An Amazing Thing Happened

A while before the annihilation of the Bursztyn Jews, we already knew that the Germans were carrying out a methodical extermination of East Galician Jewry. Very often, trains that were packed with half-dead Jews that they were transporting to be burned would travel through Bursztyn. Many Jews would jump from the running trains; some of them were killed on the spot, some of them were seized. An extremely small number managed to flee and reach the forest or a place where Jews still lived.

Those who were seized were shot right away. Once, a number of Jews in the region of Bursztyn jumped. They seized 11 Jews and brought them to the city. There was a German in Bursztyn who took special joy in shooting the unfortunate people. He demonstrated a special sadism toward the children.

At that time, too, he readied the 11 Jews to be shot. Nine of them he had already murdered; there remained a mother and her son of 7 years. The murderer told the child to turn around. He extended his revolver, only needing to press the trigger, but this is where something amazing happened. The child turned around to face the German and smiled. The murderer remained standing with the extended revolver, as though petrified. [This was] the hangman who had already murdered hundreds of people, among them many children, the beast who never had any mercy when children fell to his feet and begged for their lives. His hand [that] never quivered, suddenly grew confused by the child's smile. The revolver fell out of his hand, and he fainted. When he came to, he ordered the Ukrainian, Stek,[2] who had shot tens of Bursztyn Jews, that he should take the child to the Judenrat. He made him responsible for the child. The German lay sick for a long period of time with the tank masks. He ordered that they bring the Jewish child to him every time; this calmed him.

When Bursztyn became Judenrein, the child and his mother disappeared; I do not know what became of them.

Translator's Footnotes:

    1.   I was unable to locate this term/name in my various dictionaries. It may have been specific to Bursztyn or to the Bursztyn region. Based on the context, this is certainly not a term of endearment.
    2.   Stek appears to be a surname in this context, however, it could also mean steak or beefsteak in Polish.

[pp. 317-318]

The Journey through All Hells

The experiences of Yankl Glotzer during
the time of the Second World War

Recorded by Y. Shmulevitsh, New York

Before the war, I resided with my family in the town of Bursztyn. Together with my wife and three children, I lived on Herzl Street. I had a butcher shop and we lived not badly.

When, in September 1939, the war broke out, the Soviets entered our town two days before Rosh Hashanah. They immediately began to drive out formerly wealthy Jews and Christians. The Soviets confiscated the Jews' possessions; they confiscated my butcher shop from me. A Jewish captain from the Soviet Army then said to me that if I wanted to live calmly and remain where I was, not be driven out, then I should leave and go work for the Soviets as a simple laborer; I should forget what was before, because "among us there are no merchants." And if I did not do this, the Jewish captain said to me, it would be bad with me.

I began to work for the Soviets in a "promkombinat" of meat productions. We worked very hard there; long hours in the day, and we were paid little for the work. I received [only] so much per month, which scarcely allowed me to survive through a single week. Quite a lot of formerly poor Ukrainians from the town immediately took to collaborating with the Soviets and informed on Jews.

Yankl Glotzer and his wife

Many Ukrainians pointed out for the Soviets the former Jewish shopkeepers; that before the war, they had taken high prices from the populace for various merchandise. These Jews were driven out, deep into Russia, likely into Siberia. Many Ukrainians were also active in the Soviet militia in the town.

This is how it went until the outbreak of

[pp. 319-320]

the German-Soviet War, during the month of June 1941. After the German-Soviet War broke out and the Hitlerists advanced in various areas, the Soviets were still in our town for a week's time. The Soviets left our town in a calm manner, and many Jews who had previously collaborated with them left Bursztyn, along with the despicable Soviets. After the Soviets left, the town was free for three days without the Soviets and without the Germans, who had not yet entered. This lasted as such from Monday until Thursday. The Ukrainians from the town, many of whom had previously collaborated with the Soviets, began to go around to the Jewish houses and rob [them]; and they said to us Jews that soon the Hitlerists would enter; the time had come when they would slaughter all the Jews.

Thursday in the morning, the third of July 1941, I was standing in a field beyond the town and was pasturing my cows. I could see from the distance a military but did not know who it was. When the military drew nearer, I saw that there were Germans. They did not know that I was a Jew, and asked where the road to Jnaszkow was, so I showed them. Just as soon as I saw the Germans, I left the field with the cows and went home. On the way, a familiar Ukrainian, a wealthy peasant, encountered me, and he began to beat me. When I came home, I lay in bed for two weeks from the beatings, which I had received from the peasant. Just after being beaten by the peasant, I went to the Ukrainian lawyer, Skolski, who had been a good acquaintance of mine before the war. The Germans were still not in the town then, and I wanted the lawyer acquaintance to take me on [concerning] the peasant having beaten me. When I told my lawyer acquaintance, Skolski, "Save my life," he responded to me, "Go away; if not, I will kill you myself." That was the reply from my best friend!

Lying in bed for two weeks' time, I left my house and went out to the street. I met, standing there, a baker from Bursztyn, Yankl Pilpel, who said to me: See how they are leading [away] the rabbi of our town, R' Herzl Landau.

While looking, I saw how the rabbi was being led [away] by the two Ukrainian brothers, Ivanchuk, who lived in the village, Martynow. Those were my Gentile acquaintances, so I went over to them and asked: Why are you leading [away] our rabbi?

The Gentile fellows also took me immediately and led me [away], together with the rabbi. At that, the young man from the town, Yisroel Schwartz, walked by, and they also wanted to take him along with us, but he fled. The two Gentiles began to chase the young man, and they ordered the rabbi and me to lie down on the ground and to remain lying [there] until they returned. When the two Gentiles took after the young man, Yisroel Schwartz, I stood up from the ground and began to flee. R' Herzl Landau, as well, stood up and began to run with me. I then ran into the garden of the Ukrainian, Ilki Goy; the rabbi also ran in the same direction. At that moment, other Gentiles arrived, seized the rabbi, and led him away with them.

When I lay in the garden of the Ukrainian, I heard shouts from outside, "Hear, O Israel," as well as shots. This was next to the synagogue. This lasted in this manner from 3 o'clock in the afternoon until 11 o'clock at night. They then drove the Jews together into the synagogue, and the Ukrainians cut off part of the Jews' beards and beat and tormented them. At 11 o'clock at night, Minne Tobias, the leader of the "Judenrat" communicated

[pp. 321-322]

with the head of the Gestapo, who was already in the town then, and oversaw the Ukrainian militia. He promised the Gestapo man tea, golden watches, and related that they not beat and torment the Jews. They then stopped tormenting the Jews in the synagogue and allowed them to leave. The following morning, one Jew could not recognize the other in the synagogue, because most of the Jews had burned-off or chopped-off beards. When they came that same day to the funeral of Moshe the Red, whom the Ukrainians had shot, one Jew could not recognize the other, even though they had known each other since childhood on, over the course of many years.

In the middle of the night, when I lay in the garden of the peasant, I grew very cold from terror, and my teeth chattered very much, and I shook. The Ukrainian, Ilki Goy, slept in a shed in the garden, and he heard that somebody was there. He came out to the garden, spotted me, and took me into the shed in which he was [staying], and threw me into the hay. At that moment, Ukrainians who were going around and searching for hidden Jews, showed up. They asked the peasant whether he had not seen Jews moving about here; he responded that no, and further hid me. This peasant was my neighbor; the garden and his house were situated not far from my residence. The morning of the following day I went home. My wife informed me that she, together with the children, was also hidden one night earlier, in a shed of the same Gentile. However, he did not know about this.

Two weeks after the Germans had entered Bursztyn, they demanded a contribution from the Jews. They demanded that they give a half a million zlotys in silver. In the course of two days, they gave them this, which the Jews had collected amongst themselves. Minne Tobias, the leader of the "Judenrat," convinced us then that if we gave this contribution, then the Germans would no longer bother the Jews.

I did not have any money then to give toward the contribution, which the "Judenrat" had demanded from all the Jews, the sum that had been agreed upon that I should give. I then went out to the marketplace with two of my cows in order to sell them, so that I would have a donation to give toward the contribution that we had to give the Germans. But the peasants talked amongst themselves that they should not buy the cows from me, because they would, in either case, take them away from me without pay.

The following day, around 3 in the morning, Fitshe Schneeweiss came to me from the "Judenrat," and he demanded of me that I give my portion for the contribution. I took my four cows and went about with them to sell them, but I did not have to whom to sell them. I then went into the home of a Ukrainian peasant woman, Kopchinski, and recommended that she buy all four of the cows for 1,500 zlotys. The Christian woman said to me:

Take for yourself the 1,500 zlotys in silver, go redeem yourself, and continue to keep the four cows for yourself.

I immediately carried off the money to the "Judenrat." Just as soon as I had paid the 1,500 zlotys to the "Judenrat," I stumbled with such a sum; two hours later I received a slip from the "Judenrat" that I should once again contribute 1,500 zlotys in silver. I once again went to the same woman, Kopchinski, [and so] she once again gave me another 400 silver zlotys, which she still had, and I carried this off. In the "Judenrat" in Bursztyn there were then: Minne Tobias, Philip Tobias, Wolf Granwitter, Eliasz Rosin, Yehudah Hersh Fischmann, [and] Itzik Roher. Minne Tobias was the first leader of the "Judenrat." After they had already taken the Jews' possessions, they demanded that the "Judenrat" should hand over 250 Jews to them to be taken to

[pp. 323-324]

the camps. When they demanded the 250 Jews from Minne Tobias, he called together all the Jews in the synagogue and said to them: Until now I was prepared only to take your possessions, but now, when they want Jewish lives, I do not want to be [the leader of the Judenrat] any longer. I will turn myself in to the Germans and let them kill me; I had thought that with the possessions I would be able to redeem your lives.

Minne Tobias relinquished his leadership of the "Judenrat," and in his place came Philip Tobias, his cousin, a lawyer. He handed over just as many Jews as the Germans so desired. He even turned over more; when they demanded 100 Jews, Philip Tobias handed over 125. Minne Tobias, the previous leader of the "Judenrat," grew ill and would not allow himself to be saved. He said that he did not want to live and see how they tormented Jews; he preferred to die. He died in the Rohatyn ghetto before Passover of 1943. Philip Tobias, in contrast, survived the war. He is presently in Breslau (Wroclaw). He apostatized and is a lawyer there.

The ghetto in Bursztyn was created immediately after the Germans had entered the town. The Jews were only allowed to live in the Jewish neighborhood and were not permitted to come into contact with the Christian populace. We were in the Bursztyn ghetto nearly 2,500 Jews. Every time, they would take out

Jews from the ghetto to labor at quarrying stones in the region of Tarnopol. One worked very hard there, and many Jews died while at work. The Jews were not fed, and when they became swollen from hunger, the Germans shot them on the spot. In Lakewood, N. J., today, live the two brothers, Shmuel and Itzik-Moshe Drucker, who were in the [previously] mentioned stone quarry for [forced] labor.

The 10th of October 1942, 10 o'clock in the morning; it was two days before Yom Kippur [when] the Germans' orders were hung up in the Bursztyn ghetto; that until 3 o'clock that afternoon, no more Jews were permitted in Bursztyn; that all of them must go to Bukaczowce. Even earlier, on Yom Kippur, 200 Jews were driven out to Rohatyn. The "Judenrat" in Rohatyn then received a demand from the Germans to add 500 Jews who would be deported to the extermination camps. And so the leader of the "Judenrat" in Rohatyn, Amaranth, did the following: that Rohatyn should contribute 100 Jews, and Bursztyn and Bukaczowce should contribute up to 200 Jews. The 500 Jews were then transported to the station in Rohatyn, and from there, they were deported in wagons; nobody knew where to.

When the orders were hung out in the Bursztyn ghetto on the 10th of October 1942, all the Jews from there left at the designated time for Bukaczowce. When we arrived in Bukaczowce, they brought us to a small place [or square] where in one space they were already holding all the Jews from Bukaczowce. The Jewish streets there were small, and we, the arriving Jews from Bursztyn, did not have where to place ourselves. So, the mayor of Bukaczowce called the Gentiles together and ordered them to leave their residences on one street; that they should go to their families, so that they could hand over the street with the emptied-out residences to the [newly] arrived Jews from Bursztyn; that one should not remain outside on the street. The Gentiles, however, did not want to heed the mayor. So, the mayor telephoned the German councilor of the land [i.e., the highest official of an administrative district] in Rohatyn and inquired what he should do.

The Gestapo leader of the administrative district in Rohatyn immediately came down, on the spot, to Bukaczowce, and he called together the Gentiles for a meeting in the middle of the street. He said to them that the Jews were destined to be annihilated in eleven

[pp. 325-326]

days' time; moreover, they needed to give them residences in which to remain, in the meantime. We, the Jews of Bursztyn, then lay next to the marketplace in Bukaczowce, in which the meeting took place; and we ourselves heard the words of the Gestapo leader of the councilor of the land when he uttered them to the assembled Christians. He spoke to them in German, and a translator translated into Ukrainian. After this, the Gentiles immediately evacuated their residences on one street, into which the brought-in Jews from Bursztyn were settled.

In 11 days' time, just as the Gestapo leader had promised, there was indeed a slaughter of the Jews at the spot at which they were assembled in Bukaczowce. Germans arrived and began to pursue and drive out the Jews. The remaining Jews who attempted to flee were shot on the spot. Fifty percent of the Jews who found themselves in this place [or in this square] were shot then by the Germans. The same day such a slaughter also took place in the Rohatyn ghetto. Many Jews were driven out, and many Jews were shot on the spot.

When the Germans arrived and the slaughter began in Bukaczowce, I left for my acquaintance, Yisroelke Dawid [David], with my wife and children. This Jew lived in Bukaczowce and had a restaurant; I knew him well from before the war. He drove me, with my wife, and three children to a neighbor, a Jew with the name Wolf, from the village of Czahrow. This Jew had, even earlier on, built a bunker in his residence between two walls into which one entered through an opening in the attic. I paid this Jew to allow my wife and our two girls and a neighbor, Minka Schumer, into the bunker. My boy and I could no longer get in there. I led my wife and the two girls into the bunker, and my boy and I fled to the woods. I fled to the woods of Witany.

While in the woods of Witany, I took off from there for the Ukrainian peasant, Ivan Shkurlak, and gave him 15 dollars, two pairs of gold earrings, and my wife's engagement ring, so that he would take my son and me and hide us at his place. This was on the 22nd of October 1942. The peasant took all of this from me and led my boy and me into a separate empty room, which was situated in his house. An hour later the peasant brought in 13 more Jews to hide, from whom he took everything that they owned; they themselves handed it over to him, so that he would save them. He held us there from Sunday morning until Monday night. I then paid the peasant's wife separately, so that she would go to Bukaczowce and find out how my wife and children were doing in the hiding place at the Jew's place. She returned and brought me a sign from my wife.

When the Gentile by whom my boy and I and 13 other Jews were hidden saw that the Jews were giving him money and gold, he understood that the Jews had more of these things, but that they were not handing it over. He planted his brother, Mikhailov Shkurlak, who came Monday night (it was the third day that we were hidden at the peasant's place) into the room where we were. He said to us that they had sent him to bring us to the transport of the Jews in Bukaczowce. They were being deported from there. However, if we gave him money or gold, Mikhailov Shkurlak said, he would leave us alone. But I did not want to give [him] anything, because I understood that this was just a

[pp. 327-328]

threat. While the peasant was haggling/debating with the Jews [as to] how much they should give him, I was standing right next to the window. I kicked out the windowpane with my foot and jumped out with my boy through the window. The small house was situated on a hill, and we jumped down into a field.

In the dark night, my son and I found our way to Bursztyn, to my hometown. When I arrived in the town, I went up into the attic of the house of the previously mentioned peasant, Kopchinski, and he did not know that I was hidden there. Kopchinski was a wealthy pig breeder. In his home there was a servant, a Ukrainian girl, Krisia, who then had a Jewish lover from the town, Yossel Bigel. This Ukrainian girl greatly aided the Jewish young man; she hid him and took care of getting him food; and Yossel Bigel was still there in Bursztyn. This Ukrainian girl did [indeed] know that my boy and I were hiding in the attic of her boss; and I asked her that she let Yossel Bigel know where I was – that he should, through her, let me know where things were holding with the Jews in the town – and what I should do.

This Christian girl, Krisia, returned and told me that Yossel Bigel said to tell me that he was going to Bukaczowce to hear what was happening with his mother; he asked that I await him next to Shpak's Woods (we called the woods by this name, because Leszniczi was called Shpak) and we would see there what to do further. Kopchinski did not know that I was in his attic, and [that] the servant was in constant contact with me. Thursday at dawn, my son and I came down from Kopchinski's attic and left for the agreed-upon place, to Shpak's Woods. I, however, did not encounter Yossel Bigel there; I waited, and he did not arrive. I met a Jew from Bursztyn there, Shmuel Haber, who was coming from Bukaczowce, and I asked him about my wife and two children, but he did not know anything about them. The Jew told me that in Bukaczowce they had shot a lot of Jews, and that for them it was already far better than for the living; so said Shmuel Haber to me.

I left the woods with my son and set out for Bukaczowce. When I arrived in the town, I went to the restaurant of my familiar friend, Dawid. When I entered the restaurant, I met my wife and our two girls.

We could not remain in Bukaczowce, because there was an order that all living Jews must go to the ghetto in Rohatyn, and [that] everyone had a right to bring with him a bundle of 10 pounds. My wife, three children, and I also left for Rohatyn; this was on the 22nd of October 1942.

In the Rohatyn ghetto to which my wife, three children, and I had come, were the then-remnants of living Jews from Rohatyn, Bursztyn, Bukaczowce, Bolszowce, Knihynicze, and Zurow.

They assembled [themselves] together after the Jews had been driven out of these places, or one found these Jews hidden in various places. All the Jews were found on the street, because the ghetto in Rohatyn was by then already smaller and was situated in a small area. My older brother, Moshe, was a good friend of the leader of the Rohatyn "Judenrat," Amaranth. My mother had given Amaranth 500 zlotys, and for this reason, the "Judenrat" allowed my wife, three children, and me into a room in which there were already 15 Jews, aside from us five. When my family and I entered the room, a Jew named Skolnik who lived next door to the house where we had been and had had a printing house in Rohatyn, came over to me

[pp. 329-330]

and said: Make a dug-out for yourself, because every minute they can grab us and kill us.

We went around inside the room [or house] and did not know where to make a hiding place. At night we began to dig a ditch inside of the room, next to the wall that led outside to the river, "Gnila Lipa." The soil from the ditch that we had dug we threw into the water, so that there would not remain any signs. Three weeks' time we dug that ditch, [but] only during the nights. This was supposed to lead to the river, so that in the instance of danger, we would be able to flee. There was just then a period when the Germans were bothering the Jews less. The "Judenrat" in Rohatyn at that time voluntarily handed over 100 Jews every week to the Germans, who were shot in the cellar of the "Judenrat" [building, office] in Rohatyn. During the day we would leave our room, be outside, and also do various [forms of] work.

Once, we heard that the Germans were running around, seizing Jews. So, we ran into the ditch, which we had dug out in the room, and which led to the river. We hid ourselves there. Until Chanukah of 1942, the Jews who were capable of working had [a state of] calm in the ghetto. The Jews who were not very capable of working, sick, and elderly people, were led out [of the ghetto] and shot. The Jews who were led out, worked on the roads and aircraft runway. This is how it went until May of 1943. Over the course of time, there were "actions," and they also led out those who were able to work, from the ghetto. From the room in which we were, they led out six Jews, men and women. Over the course of time, two women also died in our hiding place; they were: Ita, the wife of Yisroel-Leizer Blecher, who left behind three children, and Minka Schumer. We became fewer people in the hiding place, in the dug-out ditch in the room, and it later grew more comfortable. When we were in the bunker, a Jew, Yisroel Stander, from Stratyn, ran up to the attic of the same house in which we lay, so as to hide himself there. We heard his groans from on high. He said that on account of a bit of water that he did not have, he was expiring. Indeed, he died in the attic; we were unable to help him.

Sabbath night, on the 6th of June 1943, the last resettlement [i.e., a euphemism for deportation, usually to the extermination camps] of the Rohatyn ghetto took place. Germans and Ukrainians arrived and laid siege the ghetto and began shooting into the residences in which the Jews resided. In the ghetto there were still close to 3,000 Jews. Half of this quantity was then shot in the ghetto, proper, and the other half was led out [of the ghetto] for extermination. The 1,500 shot Jews were buried in the ghetto, proper. I recall that the husbands of the shot women and children dug graves and buried their nearest ones.

Among us, in the bunker, it was very hot then; people would simply suffocate. There was a young man with us in the hiding place from Bursztyn, Moshe Bigel. He grew insane in the bunker and began biting everyone. He also began shouting, and we were afraid that the hiding place would be discovered. Moshe Bigel left the hiding place with his two sisters for the ghetto, and we heard how all three of them were shot by the Germans.

When the last bloody "action" took place in the Rohatyn ghetto, my wife, three children, and I left the ditch of the bunker for the river, the "Gnila Lipa." The Germans pursued us, shot at us, but we entered the river and swam across to the other side. Other Jews from the hiding place who had also fled then, but did not enter the water; rather, fled by [way of] land, were shot.

[pp. 331-332]

My family and I came out onto dry land and did not know where to go. We lay a week's time in the fields and ate the kernels of the corn, which was then in bloom. In the end, we found our way to our hometown, Bursztyn. We entered the town at night, and once again, we went up to the attic of the previously mentioned peasant, Kopchinski. He did not know that my family and I were there. We lay in his attic for a night and a day; there was a major heat [wave] and we did not have what to eat. Even earlier on, before we went up to the attic, our 11-year-old girl, Dreizsha, lost [her way] from us, and she was together with my older brother, Moshe. As we lay in the attic, we heard our daughter shouting from the distance, along with my brother, Moshe, and his four children, and my wife's sister, and her husband. They were all seized by the Germans, who beat and tormented them, and were later on led out for extermination. We heard the shouts of our nearest, but we could not help them.

Lying in the attic with my wife and two children, a boy and a girl, we felt that we would starve to death; we could not endure it anymore. At that, I climbed down from the attic and went into the peasant, Kopchinski's house, to beg for something to eat. When he saw me, he was frightened by me, and asked me where I was situated. When I told him that I, along with my family, were hiding in his attic, Kopchinski began to shout at me that I wanted to, that on my account, he and his entire family should go into the ground [i.e., go to their graves]. Then, Kopchinski's youngest daughter, Danka, called out to her father with these words:

Such a good man as Yankl we must help; perhaps we will save his life. Let's pretend we don't know anything about [the fact] that he is up in the attic with his family.

Kopchinski then permitted me that my wife, two children, and I remain by him, up in his attic, another couple of days, not more. But we were hidden there for three months. He and his family members would bring us some food from time to time. During the nights I would go down from the attic into the fields and garden and collect cucumbers, radishes, and apples; and from this we survived.

When the three months had passed and it grew a bit quieter insofar as the searching for and seizure of Jews, since nearly all [the Jews] had been led out to be exterminated or shot, I came down from the attic and went into the town, wanting to procure food from familiar peasants. Immediately, though, the Christians began speaking amongst themselves, that moving about in the town was a Jew, the sole Jew who had survived. The Germans began to go about with scent dogs and searched for me. I was once again hidden in the attic with my wife and two children. Once, the Germans came to the Ukrainian pig breeder, Kopchinski, and asked him whether there were any hidden Jews around. The peasant responded that no, [there were no Jews,] although we were then up in the attic. When the Germans moved about next to his house, searching for Jews, Kopchinski's wife paced back and forth, wringing her hands, and begged God that the Germans should not find us. In the end, we needed to leave that place.

My wife, two children, and I went at night into a garden in which an elderly Ukrainian priest resided. We went up into the attic of his small house, and he did not know that we were hiding there. My wife, two children, and I were hidden in this attic for two months' time, and the elderly priest did not know about this. During the

[pp. 333-334]

nights, I would go down from the attic and into the fields to search for food. However, I would go to other villages where they did not know me. I swam across a [body of] water and ran to the villages of Jnaszkow [and] Kuropatniki, where nobody knew me, and brought food up to the attic for myself and for my family.

Returning home one time to the priest's attic after having gone about among the villages searching for food, I did not meet my wife and daughter. My boy was then with me, searching for food. While I was gone, the priest's son came up to the attic, so as to repair the roof, and he suddenly saw my wife and daughter there. He said to them: "I did not see anything, I do not know anything," but he asked them to immediately leave the attic. That same day before nightfall, my wife came down from the attic and went into the garden, where they hid themselves.

When I did not meet my wife and daughter in the attic, I went around at night searching for them. While moving about in this manner from place to place, I met them in the garden where they had hidden. However, we were afraid to remain there. We again returned to the courtyard of the peasant, Kopchinski. There, we entered an ice cellar, and the peasant did not know that we were there. We lay in that cellar for a week's time. Right over there lay potatoes, so we broiled and ate them. I would also go out during the nights to the fields to procure food. A week later, Kopchinski came to the ice cellar and met us there. Kopchinski told us to leave the place, and with that, he said: I do not see an end to the war; I had thought that I would be able to hide you, but I do not want to be killed with my family.

Sabbath night I went with my boy to the forest, and persuaded Kopchinski that my wife and daughter remain in the ice cellar on-site for another week's time, where we could hide ourselves.

I went to the Witany woods with my son. There, I went to the home of the peasant, Shkurlak, where other Jews and I had been hidden initially for money and gold. Upon entering the peasant's hut, I saw two Russian partisans there with rifles. Both Russians were drunk and began to badly beat up my boy and me. They knew that I was a Jew, but they said that I was a spy, since in that place there were only partisans (Russians), and [so] how did I come to be there? Suddenly, a Jew from Bukaczowce, Shmuel Grossnoss, who was in the partisans, together with these two drunken Russian partisans, entered the hut. He recognized me and asked the Russians that they stop beating me up. So, the two partisans said to Grossnoss that if he continued to talk, they would disarm him and shoot him, along with me.

A few minutes later another Jewish partisan, Kalmen Streger, a baker from Bursztyn, entered the hut. He, too, began begging the two Russian partisans that they not beat me up. He persuaded them and took me off their hands. Kalmen Streger led my boy and me deep into the woods, and there I met a lot of Jews who were in the partisans. The partisan group in the forest consisted only of Jews who hailed from Bursztyn and Bukaczowce; all of them had weapons. The group of Jews numbered 130 persons. The leaders of this partisan group were three Russian soldiers who had fled from German captivity. Two of these three Russians were indeed those whom I

[pp. 335-336]

had met in the peasant's hut and had beaten me up. Two of the three Russian leaders of the Jewish partisan group were called Sashke and Bashke; I do not recall the name of the third Russian. "Bashke" was a Russian Jew, but he did not reveal that he was a Jew. In the partisan group in the forest there were also Jewish women, as well as entire families: fathers and children.

Several days later, after I had arrived in the forest [at the site of] the Jewish partisans, I left for Bursztyn, for the peasant, Kopchinski, so as to bring my wife and daughter from there, where they were hidden, into the forest. I left to go there, accompanied by several armed partisans. Kopchinski did not know when the armed partisans and I had entered his courtyard, and when we had left there with my wife and daughter. Going into the forest, my wife was so weak; her feet were numb, so it was necessary to carry her on my back.

In the woods they gave me a rifle, and I took part in the partisan group. We would go out at night to the villages and appropriate pigs and cows, as well as other products from the peasants, and bring this to the forest, from which everyone had [something] to eat. The first time, when I was still not in the forest, the partisans had ventured into Bursztyn, attacked the policemen's station, and appropriated 9 rifles there. There were then two old policemen at the station, and they did not put up a fight. They did not do anything to the policemen. Later on, on the road near Bukaczowce, they attacked Germans who were traveling through, and having shot them, appropriated their weapons and boots. In this manner, the partisans procured weapons and clothing, as well as food.

Following the three weeks when my family and I were in the woods, the Germans staged an ambush on the partisans in the woods. The Germans then shot 9 Jewish partisans and took with them 21 living Jewish partisans. When the Germans had completed their raid in the woods, I fled with my family, and along with us also fled one of our neighbors from Bursztyn, Mrs. Ita Mandelberg. When we realized that the Germans were encroaching, we threw ourselves onto the snow and closed our eyes, so that we would not see them shooting us. When the Germans approached the spot where we lay, Mrs. Mandelberg got up and asked the Germans why they wanted to shoot her. Just as soon as she had finished uttering these words, the Germans immediately shot the woman on the spot. Then the two Germans looked at us, and one said to the other: Leave these!

Once the Germans had left, we got up and returned to the dense woods.

My son, who was then 17 years old on the 8th of January 1943 (yet before the German raid), left the forest with several other boys; they went to search for food. It was a well-lit night, and the boys were captured by Ukrainians. The boys fled and were pursued by the Ukrainians, who were also shooting [at them]. The other boys were shot by the Ukrainians, and my boy they caught, alive. They led my boy off to Rohatyn, and they investigated and tormented him, so that he would reveal where in the woods the partisans were situated. When my boy did not want to reveal anything, they shot him.

[pp. 337-338]

My wife and daughter and I were in the woods with the Jewish partisans until the 23rd of August 1944, when the Red Army began to advance and drove out the Hitlerists.

Following the liberation, my wife, daughter, and I returned to our former hometown, Bursztyn. There, we saw a great deal of destruction, and encountered only 13 Jewish survivors from the former Jewish settlement in Bursztyn. The Soviets, who were among us in the town, constantly took the Jews to do various [types of] work, and the

Mechele the butcher and Meir Gittel-Leah's

able ones were taken into the Red Army. I was exhausted and utterly tormented from the experiences, and when I saw that the Soviets wanted to take me into the army, my wife, daughter, and I left Bursztyn. The remaining 13 surviving Jews also left the town then.

My wife, daughter, and I left for Poland, to Lower Silesia, and we settled in Richbach. I was a butcher there, and we had it not bad [there]. However, when in July 1946 the pogrom in Kielce took place, we no longer wanted to remain in Poland. We left Poland illegally and arrived in Berlin, in the American zone. We were in the Schlachtensee [DP] camp there, until 1948. From there, we left for Landsberg, where we were in a camp for Jewish refugees; and from there, we immigrated to America in 1949.

We arrived in New York on the 23rd of August 1949 with the ship, "General Muir;"[1] we have lived the entire time in Coney Island, and we do not have it bad [here]. I work in a large meat manufacturing store. Our daughter got married here in 1951, and we already have two grandchildren. Our daughter married Irving Abramowicz, who hails from Zhetl, Poland. They have a grocery in New York and live well.

My wife and I live in four rooms that are nicely arranged. We belong to the Bursztyner Society; we have many familiar kinsmen with whom we get together from time to time. We read the "Tog-Morgn Zshurnal" ["Day-Morning Journal"], sometimes also the English newspapers. We are already American citizens and are happy with our present-day lives.

New York, the 16th of April 1955

Translator's Footnote:

1.   I have found references to a ship by this name: the General C. H. Muir, which transported displaced persons (Jewish and otherwise) from Europe to the United States in the postwar era, but I cannot definitively confirm that this is the same ship being described here.

[pp. 339-340]

Through Rivers of Tears and Seas of Blood

The experiences of Pola Tichover during
the time of the Second World War

Recorded by Y. Shmulevitsh

When the war broke out in September 1939, I was eleven years old. At the time, I was in the village, Nastaszczyn, which is four kilometers from the city of Bursztyn, in eastern Galicia. I was my parents' only daughter. My father was a merchant; he dealt in cattle/cows, grain, and related goods. In the same village lived two other Jewish families: my grandmother and my uncles, and another Jewish family. Together, there were three Jewish families living in the village. My grandfather died yet before the war. I learned then in the public school in the village.

I recall that when the Soviets entered, they appropriated everything that was to be had in the warehouses from my father, as well as from other Jews, and non-Jews. Under the Soviets, my father no longer traded. He worked in the fields that belonged to my grandmother, but the Soviets came and appropriated everything that my father had harvested from the field. They only left us a little bit to eat. I also went to school under the Soviets, and this is how it proceeded until June 1941, when the German-Soviet War broke out.

When the Hitlerist army passed through along the way, a few Germans remained stationed in our village. They drove my father out to do various [types of] work, and the Germans wanted to shoot him, because he did not work as quickly as they, the Germans, wanted him to [work]. A few weeks after the Germans had entered, Ukrainian peasants entered our house, and they beat my father severely; they split open his head. The Ukrainians also beat my mother, and they then killed our only horse. The Ukrainians wanted us to leave the village, leave our house. We continued to stay in the village, but the Ukrainians made a great deal of trouble for us. In the end, we had to leave the village. The Ukrainians drove out my parents, as well as the other two Jewish families from the village. When we left the village, they pummeled us with stones. We then all left for Bursztyn.

In Bursztyn, my father rented a house, and we lived there. My mother would go into the village, exchange a bit of merchandise that we still had, and with that, brought [back] food, from which we had on what to live. My father did not dare show himself on the street, because at that time they were seizing Jewish men to do various [types of] labor, and they made lots of trouble for them. My father was then hidden in

[pp. 341-342]

a cellar. We needed to hide ourselves in this manner until an "action" took place in Bursztyn; this was after Yom-Kippur; I do not recall which year [it was]. In general, it is difficult for me now to recall the dates, because I was then still a child. They then drove out my parents and me, as well as our entire family, along with other Jews, to Bukaczowce.

When they brought us to Bukaczowce, they let us off in the street next to a small chamber. Our family went into that small chamber, and we were in dire straits. Also, a few days later, an "action" was staged in Bukaczowce, and Jews were deported. Our family, though, managed to hide ourselves then. In the small chamber where we were, we dug a deep ditch, and hid inside of it. After the "action," we left the small chamber. There were other Jews in Bukaczowce who had managed to hide themselves during the "action." Our family then received a room that the "Judenrat" allocated for the remaining Jews. In that room, were several families; there were also children there. We were in that room nearly two weeks.

Immediately after we entered the room, following the "action" that was carried out in Bukaczowce, my father and mother began to dig a ditch, a bunker, so that we would have where to hide in case of danger. The ditch was made in the kitchen, and there was a path leading outside, through the other side of the house. My mother and father, as well as the other Jews, worked for eight days' time at digging this ditch.

Two weeks later, another "action" took place in Bukaczowce. All of us from that room, which was nearly 20 people, adults, and children, then went into the bunker, which had been prepared previously, in the kitchen.

Ukrainians and Germans entered the dwelling; they searched in all the corners, but they could not find us. The Gentiles banged on the floor and the earth poured down upon our heads. The peasants, in either case, did not want to relent, and said that there must be Jews hidden here. Every second we thought that we would be discovered, but God helped us; the peasants left, and we left the bunker and went back into the house. During this "action" they also led my grandmother and aunt, along with other Jews, to be exterminated. They were not together with us then. They had hidden themselves somewhere else. After that, we left the hiding place and the house. We hired carriage drivers and left for Rohatyn.

When we arrived in Rohatyn, we entered the ghetto there. I was together with my parents. In the Rohatyn ghetto, a Jew, a certain Shmuel Acht took us into his residence. He gave us a small corner in his room, and we three remained there. Eight days later, after we arrived in the Rohatyn ghetto, an "action" took place there. It was winter; unfortunately, I do not recall which year. Shmuel Acht had, however, previously prepared a bunker in his residence; [and so] all of us, nearly 20 people, went into the hiding place. At the time, it was not a big "action," and we survived [by] remaining inside the bunker.

During the time when we were in the Rohatyn ghetto, a peasant from our village would gradually bring us food. My father had given him money, earlier on, so that he would help us, should we be in need. I was a small girl, [so] my parents would give me a little bit of money, and I would steal my way out of the ghetto and go buy a bit of wood, so that there would be with

[pp. 343-344]

what to heat up [the place]. Once, a Jewish policeman from the ghetto; I do not recall his name, detained me at the gate of the ghetto, and he appropriated some of the wood from me, which I was carrying into the ghetto. He also beat me. But God, therefore, punished him. When the Germans led all the Jews out of the ghetto, that Jewish policeman went to a peasant to hide. He lay in a hiding place in an attic. But in the hiding place [his body] began to decay; pieces of his body fell off, and in the end, he died.

We were once again in the ghetto. I then grew ill with spotted typhus, but no doctor wanted to come to [treat] me. The Jewish doctors in the Rohatyn ghetto did not want to concern themselves with newcomer

Jewish refugees from the other towns. I was then already on the verge of dying, and my father and mother began to sob over me. But I became well/recovered.

On the 6th of June 1943, the last "action" took place in the Rohatyn ghetto. The "action" lasted a day and a night. My mother and I were hidden in the bunker, in Shmuel Acht's room. Together with us were yet other Jews. We were in the hiding place for two days' time without a drop of water or food; there were also small children, and we nearly expired.

One day before the liquidation of the ghetto in Rohatyn, my father left for a village to search for a place in which we could hide ourselves. When he learned that the liquidation was taking place in the ghetto, he no longer returned [there]. He went to the fields and lay there for eight days and eight nights. While the "action" was taking place, my mother and I dressed up as peasant women, and we left the ghetto. The Germans did not recognize us at all. When we went at night through the streets of Rohatyn, the peasants looked at us and said amongst themselves that we were Jews. But God helped us, everything turned out alright, and we left for the fields. Other Jews also stole their way out of the ghetto then. However, they carried goods/belongings with them, and when they went about across the streets, they were recognized by the peasants, and seized and handed over to the Germans.

My mother and I were in the field all day. At the time, it was thundering and lightning very hard and pouring rain. The next day we left for the village to which my father went from the ghetto, so as to find a hiding place at a peasant's home, for us. When my mother and I came to the Ukrainian peasant; he was an acquaintance of ours, and I asked him where my father was, and so the peasant said to me:

Get out of here, dog; you have no reason to be here.

[And] so my mother and I left for another Ukrainian peasant, Mikolaj Matschke, who, prior to the war, was the village head of our village. He took us both in, gave both of us [something] to eat, following our not having eaten anything for several days. We stayed at the peasant's home for several days; he helped us dry out our clothes, which had become drenched from rain, when we lay in the field. The peasant, Mikolaj Matschke, said to us that my father was hidden in a field beside the brickyard. At night he led us to this field. In addition, Matschke gave us bread and other food for the road. When we arrived at the field near the brickyard, we did not, however, find my father there. My mother and I went around for eight days in the field and searched for my father. We lay hidden in the grain. I, however, was hungry and thirsty, and could not lie still, so I stuck my head out of the corn. The peasants who were working

[pp. 345-346]

in the field saw me and recognized me; they were from our village. When the peasants left for lunch, my mother and I left the field and went to another field.

Wandering about in this manner, not far from our former home in the village, we encountered my father, who was hidden in a garden. My father took my mother and me into a stable with hay, and all three of us hid. Thereafter, my father left to go search for food. The peasant to whom the stable in which we lay belonged, did not know that we were hidden at his place. He came into the stable, stabbed with the rakes at the hay, but did not find us. When my father returned from a village where he had procured a little bit of food, a German chased after him, but my father hid, and the German did not catch him. When my father came to us, he said that we needed to leave this place. Indeed, all three of us left for the fields and lay there an entire summer in the rain. During the day I would go out to peasant acquaintances; they knew me, and they would give me food. The Gentile girls, my former girlfriends from school, gave me [food] to eat.

Later on, all three of us left for the village, Zwirincy, where my father had a peasant acquaintance. My father asked the peasant to hide us, but the peasant did not want to; he was afraid. The peasant said that we should hide in the field, and that every time he would bring us [food] to eat. We went to the field, hid ourselves there, and the peasant did indeed, over the course of several days, bring us [food] to eat. He would not bring the food [directly over] to us; rather, he would throw it into the field, as one would throw it to a dog, and we would later collect it.

When my father, mother, and I lay in the field, there were then three peasants with rifles; and with a dog they would go around in the fields, and sought out Dr. Schumer, who had fled during the "actions," and had hidden himself somewhere. The peasants happened upon us. At first, one peasant came over and began to beat my father severely. But my father beat him back and wanted to tear the rifle away from the peasant. Immediately, though, the other two peasants came [on the scene], and all three took to severely beating my father. They split open his head; the peasants also beat up my mother severely, and they made her deaf.

Just as soon as all three of the peasants approached us, they gave us a shovel and ordered us to dig a grave. My father, however, did not want to; he defied them. The peasants also beat me. When I begged one of the peasants that they not beat me, [that] I was young and still wanted to live, the peasant said to me:

What are you waiting for, for the Americans, for the English, that they should come and liberate you?

In the end, the peasant said to me that I should choose which one I wanted, my father or my mother, and they would kill the other one. But I said to the peasant that they should leave all three of us alone or shoot all three of us. Following a half hour of arguing, the peasants left us three alone, and at that, said:

They will kill you, either way!

The three peasants led us out beyond Bursztyn, near another field. From there, we entered the field that is situated next to the village in which we had lived, prior to the war. It was already autumn. Next to the forest where we had been, lived a Ukrainian peasant, Florke, who had hidden Jews at his place; although at the time, we did not know this. The peasant said to us that we should dig a bunker in the forest and hide ourselves there. The former leader of our

[pp. 347-348]

village, Matschke, brought out a shovel, and my father and mother dug a ditch in the ground, beside the pine trees. The bunker was covered from above with shrubs and leaves; we also placed a small box on the ditch, and we lay there for two weeks' time.

Once, when I left the bunker in order to procure a bit of food, I encountered next to the brickyard, a girl from Bursztyn, Vitele Kodar, who was one year older than I. Already then, she had nobody; they had led away all her nearest ones, and she was wandering about on her own. So, I brought her to our bunker, and she was together with us. (She is alive; a year ago she got married and now lives in Carolina,[1] the United States). We were in the bunker for another two, three months. This girl and I would always go out to search for food. My father and mother did not leave the forest; from the bunker they would, though, go out. The Gentile girls from the village knew that we were hidden in a bunker, and from time to time, they would give me food.

Once, a Jew from the village of Czahrow approached our bunker. The Jew's name was Mordechai; unfortunately, I do not recall his surname. Mordechai told my father that they should dig a larger bunker, because he wanted to hide together with us. He was hidden then in another place in the forest; a raid had taken place there, and he had needed to leave there. This Jew, Mordechai, brought his wife, as well as three other Jews, the two brothers, Fitshe and Davidye Schiffer, and Mottel Messinger. All of them dug a large ditch, where we remained together. Mordechai and the other Jews who had come to us in the forest had some money with them; they also had a rifle with two bullets and two revolvers with six bullets. We all lived in that bunker for nearly six weeks' time. The former small bunker in which my parents and I and the girl had been together, we left free.

Once, at dawn, when everyone in the bunker was asleep, and Vitele and I were sitting and inspecting our clothes and removing the lice, Ukrainian policemen came running and began to shoot in the direction of where our bunker was situated. Vitele and I quickly woke the people in the bunker. Mordechai grabbed the rifle and shot out to the Ukrainian policemen, who fled from the forest. Immediately following this we all got dressed and climbed up and hid ourselves in the pine trees, because we knew that the Ukrainian policemen who had fled would bring Germans. It was then winter, there lay snow, and we made footprints [leading] to the old bunker, where we had been in the beginning, so that the Germans would think that we were there. Mordechai did not climb up into the trees; he lay down on the ground and lay outstretched with the rifle. Fitshe and Davidye Schiffer also lay on the ground with the revolvers in their hands. We, the other [members] of the group, all climbed up into the trees.

A few hours later many Germans arrived in the forest with a dog. The dog followed the footprints and approached the bunker, which was empty. When the German who was leading the dog bent over, peering into the bunker, Mordechai shot out from the rifle and shot [dead] the German. The remaining Germans became very frightened and retreated from the forest. The Germans began to shout at the Ukrainian policemen, [as to] why they had not said that there were armed partisans in the woods. As they were pulling out, the Germans strongly shot up the forest, and two bullets struck the Jew, Mordechai. One bullet in his foot

[pp. 349-350]

and one in his hand. At night, we went to a familiar peasant woman; we took a sled from her and led Mordechai away on it to another forest, to the Bukaczowce woods. We, the others, went on foot. Mordechai was limping on his foot and the shot-through hand began to decay on him. Then, his wife and I chopped off the rotting hand from him with a razor and buried it in the forest. The amputated arm we bound up with

rags and washed with water. Mordechai's arm healed, but he limped on one foot. He was later killed when there was a raid in another spot in the forest. During a shoot-out on the part of the Germans, the Jew was shot [dead].

In the Bukaczowce woods we were in a large bunker; we were nearly 15 persons there. There were also children hidden there. My cousin, Yankl Glotzer, and his daughter (he now resides in Brooklyn, N. Y.) were hidden in the same bunker. We were also later in other parts of the forest, and we encountered yet other hidden Jews. While in the woods, we did not, however, have what to eat; our hunger was great. Once, my father and Yankl Glotzer's son left the forest with another Jew, a certain Fogel, so as to procure food. But they never again returned. They later told us that all three of them were captured by Ukrainian peasants, and [that] they killed them with hatchets.

We later entered the Czahrow woods. There, again, we were shot at by White Russian deserters who had gone over to the Germans. At that time, 7-8 Jews were shot. We went about in this manner from place to place, hiding. In the end, we dug a large bunker in the woods, and lay there until the liberation by the Red Army, in the summer of 1944.

On a winter's day

In the group: Two sons of Leibush Hornik, Mandelbaum, Ida Heller, and T. Fenster

Following the liberation, my mother and I went to the village in which we had lived before the war; we wanted to find the spot where my father had been buried. But a peasant woman told us that we ought to leave the village, because the adherents of Bandera[2] would kill us. I was later in Bukaczowce; we were in Germany, and on the 8th of December 1949, we arrived by plane in America. In 1945, I married Walther Tichover, who hails from Katowice. My husband is in the butcher business here, and we do not have it bad. We live in a four-room apartment that is decently arranged, and we are very satisfied with our life. We do not belong to any organization. We only read English newspapers; we hardly read any Yiddish.

Translator's Footnotes:

1.   The original Yiddish text does not indicate whether this was North or South Carolina.
2.   This is a reference to Stepan Bandera (1905-1959), a Ukrainian politician and leader of the Ukrainian nationalist movement in Western Ukraine that fought for Ukrainian independence. Toward the end of and just following World War II, in racial cleansing efforts, adherents of Bandera took to murdering Poles and Jews in eastern Galicia.

[pp. 351-352]

Across Bloody Roads

My experiences during the years 1939-1945

Miriam Ginzburg-Allerhand

When one tries to recall all the experiences over the course of the several years from 1939 until 1945, it is simply difficult to believe that we were able to survive all of this, so much horrible anguish, pain, and death. And now, once again, one lives, works, is busy, the daily worries. Is it possible?...

Often, I am overcome by such sad thoughts; they take away my [sense of] calm and the sleep from my eyes.

Chaim Ginzburg, the son of
Rabbi R' Yoel Ginzburg

In such moments, I relive the pictures of my former childhood in the town, my father and mother, the Jewish holidays, girlish memories, when I first met my husband; there, he stands before me, as though alive, the young Chaim Ginzburg, when he came that first time to our town (Krzeszowice), having come down to disperse Yiddish and Hebrew culture. He organized courses for Hebrew. The youth from our town, thirsty for knowledge, came en masse to the courses. They taught Hebrew, sang Hebrew and Yiddish songs, and dreamt of Zion. We fell in love. He was the leader, the teacher. A fiery speaker, writer, co-worker of the Yiddish and Polish newspapers, "Nowy Dziennik," correspondent of "Haolam," in London. He received a position as a professor of Greek, Latin, and Hebrew at the Jewish gymnasia in Krakow, a respectable position. In 1936, we got married.

Here [i.e., at this point] I am again struck by the memory of my father-in-law, Rabbi Yoel Ginzburg ZT"L. He stands before my eyes with his impassioned figure, [his] patriarchal majestic appearance. My brother-in-law OB"M, Gershon, the younger son, the prodigy, one of the leaders of "Beitar." (For his idea as a revisionist, he was also later murdered in Lemberg, when the Bolsheviks overtook that part of Poland).

How great was the joy when our son, may his light shine, was born a year later. We gave him a biblical name, "Amram," spoke Hebrew with him,

[pp. 353-354]

which sounded so nice [coming] from his childish mouth.

This ideal did not last long. In September 1939 the war broke out, and already the next day the chaos began. Everyone began to flee. People ran to the east, as far away from the border [as possible]. Usually it was the men, because one believed that the German would indeed not kill any women and children.

My husband Z"L also fled. He was even more afraid, because as a journalist he had often written against Hitlerism. In this manner, we parted [ways] – forever. My child and I remained in Krakow. He went to Lemberg and afterward to Bursztyn. The Russians were there. They began to confine us to ghettos, forced us to wear special signs, and so forth.

In 1941, the German-Russian War broke out. The last chapter of Polish Jewry had begun. The exterminations had begun.

In 1942, the Krakow ghetto was liquidated. I managed, through a Polish acquaintance, to obtain Aryan documents for my son and me, under the name Maria Jawsrewska. We then fled to Warsaw, where

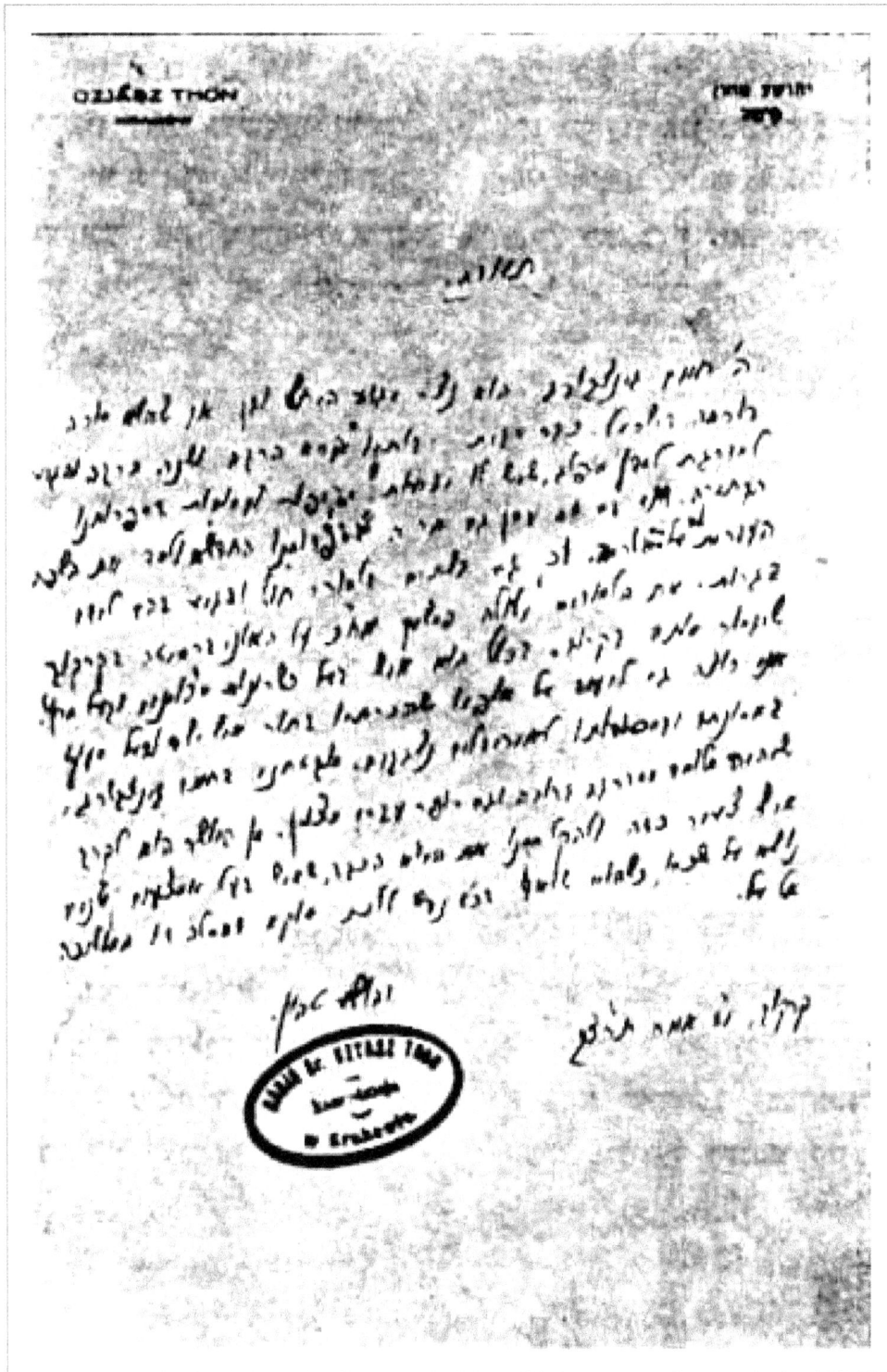

The certificate given by Dr. Yehoshua Thon Z"L to Chaim Ginzburg Z"L

[pp. 355-356]

our thorny road first began.

Every moment, we looked death in the eye. Where we spent the day, we did not spend the night. We were afraid of every gaze; indeed, everyone could betray a Jew, and furthermore, be rewarded. So, the Poles took advantage of the opportunity. At first, they threatened, extracted money, and when there was no longer any remaining money – they denounced – one nearly had to pay with gold for a residence, because the landlord was indeed risking his life; for hiding a Jew there was indeed a death penalty. If one were thrown out of one's residence one would have to find another one, by [some] miracle, and sometimes, would also need to flee from there the [very] next day. A denunciation following a denunciation, one threat after another yanked the marrow from one's bones and one's last groschen.

It was all the more difficult for me with a little boy. One could see right away for oneself that he was a Jew.

Once, following a night of frights, when the Gestapo carried out a raid near me, I thought that the end had already come. There were two agents; they examined my child and could see that we were Jews. They beat me dreadfully with their revolvers. My child cried terribly. Here [i.e., at this point], as though by a miracle, one of the two said to his companion that he could not shoot the child, because he reminded him of his child back at home. They allowed us to live; however, they appropriated everything, even my coat, and announced that we should get out of there immediately.

Once again, I amazingly acquired a residence in a decrepit house, with a broken roof, from which it [i.e., water, rain] would run in; however, there, they already permitted me to reside. All my money ran out, so I began to work as a presser in a factory for uniforms, not far from the "ghetto." Twelve hours a day I ironed for hunger wages; my child lay wrapped in rags behind the table. I could relate such episodes without end. From my husband I initially received letters via the intervention of a Ukrainian, until I received word, at some point, not from him, that I [no longer] had any reason to write.

I saw through the window of the factory the uprising in the Warsaw ghetto, witnessed the joy of the Poles, that they were ridding themselves of the Jews. There is much to tell, but that is a separate chapter.

I also lived through the Polish uprising. I witnessed the Germans fleeing. But we had lost too much for me to reap joy from this.

For me there remained only one purpose: to give my son, may he live [and be well], a Jewish education, to make from him a proud, national[istic] Jew, which was the holy wish of his father, of blessed memory.

[pp. 357-358]

Inhuman Suffering and Pain

The experiences of Dr. Lipa Schumer during the time of the Hitlerist murders

Recorded by Y. Shmulevitsh, New York

I was born and raised in the town, Bursztyn, East Galicia, where I lived until the outbreak of the Second World War. After completing my degree in the Department of Medicine at the University of Vienna, I was the popular city [town] doctor among Jews and non-Jews. I lived in Bursztyn with my wife and daughter.

When the Soviets entered Bursztyn on the 17th of September 1939, they dealt with the populace without [making any] distinction between Jews and non-Jews. The local Ukrainian opponents began to stir up an incitement against the Jews. The Ukrainians began to inform on the Jews to the Soviets that every Jew was a bourgeoisie, that the Jews were connected to the Polish "Pones," and so forth. As a result of this, the Soviets began to issue passports with paragraph 11 to the Jews; that they were not permitted to live in certain cities, they were not to travel from place to place, and that one was, in general, a harmful/destructive element. These passports were issued mostly to wealthy Jews. Wealthy Ukrainians, in contrast, received good passports because they were informers for the Soviets. The Jews who received passports with the paragraph nr. 11 were also the first on the list to be sent to Siberia.

Officially, the Soviets did not run an anti-Semitic course in the town, but Jews received separate laws and orders. Many Jews from the town, among them Zionists, said then that in spite of everything, the Red Army was a salvation for the Jews, and it was fortunate that one had not fallen under the Nazis. At that time, we already had greetings from Central Poland regarding troubles, which the Jews there had to bear from the Hitlerists; and at that, we must remember that this was just the beginning. In Bursztyn lived close to 2,600 Jews. Only 60 Jews received bad passports (one must remember that there were also many underage people), because our town was a poor town. There were many impoverished people, and only a small number of wealthy people.

When the Soviets were by us in the town, the Jews were afraid to barter/conduct business; they were threatened with jail [i.e., with a jail sentence]. Indeed, in Bursztyn, the Soviets also arrested Jewish

[pp. 359-360]

youths, the leaders of the Zionist youth organizations. These [individuals] were taken away to Lemberg and killed there, together with the Ukrainian nationalists, or sent to Siberia. They also sent away wealthy Jews and former community activists. I, indeed, worked as a doctor in the hospital, which the Soviets had created. I worked nearly 20 hours during a twenty-four-hour period, and thereby received a small salary; however, I was happy that at least nobody bothered me. My wife then sold off everything that we had from before in our house and lived on this. I also had a mill before the war, [so] the Soviets confiscated the mill from me, and I still had to sign off [on the fact] that I was giving this away to the Soviet government.

The Ukrainian informers at that time specially informed on wealthy Jews; that these [individuals] should be sent away to Siberia, so that they, the Ukrainians, would later be able to steal the possessions that the Jews had left behind, since indeed, the Soviets did not allow one to take too much with one when leaving. The Ukrainians informed on me to the Soviets that I had collaborated with the Polish government and had given advice to the Polish government as to how to oppress the Ukrainian populace. In the meantime, however, the Soviets did not bother me, because they needed me as a doctor. This is how it proceeded until the 22nd of June 1941, when the German-Soviet War broke out.

The Red Army retreated from our town in great panic. Around the town, major battles took place with the first German patrols. The bridges were also torn up. When the Soviets retreated, certain Jews also left with them. This was mostly Jews who had positions with the Soviets, and they were afraid to remain [behind], on account of the Ukrainians, and also because of the Germans, who needed to enter. During the fights around the town, German pilots were shot down by the Soviets, and they were brought to me, as a doctor, and I healed them.

Just as soon as the Soviets left the town and the Germans had not yet entered, they created a Ukrainian military. The Ukrainians were looking out, in general, that the Hitlerists should already enter. Among the Ukrainian militiamen, there were those who had been big shots under the Soviets, and they shouted: "Long live Stalin!" When the Soviets retreated, these same Ukrainians became big shots with the Hitlerists, and they shouted: "Long live Hitler!"

Certain Jews who had left with the Soviets returned to the town. The Ukrainian militiamen detained these Jews along the way; they robbed them, beat them, and many of them were killed. Even before the Hitlerists had entered Bursztyn, the Ukrainians sent off a delegation of 12 distinguished Ukrainians to their captain countryman in Rohatyn, and related to him that the Jews from our town were wealthy; that in their residences they had silver, gold, and reserves of produce, coffee, and tea, which was difficult to obtain then. The delegation also told the Hitlerist captain in Rohatyn that the Jews in Bursztyn were laughing at Hitler, and that something should be done about it, that these Jews should not behave so impudently…

Right away, the following day, it was Tuesday, the 20th of July 1941; I was standing in my medical office, dressed in a white apron, and tending to a sick Ukrainian, [when] a Bursztyn Jew approached me, [it was] a certain Minne Tobias. He was pale as the wall, he held a slip of paper in his hand, and said to me: Listen, doctor; unfortunately, you must

[pp. 361-362]

go with me into the community [building]; they are waiting for you; it is an order.

The Jew who had come to me, Minne Tobias, was a community activist in our town, and he had some good, small assets in a bakery. The Ukrainian militia had approved him then as their liaison with the Jews, and whatever they wanted taken care of with the Jews, they achieved via Tobias, considering him the representative of the Jews.

When he told me this, I was stunned, and went with him. When I came out outside, there were several Ukrainian militiamen standing in front of my house. One of them came over to me and ordered me to start running. When I began running, the Ukrainian began to beat me with a whip. My wife and daughter witnessed this. My daughter then cried out to the Ukrainian – You are not ashamed of beating an old, devoted doctor who saved thousands of Ukrainian mothers when they needed to give birth?

The Ukrainian grabbed his revolver and wanted to shoot my daughter, but my wife still managed to drag my daughter into the house and closed the door behind her. As the Ukrainian was beating me with the whip, I tore open the shirt upon my body, and said to him that he should not torment me; rather, it would be better if he shot me. So, he ordered me to run, and he beat me further. As I ran and received beatings, I ran to the town's community [building] (magistrate).

When I entered the community [building], I encountered Ukrainian members of the intelligentsia, judges, lawyers, and those notaries whom I used to heal and who were good friends of mine before the war. When they saw me, they pretended that they did not recognize me. As I was standing there, somebody pushed me into a room. Just as soon as I entered that room, I immediately heard a lamenting shout. The door opened, and the rabbi of Bursztyn, Rabbi Hertz Landau, who had been beaten and bloodied from the beatings of whips, was thrown in. A few minutes later, under the same scene, the old religious law adjudicator, R' Yoel Ginzburg, was thrown into the room. This picture was replayed several times; 8-10 distinguished Jews from the town were in this manner thrown into the room in which I was, inside of the community [building].

When I saw in the room that Minyan of beat-up Jews, I said to them:

Jews, do what Jews did when they underwent fire and water; do not give the enemy any pleasure!

The Jews in the room began clinging to me, as though I had some power to protect them, but at that time, I felt a great deal of powerlessness within myself.

The door opened, and a German sub-officer who was the commandant over the formed Ukrainian militia in the town; the regular German army had not yet entered. The German officer entered, accompanied by several Ukrainians. All of them were armed and with whips in their hands.

One of the Ukrainians went over to the old adjudicator, cut off his grey beard, and threw the hair in his face. At that, the Ukrainian said to the adjudicator: "Damned Jew, now the time has come when we will be rid of you and pay you back for all times." The adjudicator's tears poured over his face, and he said nothing. At that moment, I went over

[pp. 363-364]

to the German sub-officer, and said to him:

I studied in a German university, I am a Jew, and I benefited from the German education; all my educators were Germans. During the First World War, I fought together, shoulder to shoulder, with Germans, worked with German doctors, and treated sick Germans, along with Austrians. [And so] I am appealing to you now as a German, and I do not want to speak to the Ukrainian; do not torment these guiltless people. As a doctor, I have good things at home, and I also know what other Jews have; we do not need these things. You will receive fine schnapps from us; I have a good camera, a "Leica"; you will have everything, but let me out, so I can bring it to you.

The German contemplated this for a minute and then said that I was free [to go], that I should go bring him the promised goods. I responded to him that alone, I would not be able to procure/access anything; I could not leave behind the other Jews, so they should go with me to procure/access all these goods. The German sub-officer said to me that the other Jews may go with me; however, I was responsible with my head [i.e., it was on my head] for them; if one of the Jews did not return, I would be shot. The German said to me that we should return within an hour with the promised goods. Later on, he would search us, me and the Jews who had gone with me, and if he found anything, he would shoot us. The sub-officer did not want to let the rabbi and the adjudicator out.

When the other Jews and I went out of the room, I saw behind me how the Ukrainians had bound twine around the throats of the rabbi and the adjudicator and bound them with twine to the iron grates of the window. I wanted to turn around and go back to the room, but the other Jews begged me not to leave them alone, because they would be killed. I ordered the Jews to stand together in one place and promised them that I would soon be back together with them. I returned to the room of that community [building], went over to the German sub-officer, and begged him to not allow the rabbi and adjudicator to be tormented. The German said to me that I should get away, "The rabbi and the adjudicator will not croak [die]" – he shouted at me. I begged the young German that he permit me to go over to these two Jews and say something to them. The German allowed me [to do so]. When I went over to the corner in which the rabbi and the adjudicator stood, bound to the window grates, both of them were terrified and saying Viddui. I said to them: "God is with you; I will return soon."

I left with the other Jews for the city [town]. I went back to my residence, gathered together whatever I had there, and sent the other Jews off, across the town, and told them to announce to the Jewish populace that they should bring preserves, schnapps, sugar, conserves, coffee, tea, and other items to the community [building]. The Jews heeded my call and Jewish women and girls and men began to carry these items into the community [building]. On the way, however, Ukrainian attacked these Jews and beat them up murderously.

I, alone, took a sack from my home, filled it with costly goods, with a camera, several bottles of good wine, comfitures, sugar, tea, and so forth. The sack was heavier than I. I took the full sack upon my back and went like this into the

[pp. 365-366]

community [building]. On both sides of the street stood Ukrainians and Poles who had been my patients over the course of [many, several] years, Gentile men and women whom I had delivered to their mothers, and they laughed at me. They looked at me with a [look of] joy on their faces, as if they did not know me at all. The other Jews and I brought in the goods to me in the community [building], and I begged the German sub-officer that they not beat the Jews.

In the meantime, the Ukrainian members of the intelligentsia in the town, judges, lawyers, and simply well-to-do people, organized a pogrom against the Jews. It was at the same time, on the 20th or 21st of July 1941. I was then standing before the community [building], and a Ukrainian doctor arrived, the son of a priest, a former neighbor of mine, Dr. Komariatsky. He arrived at the community [building] in an automobile, upon which were the colors of yellow-blue. Along with Dr. Komariatsky, the judge, Klysz, a former patient of mine and a good friend, and several other local intelligentsia [members] arrived. The automobile in which they had come remained standing beside me, and they came out and happily amused themselves.

Then, a young Ukrainian militiaman of 16-17 years [of age] came over to me with a whip in his hand. I was dressed in the white doctor's coat, just as I had been when they had taken me that same morning from my medical office. The younger Ukrainian said to me: "Damned Jew, what are you doing here?" I responded to him that the German sub-officer had ordered me to stand there and see to it that the Jews brought the demanded goods. The younger Ukrainian took the whip and began to beat me. He gave me 5-6 whippings. I stood straight, calmly, not moving from my place. This, apparently, surprised him somewhat, and he left.

My formerly good friends, the Ukrainian [members of the] intelligentsia who were standing next to the automobile, witnessed this scene. I went over to Dr. Komariatsky and asked him: "Perhaps you know why they are beating me?" And so, he responded to this that he had not seen anybody beat me. Then, I left the community [building] and went home to see what had happened to my wife and daughter.

My daughter had gone to another place, far from Bursztyn, where she had hidden herself among Christians. When I entered the house, I met my wife, who had been crying, praying; and she did not know whether I was still alive. I no longer returned to the community [building]. I went up to the attic in the house of a Christian neighbor, who did not know about this; there I sat, like in a hen pen, not knowing what was happening with me. I sat like this an entire night until the next day, nearly deafened; lying at night in that attic, I heard shooting, and simultaneously, the shouts of desperate and tormented Jews. On the other hand, I once again heard laughter, music, and the Ukrainians' amusement. The following day, I went to see the rabbi and the adjudicator; both were at home. They lay in bed, clad in their Tallit and Tefillin, battered and beaten-up. I looked at the wounds that they had upon their bodies, and I showed them my [own] wounds. The rabbi and the adjudicator told me, and I heard the same thing from other Jews, what had been perpetrated the previous night, when I lay hidden in the attic. A pogrom was carried out against the Jews. They ordered all the Jews from the town to gather together in the synagogue. They drove them into the synagogue, as one drives sheep to the slaughter. On the way, they murderously

[pp. 367-368]

beat them. The sub-officer and the Ukrainian militiamen, who consisted of 15 men, were armed with machine guns, and they ordered the assembled Jews into the synagogue to pray. The Jews said the evening prayer. So, the German officer and the Ukrainian beat them, because they were not praying loudly enough. When the Jews began to pray loudly, they were ordered to pray with their hands raised upward. Since some of the Jews were weak, tired, and broken, they wanted to lean a bit on the wall. So, the Ukrainians murderously beat them, because the Jews were leaning on the wall. They told the rabbi to go up onto the podium; and if a Jew did something that did not please the German sub-officer and the Ukrainian, they would beat that designated Jew and the rabbi.

At a certain moment, the German sub-officer noticed that Dr. Schumer, I, was not among the assembled Jews in the synagogue. He grew wild with murder and ordered that I immediately be brought into the synagogue. One of the Ukrainian militiamen then said to the German sub-officer that there was a Ukrainian mother in grave danger in the process of giving birth; so, they told me, as a doctor, to go to this woman in the village. The sub-officer gave an order that when I returned from the sick [woman] I should report to him; but as I already related, I was hidden at that time in the peasant's attic, about which the peasant did not know.

At the same time that they were tormenting the Jews in the synagogue, the Ukrainians in the town were carrying out a huge ball. The Ukrainian intelligentsia, officials, peasants, common folk, young and old, were there. They danced, sang, and reveled in the schnapps and drinks, which the Jews had turned over during the day, inside of the community [building]. Late at night the Jews were allowed out of the synagogue, that they may return home. When they returned home at night, the Jews were attacked on the streets by Gentiles, who took to beating them murderously. Thus, the Jews returned to the synagogue, and remained there until dawn. In the meantime, the Ukrainians robbed the Jews' abandoned homes.

The Ukrainians in the town began to say amongst themselves that it was wrong that I had been beaten, since I had never done anything bad to anyone; everybody knew me. I had healed thousands of Gentiles. The following day, two representatives of the Ukrainian intelligentsia, the lawyers, Skolski and Trocz, came to me. They apologized to me and said that my getting beaten up had been a misunderstanding. The two said that I should not flee from the town, I should stay, that they would protect me.

When the Ukrainian priest, Jaciew, from the nearby village of Baszow heard that I had been beaten, he said in church that were he to die, he would want to lie beside me, that I had not merited being beaten. The priest's words made a major impact on his community's populace.

Fourteen days later, after the Ukrainians had partied in the town, the regular divisions of the German Army entered. In the interim, before the Germans had entered, they drove the Jews out of the surrounding villages into Bursztyn. On the way, many Jews were killed; only a small number of Jews that had been driven out of the villages reached Bursztyn. These Jews arrived in the town naked and barefoot, having been robbed along the way. We then learned that Bandera, the main leader of the Ukrainian nationalists, had given an order that they murder as many Jews as possible, even before the Germans took over the places in which Jews resided.

The Hitlerist occupants came

[pp. 369-370]

into Bursztyn in the beginning of August 1941. An order was issued that all Jews should register immediately. Jews had to don white-blue armbands with Stars of David on their arms, a restriction was issued against Jews leaving the city, [and] an order [was issued] to the Christian populace against buying from or selling to Jews. An order was also issued to create a "Judenrat" of eight people, which would need to oversee all the orders and be beholden to the Germans. I also joined this "Judenrat," and became the chairman. I joined the "Judenrat," because I was also forced and threatened with deportation. I was, however, [only] in the "Judenrat" for a short time. I fled, about which I will relate, later on. In the "Judenrat," were also [present]: lawyer, Philip Tobias, Minne Tobias, Yehudah-Hersh Fischmann, and other distinguished Jews of the town.

Three days after the "Judenrat" had been created by us in Bursztyn, the "Judenrat" of Rohatyn, upon the order of the Germans, ordered the "Judenrats" from all the towns in the region to send up to three representatives to Bursztyn. Philip and Minne Tobias, and I were the delegation of the Bursztyn "Judenrat." When we arrived at the "Judenrat" in Rohatyn, there were already assembled representatives of the "Judenrats" from all the towns in the region, which belonged to Rohatyn.

At the gathering of all the representatives of the "Judenrats" from the towns, the leader of the "Judenrat" in Rohatyn, Amaranth, spoke. He presented an order of the Germans, in which had been calculated that the Jews must pay a compensation of approximately 8-10 million rubles for the damages that Jews had caused. It was not demonstrated to whom and how about the Jews had caused damages. Upon our town of Bursztyn was placed [an order] to pay the sum of 2-3 million rubles. When I heard this, I became depressed, because our town was impoverished, squeezed out like a lemon. For a potato one needed to pay with gold, if one could get such a thing, and then here [I was to] go to our impoverished Jews and say that we needed to have millions! I cried and begged that they decrease the contribution [amount] for the Jews of Bursztyn. However, they told me that I should not needlessly lose my [right to] speak; should we not donate the proper sum, the entire Jewish population of Bursztyn would be slaughtered.

Philip, Minne Tobias, and I returned home that same day, broken up. We called together the Jewish populace in the religious study house and conveyed the sad news to them. The following day a committee was formed, and a list was put together of all the Jews, how much each individual needed to give for this contribution, which the Germans had placed [on us].

The put-together list with the submitted sums that everyone needed to contribute had a terrible effect on the Jews, because they were very poor. But the Jews began to sell off everything they had, until the last [item], so that they could put together the money that they had to give. The Gentiles were happy that they could purchase everything from the Jews for groschen; furthermore, the Jews were still grateful to the Gentiles, because according to the Hitlerist law, they were not supposed to buy from any Jews. Over two-three times we assembled the demanded sum and turned this over to the "Judenrat" in Rohatyn.

Every day, though, new laws were issued. Once, Saturday during the day, two Gestapo officers came to Bursztyn and ordered that in the course of two hours the Jews should amass for them: 100 silver coffee spoons, a certain number of silver tea pitchers, 200 pounds of coffee, 100 pounds of tea, 150 covers,

[pp. 371-372]

sheets, blanket covers, and tablecloths. Once again, the Jews took out the last of what they had, a bit of jewelry or a bit more money that one had, and one purchased from the Gentiles all the goods that the Gestapo men had demanded. Aside from the Gentiles, one also purchased these goods from the Russian priest, Gutkovsky, who had [already] stolen for himself many Jewish possessions, which the peasants had brought him. Gutkovsky was a well-known anti-Semite. We assembled the demanded goods and handed them over to the two Gestapo men, and such demands of the Jews were then made in Bursztyn every couple of days.

We always lived with troubles. The Germans did not create a ghetto in Bursztyn, but the entire sector where the Jews lived was converted into a ghetto. The Jews were ordered to leave their residences on the leading thoroughfares; they were not permitted to reside among Christians. In the neighborhood in which the Jews resided it was very congested; up to 20 people lived in a single room. Jews were not permitted to leave the neighborhood; one was not permitted to walk on the sidewalk, but rather, in the middle of the road, like the horses. One was also not permitted to enter the town's shops, not even one's own shops, in which Gentiles had been placed. It was a terrible picture to see the Jews swollen from hunger, children with thin legs, and bellies swollen from not having eaten. I was then the doctor among the Jews, and also for the sick Gentiles, for the entire town; and therefore, I had a right to leave the Jewish neighborhood and also go to sick peasants in the villages. I, however, had to wear the white-blue armband with the Star of David on my arm.

When I would go and treat sick Gentiles, I would not take any money then from them for this; but rather, produce, various foods, which I would later distribute among the Jews. The Germans then sent many Jews to the camps to do [forced] labor, but none of these Jews who had been sent out ever returned. These camps to which they sent the Jews were situated near Zaborow, near Lemberg, where one did not last more than 2-3 weeks. The Germans sent demands to the "Judenrat" that they should be sent Jews in groups, men, women, and children, to do [forced] labor. We really believed that Jews were being sent to do various [types of] labor. These Jews were led to the station; up to 120 men per wagon had been demanded, and after having been sent off, many Jews suffocated along the way in the wagons from the crowdedness or died from hunger and thirst. These Jews were sent to Belz and burned there, in the crematoria.

Once the transport had left, it stopped along the way at the station, Chodorow. A Jew then extended a gold watch through the gratings of the wagon, and begged a Gentile that if he gave him some water, he would give him the watch. The Gentile then took a petroleum/kerosene bottle and drew water from the gutter [that had] mud and handed it to the Jew inside of the wagon. Around the bottle of dirty water, the Jews in the wagon beat each other. Many Jews were even killed during this beating.

The following day, in the morning, after the transport of Jews had been sent out, the Jewish tailor from the town, Drucker, came to me and told me that up in his attic sat a naked Jewish doctor from Kosow, who had jumped out of a transport wagon. The Jewish doctor had come in a naked condition from the village into the town, at dawn, walking in this manner four kilometers. I sent a suit with the tailor for the doctor, and went at once

[pp. 373-374]

to visit him. The doctor related to me that he had jumped from a transport, because he wanted to die; he had thought that he would be killed when jumping. Jumping from the wagon, he fell on wet grass, began to drink the dew, and in this manner, recovered and reached the town.

On the 15th of October 1942, the Germans gave an order that all the Jews from Bursztyn must leave for Bukaczowce, a town that was situated next to the station. All the Jews left for there, and they were placed in peasants' houses there. By us, in the town, there only remained 30 male Jews who were working on the road. With these Jews, by whom a camp was created and all of whom were situated in one place, there also remained two doctors: Dr. Samuel Katz and I, as well as the primary [figure] of the "Judenrat," Philip Tobias, and two other Jews from the "Judenrat." Four weeks after that, Gestapo men arrived at the camps, and they sent these 30 Jews away to the Rohatyn ghetto.

The Jews of Bursztyn who had been sent to Bukaczowce, as well as the Jews from Bukaczowce proper, in addition to Jews who had been brought from Bolszowce, were loaded onto wagons on the 26th of October 1942, and sent to Belz. Many Jews then fled, and wanting to hide, were later found by Ukrainian militiamen, and these Jews were killed on the spot. The Germans drove out the Bursztyn Jews together to Bukaczowce, and also brought Jews from other surrounding towns, because there was a train station nearby where it was easy for the Jews to be loaded onto the wagon and sent off to Belz.

When the Gestapo had liquidated the camp of the 30 Jews in Bursztyn and sent them off to the ghetto in Rohatyn, my daughter had already left for another place outside of Bursztyn where she hid at [the home of] Christians. I was not at home at the time, and a Jewish boy came running in, who told my wife that the camp was being liquidated. My wife immediately left for a nearby village and hid at [the home of a] a Polish peasant acquaintance.

The Gestapo later came to me and asked me where my wife and daughter were. They then came to take me at the time that the ghetto was being liquidated. I told them to wait and said that I was going into the other room to change, because I was wearing the white smock. When I went into the other room to change, I took a bottle of rum (alcohol/liquor) from there and brought it in to the Gestapo men. I gave this to them to drink, until I was done changing. The Gestapo men sat and drank the rum, and I, in the meantime, exited through the back door in the other room. I went in to the [home of the] closest neighbor, a Ukrainian, and begged him to hide me. He, however, was afraid to hide me at his place. I then quickly went up to the roof and into a stable, crawled into the straw; there was then a terrible frost. I lay there for nearly eight hours, until the morning.

At night, I crawled out of the hiding place, so as to find out what had happened with my wife. I went into the garden that belonged to my house, crawled around there, and went in to the [house of the] Ukrainian peasant, Bilo, who was a big anti-Semite. I asked him whether my wife was alive, so he told me that I should run away, quickly. I went up into the attic of his house and hid myself there. The peasant did not

[pp. 375-376]

know that I was hiding there. Gestapo men immediately entered and said that they had seen somebody creeping in the garden, that this was a Jew, and that he should turn me over [to them]. The peasant responded that there was no Jew in his home; perhaps in the attic – he said – but he did not know anything about this.

The Gestapo men went up to the attic and found me. When they led me out of the attic, they asked me where my wife was. I responded that I did not know. I genuinely did not know. So, one of the Gestapo men took out a revolver, pointed it at my heart, and ordered me to tell where my wife was – if not, he would shoot me on the spot. I said to the Gestapo man: Please, do me the favor and shoot me!

The Gestapo man returned his revolver and slapped me, such that I had stars before my eyes. He took me away into custody. In custody, I encountered a Jewish woman, Maltche Fischmann, who had been in a hiding place, and the Germans had caught her. I asked the Gestapo men to shoot me.

Sitting there in custody, I knocked at the door, with the hope that the Gestapo men would thus come and shoot me; I wanted to put an end to the pain. But they did not respond to me; the Gestapo men were sitting high up in other rooms, amusing themselves. At a certain point, I leaned against the locked door, and the door opened; the lock had broken. Even then, none of the Gestapo men came. I went through the narrow corridor of the custody [area] and did not see anyone. I was outside and began to run down the road. It was nighttime, and along the way, I went in to [the home of] a Christian acquaintance, Milner, where I lay hidden for three days and they gave me to eat.

Lying at Milner's place in the attic, I sent word to a Polish acquaintance of mine, a former policeman, Stowarowski. He came to me in the attic and later took me away to his brother-in-law, Jozef Losek, where my wife was hidden, in a flower greenhouse, in the town of Bursztyn, proper. The situation of the peasant was then a dangerous one, because the Gestapo men together contended that it had never before happened that a Jewish doctor should escape from their hands twice in one day.

The night that I fled from custody, the Gestapo men sent out patrols along every road; they searched for me, and an order was issued that the family that hid me would be annihilated, along with all of their possessions. The Gestapo men also promised that whoever brought Dr. Schumer, me, living or dead, would receive 25,000 zlotys and two liters of genuine spirits, which was difficult to obtain then.

But notwithstanding the danger, the peasant hid me and my wife at his place, over the course of several months. My wife and I were in separate places, and later on we left to go hide in the woods.

We went into the woods next to Czahrow. On the 9th of July 1943, when we were in the forest, we heard strong shootings in the distance. The Germans had liquidated the ghetto in Rohatyn then and shot every Jew whom they found somewhere. In the woods we made bunkers, in which we

[pp. 377-378]

hid ourselves. We also went from place to place, so as not to be caught. In the end, we dug a bunker in the field amidst corn, and lay hidden there. We suffered from great hunger and thirst, lay in wetness, and were eaten up by lice. Later on, peasant acquaintances began to bring us food; these were mostly followers of the "Jehovah's Baptists" [i.e., Jehovah's Witnesses].

We were in the woods and fields for nearly two and a half years. The peasants who brought us [food] to eat told us that in the same woods there was another group of 6-7 hiding Jews. We knew about these Jews, and they knew about us, but we never saw each other. Later on, these Jews were captured by the Ukrainians and Germans when they went into the villages for water or to procure food.

The peasants who brought my wife and me [food] to eat gave me everything that they had; the shoes and clothes that we still had on; later on, a Jewish butcher from Bursztyn, Yankl Feldman, whom we encountered in the field in which we were hidden, was also together with us. He helped my wife and me a great deal. He knew all the paths well, and he was bold, [so] he would go to the peasants, carry off goods for them, for which they gave him produce. The peasants knew that this Jew was with me in my hiding place, and therefore held him in esteem, and did not do him any harm.

We were hidden in this manner until May 1944, when the Soviets entered and pursued the Hitlerists. Following the liberation, my wife [and] daughter – who had survived the war as a Christian, and we did not even know whether she was alive – and I, left for Poland, and from there, for Germany, and arrived in Ranshofen, near Braunau [Austria]. We were in a camp of liberated Jews there, and in 1946 we immigrated to America; in the month of July 1946, we arrived with the ship, "Marine Perch," in New York, where we have lived the entire time [since coming here].

We are happy with our life in America. In the beginning, we went through difficult times, because we arrived here broken and hungry. I passed an examination, and now, as you can see, have my own medical practice.

My wife and I are sick people, and furthermore, we do not have time to belong to and devote ourselves to certain Jewish organizations. We belong to the community center in our neighborhood. From time to time, we visit with our kinsmen. They come to our home; they know that it is difficult for me to come to them.

Our daughter is married and lives in the province [area]. She is a medical social worker, and her husband is studying medicine. I read the "Forward" and the "Times" every day. In my free time, I read religious books, I study the Zohar, Talmud, Gemara, and Kabbalah.

New York, 23rd March 1955

Dr. Lipa Schumer, unfortunately, did not merit to see this Bursztyn "memorial book." He died on the 18th of Cheshvan 5720 [19th of November 1959]

May his memory be blessed

[pp. 379-380]

Through Horrors and Fears

The experiences of Hersh, son of Moshe-Aharon Weissmann
during the black night of the Hitlerist occupation

Recorded by Yosef Schwartz, New York

The family: My father, mother, and 9 children lived in the village of Kuropatniki; after the Germans arrived, we lived for another 3 months in the village. The young Ukrainian Gentiles often threw rocks at our house. During the time that we lived in the village, the adults forced us to do hard labor every day.

Hersh Weissmann

The village head, as well as other older Ukrainians, did not coerce us to leave the village until there was an order [issued] by the German commander. When we still resided in the village, they once held an inspection by us and found a piece of butter. Given that there was already an order to supply butter-goods we were threatened with a very extreme punishment for this. They dragged all of us to Bursztyn, to the Ukrainian police, and they would surely have turned us over to the Gestapo. The Judenrat, however, bribed the Ukrainian police commandant, and they let us go free.

In 1942 I worked in the Kuropatniki courtyard, where the manager was a Volksdeutscher. Moshe Blecher's two sons, Shlomo and Lantzi, also worked there. In the interim, an order came from the Judenrat that we should be presented for the transport, which was going to Tarnopol, and to the labor camps. I managed to flee to the woods, and in this manner, remained in the village with small interruptions. Given that I knew the peasant [lines of] work well, I would work illegally for peasants in the village, here by one, there by another. Once, two neighbors got into a fight. I worked for one of them. So, a small Gentile singled me out/identified me. Right away, 2 Ukrainian policemen came, [as did] one German. I was in the middle of doing farm/day labor. Having seen that they were coming, I left behind my work and went to the woods. The peasant woman for whom I was working was called Faranka Sarncka. When I came [back] in the evening, I found her in bed, sick [and] beaten up. She had been beaten because I had fled.

My sister, Mani, worked at cleaning

[pp. 381-382]

the Gnila Lipa, and my sister, Eltzie, worked illegally like me, for peasants.

When they had already liquidated Bursztyn, and it was no longer possible for us to remain in the village, we went by our own volition to the Rohatyn ghetto.

Once, during an action in the Rohatyn ghetto, I, and another 20 people, approximately, hid ourselves in a bunker, which we had previously prepared. The day after the slaughter, they took us to bury the dead and collect all the remaining items [belongings]. Two weeks later, they caught me and sent me away to a work camp, Gleboczek Wielki, near Tarnopol. My brother Simcha, who was still living with my two sisters in the Rohatyn ghetto, lured the militant Shaike Granwitter (Wolf's son) during an action into a house/room, supposedly to give him bread, and he was shot, along with us Bursztyn Jews, by the Gestapo.

Following the liquidation of the Rohatyn ghetto, my two sisters, Eltshe and Mani, fled to a village. They hid the entire time in the forest, where male and female peasant acquaintances would bring them food from time to time.

In Gleboczek we worked in stone quarrying. With me were Yaakov Stryzower (Chaim's son), Mendele Schurtman, David (Strelisker's son-in-law), and 40 other Bursztyn Jews. Following 3 weeks of hard labor, a few of us Bursztyners discussed fleeing. Somebody informed [on us] to the Gestapo. They right away made all of us stand in a row, and every tenth [person] they shot. The camp commandant was an S. S. man [named] Frommer.

One day, a German overseer, Hammer, took me and others to another [form of labor] in the village. Over the course of 6 months, during which I was in the labor camp, people were punished every day. For the littlest thing that did not please the camp overseer, they would hang or shoot. If they found money on somebody during an inspection, or they caught somebody speaking to a Gentile, that person would be shot right away.

After 5 months, the camp overseer, Frommer, was taken away. In his place came an S. S. man [named] Tomanuk. When Tomanuk took over the camp, he sorted the people. Whoever did not please him, he ordered to go to the left – to be liquidated. He would send in the Ukrainian police, and they would advise the Jews: If you can't, you may go more slowly. Jews believed [them] and would go slowly. At the gate stood Tomanuk, [who] detained nearly 100 slow moving Jews, sent them away, and liquidated them. This is what he did a couple of times. Once, from the middle row, once from the back, he took them away and liquidated them, not far from the camp.

From the 22nd into the 23rd of July 1943, a Thursday, during the night, the increase in liquidation of the entire camp, began. At first, the Jewish police came in. [They] right away awoke us and shouted: "Jews, move more quickly, let's save ourselves; they are going to liquidate us." We were approximately 1,600 souls.

We grabbed whatever we could get our hands on, and made for the closed gate, where the camp overseer, Tomanuk, and armed Germans and Ukrainians stood. They began shooting at us through the wires, which resulted in a few hundred dead Jews. Later on, they brought in a few hundred women from a not [too] distant women's camp. Then, Ukrainians arrived with wagons, and right away, they loaded up all the dead and wounded, and sent them off to the mass grave, not far from the camp. Then, they made us stand 4 in a row. From both sides, armed Gestapo and Ukrainian police guarded us. [They] sent us to already previously prepared large graves and began to shoot at us. I began to run. I received two shots. One in the cheek, and one in my foot, and in this [condition] I entered a field

[pp. 383-384]

among grain. A few other boys also managed to flee. We moved about next to Tarnopol for close to 6 weeks. During that time, we encountered good Gentiles, including a priest, who would give us food.

In the interim time, they apparently identified/singled us out. They perpetrated attacks, but every time, we managed to run away. Autumn approached, and each of us began to go into his [own] neighborhood/area.

I took a sack on my shoulder, a so-called peasant, and greeting peasants in the local manner, "Slowo misusy Krysto," and 4 days later arrived in my former Kuropatniki. They also detained me in Brzezhany regarding documents. But not being able to communicate with the German, as a "Ukrainian," he shouted: You damned Ukrainian, and let me go free, after having hit me. Walking nearby, next to a village, already not far from my goal, I encountered a Ukrainian with a cashbox on his shoulder, and he asked me who I was. So, I told him that I was a Ukrainian. This mobilized me. Now I was running back home. You! He shouted: You want to fool me? You are indeed Moshe Aaron's son from Kuropatniki. They killed all the Jews, and you want to live?! And he took his cashbox to my head. I deftly bent down and began to run into the woods.

Even before I had left the ghetto, I had conversed with a familiar Ukrainian in the village, [saying] that if anyone from our family should survive, someone should let him know and he would already be able to say whether another family member would appear/show himself. I came at night into the yard of this very Ukrainian. I noticed two shadows shifting about in the garden, and since they had apparently heard steps, they bent down. I went into [the home of] the Gentile, [and] he gave me a piece of sugar and said to me: Yours sisters are alive. They are here, by me, in the garden. Right away I went out and met my two sisters. I then dug bunkers in three separate places in the woods. At night, I stole potatoes from the gardener, which I carried to the bunkers. I also managed to steal 2 sacks of wheat. I built a kitchen in the bunker in which to cook, and in this manner, I persevered until April 1944; after we covered up the bunker in which we were living, we went into another bunker, until the end of spring, when the grain began to grow. Once, small Gentiles detected me in a potato ditch. I began to flee. But an entire horde of adult Gentiles with hammers and knives chased after me. I entered a pile of trash in the field (like a mouse), and in this manner saved myself from my pursuers, who had lost sight of me.

Later on, I sustained/provided for myself and my sisters in the field, among the grain, until the Russian military had encroached upon us. They, the Russians, at first, took us to be spies. They took us to their headquarters, where the investigator was a Jew from Kiev. When I began to tell him how we had survived and what had happened to the other Jews, he sobbed like a small child, and could not write any more. They called another [person], also a Jew, and he recorded it. Night fell, and the peasant of the house in which the commando had interrogated me, wanted to take us up to the attic to sleep. The Jewish commander ordered: You [word unclear, but seems to connote something quite negative, such as "low-lifes"] will sleep over there, and they will sleep here, in the house [or room]. The same Jewish commander took us to Brzezhany, where we encountered other Jewish survivors. From there, we rode to Bursztyn. Sometime later, we left for Poland, [and] from there, for Germany.

[In] 1951 I came to America, [in] 1955

[pp. 385-386]

I was called as a witness to Germany, for the trial of the first camp overseer, Frommer, who was sentenced to a life sentence in jail. At that same trial, I encountered the S. S. man, Tomanuk, the liquidator of our camp in Gleboczek, as well as other Jewish camps, approximately 20 in number.

[In] 1957, I was called to Germany for the trial of Tomanuk. He received 15 years.

I am married. My wife is from Krakow. We have a child of two years. My sister, Mani, resides in Paterson, not far from New York, [and] is married to a weaver from Lodz. They have a girl of 9 years. My sister, Eltzie – [is] married, has 3 children, [and] they live in Israel.

[pp. 387-388]

Deported and Murdered Bursztyn Jews
in the Soviet Camps

After the arrival of the Red Army in Bursztyn, all the shops were emptied out right away. An order was issued to buy up all the merchandise within a short time. Indeed, the shopkeepers remained seated in their stores right away, with empty hands, with heaps of empty boxes and paper. They did not sit like this for long, because they, the "bourgeoisie," were also driven out from their empty stores.

Right after that came denunciations/reports – at the merchant, at home, one found two pairs of shoes for a child, at this [other] one's [home], a piece of metal, and so forth.

The first victims were: Yitzchak Cohen, his brother-in-law, Moshe Hauptmann, Baruch Bien, [and] his brother-in-law, Yitzchak Baumring. They were sentenced by a "people's court" to 7 years of camps. Later on, Baila Brodman, Leizer Deichsler, Minter Velvl, and Volke Haber were deported.

Also deported were: Shike Kletter, Munye Cohen, Izye Hammer, and Yisroel Leib Fenster.

Our townsman, Yosef Schwartz, a former supporter of Soviet Russia, a contributor to the leftist Ukrainian journals, was sentenced in Moscow by a military tribunal to 8 years of camps for [being a] "counter revolutionary."

In 1948, he and many Polish citizens were handed over to the Polish powers that be.

The youngest son of R' Yoel Ginzburg, Gershon, was arrested by the Russians in 1940; they kept him confined in the Lemberg prison. Before the occupation of Lemberg by the Nazis in 1941, at the time that the Russians abandoned the city, the prison was set afire. Gershon Ginzburg Z"L ended his young life in the flames.

Yosef son of Yisroel Schwartz, Hershele the butcher's grandson

Polish document released following his liberation.

In Russian [the following] perished: 1) Moshe Hauptmann, 2) Levi Yitzchak Baumring (Baruch Bien's brother-in-law), 3) Leizer Deichsler, 4) Baila Brodman, 5) Shike Kletter (fell in the Red Army).

[pp. 389-390]

After having been liberated and left Russia, [the following] died, exhausted, en route to Israel: Yitzchak Cohen and his wife.

3 of the Bursztyn intelligentsia perished in the Katyn woods: 1) the pharmacist, Grinhoyt, 2) the veterinarian, Adolph Wattenberg, 3) the physician, Dr. Zusmann.

In the Woods

We do not want to be investigators, we do not wish to quibble about the souls of those who lived during that terrible time in the woods, pursued like animals, concealed inside of lairs, ditches, bunkers, the people who looked death in the eye 10 times a day.

We only wish to convey a few facts here that truthfully should and must be recorded. There were instances during those dark days when simple common folk reached the highest height of morality. They revealed in themselves everything beautiful in human beings: good-heartedness, feelings for helping another person, the willingness to make sacrifices, and belief. But also, the opposite [was true] --- people sank to the lowest abyss.

This happened among the tormented Jews in the woods, camps, ditches/dug outs, and precisely the same thing happened on the Aryan side. Among the sea of hatred, loathing, murder, and theft, which engulfed huge segments of the Polish and Ukrainian population. Among these very human snakes, there were a few Ukrainians or Poles, who, with their good deeds, saved not only Jewish lives, but also the honor of their people.

In the Bursztyn woods approximately 10 Jews remained alive, but earlier on, there were many more [of them] there. They were murdered when they came out to search for food; the peasants caught them and murdered them in a cruel manner. The Germans and the Ukrainian militia; also, oftentimes, the Russian prisoners, Vlasovites, [and] Kalmuks would conduct actions [i.e., in the German-Nazi sense of the word], during which many Jews from Bursztyn and the surroundings fell. The Jews frequently staged uprisings and fell with weapons in hand.

It is worth mentioning Kalmen Streger (Sarah, the baker's [husband]), who demonstrated the highest courage, purity of spirit, and willingness to sacrifice [himself]. He did not want to collaborate with the Judenrat, went into the ghetto, fought there, fled to the woods, aided people; and while protecting others, he fell with weapons in hand.

Mordechai from Czahrow protected a bunker of Jews in the forest. When the bunker was surrounded by Germans and Ukrainian militia, he exited the bunker, and as the first group of Germans approached, he killed a German and wounded another. He himself was badly hit in one of his hands, which they later amputated in a bunker.

During another attack on the woods, he was killed. May these very valiant Jews be honored!

Among the survivors, Yaakov Feldman, who helped many Jews at that time, exemplified himself. This was also confirmed by our Dr. Schumer in his testimony.

This must also be stated: When the first survivors emerged from the woods, the name Yehudah-Hersh Fischmann was right away mentioned for the bad. Everyone related the most dreadful acts, which he did to the harassed, tormented Jews of Bursztyn. Y. H. Fischmann had previously been a distinguished resident of Bursztyn. His wife was the daughter of Avrahamtshe Breiter. He had 3 talented children. He was a calm, stable person, and successful merchant. Our kinsman, Loncia Feffer, who lives in America, said in his testimony, [something] that was a

[pp. 391-392]

heavy accusation against Fischmann – that upon his orders, the Ukrainian police and Germans beat and murdered Jews; and he, too, Loncia Feffer, was himself murderously beaten.

Fischmann also collaborated with the Germans in deporting the Jews to labor camps and death camps.

The residents of the woods at that time, with whom Fischmann was together, following the liquidation of the Jews of Bursztyn – his wife and children were then in the Rohatyn ghetto. He, alone, was then hidden under the protection of the Ukrainian police.

Once, at night, his wife and children escaped from the Rohatyn ghetto and came to Bursztyn. They went to the militia; from there, Fischmann was notified that his wife and children were there. He did not want to leave his hiding place. He did not go to help even his [own] wife and children. They were deported and murdered.

We posed a question to the people who related all of this to us, and who had been together with him at that time in the woods: If you knew his deeds, you knew what this person had on his conscience, why did you not sentence him there, in the woods? The response was: We wanted to do that many times, but the decision was always made that we should wait until after the war, and at that time, all the Bursztyn survivors, wherever they might be – should sentence him.

In the Armies

At the outbreak of the Second World War, when the Hitler hordes attacked Poland, the Polish government in haste and in terrible disorder, mobilized the military reserves; they called the officers and tradesmen; many Jewish physicians were mobilized, [as were] veterinarians, engineers, and so forth.

From among the Jews, they called several young people, as well as officers-tradesmen, into the Polish Army.

Most of them returned after a few days because the Polish Army had broken up during the first days of the war.

A portion of the Bursztyn youths fell into German captivity, from which only individuals managed to escape.

The officers fell into Russian captivity – the Polish Army was disarmed in conjunction with the Germans and Russians.

A short time after the Germans had overtaken the town, they began to call up young people to the military, and before the outbreak of the war between the Russians and Germans in 1941, a significant number of Jewish youths left Bursztyn for the Soviet Army. The youths participated in many battles against the German enemy. Some of them fell on the battlefield, some remained in Russia until today, [and] a few came to Israel.

Reference should be made here to Shike Kletter, who was deported to Siberia. Following his liberation in 1941, when the majority of liberated Jews migrated from the far north to Middle Asia, with the hope of getting out of Russia, Shike Kletter did not want to hear of this. He went of his own volition to the Red Army in order to fight against the bloody Nazis.

He fell in battle at Stalingrad.

At the time that the Jewish state was declared, Itzik Ben Shlomo (Prochniker), a healthy young man, full of hope and desire to begin a new life here, arrived in Israel with an illegal ship. He took part in

[pp. 393-394]

various fronts in Russia and Europe and received a series of awards.

At that time, Arab bands were rampant on all the roads in the land. In the cities fights took place between the Jews and Arabs. He was then in Haifa. Itzik aspired to participate in the fight. We only begged him that he stay in Haifa; he did not want to hear this. At such a time, one ought not to sit [idly] with folded arms, he said. He left – we never saw him again.

In Tel Aviv, during an attack by Egyptian jets, he was killed while standing at the bus station.

All the young people from Bursztyn who were in Israel during the time of the War of Independence, took part in the liberation of the country.

Murdered in the Woods of Katyn

1943, in the very heat [fervor, zeal] of the Second World War, the entire world was shocked by the news that mass graves of thousands of murdered Polish officers had been found. The site: in the woods of Katyn.

During the collapse of Poland, when the Russian Army cut off the roads for the split up and disorganized remnants of the Polish military forces, several thousand Polish officers from all the [military] rungs were taken into captivity and driven into Russia.

After the Sikorski-Stalin agreement of 1941 was signed, Moscow freed all the Polish citizens from the camps and prisons. Only missing were the [previously] mentioned thousands of officers. The Polish Government-in-Exile in London began demanding them. For a long time, the Russians said that they would release them, [but] were later entirely silent [on the matter]. – Until the Germans came along and said that they had found significant mass graves in the woods of Katyn, and according to all the signs, these were the lost murdered Polish officers.

The Germans said that the Russians had murdered them. The Russians, in opposition, claimed that the Germans had shot them.

The pharmacist Grinhoyt

Among these very thousands of [the] Polish intelligentsia, who had been so cold-bloodedly annihilated, were many Jews.

Our town of Bursztyn contributed 3 victims to the woods of Katyn:

1.   The veterinarian, Adolph Wattenberg, was an active Zionist, an alderman in the Magistrate, and for a while, also chairman of the Jewish community. At first, he wrote about Russian captivity; later on, the Russians also sent away his wife.
2.   The pharmacist, Grinhoyt, an energetic [person], full of life, socially active. For a long time, he was the chairman of the Peretz Association; more recently, he had resided in Krakow. His wife and two sons live in Israel.
3.   Dr. Zusmann, an able physician; he was known for his good-naturedness and humor.

Prior to the Second World War, he resided in Drohobycz.

[pp. 395-396]

Bursztyn 1957

Reported by an eyewitness

The remnants of Jews from our town of Bursztyn, the She'erit Hapletah [literally, the surviving remnant] spread out and dispersed across Poland, following the end of the war. From there, to Austria, Germany, off to America; some came to Israel.

The synagogue as it appears today – it serves as a grain storehouse

A number of young people remained behind in Russia. A few of them came to the destroyed town of Bursztyn. They did not remain there, but rather, settled in Stanislawow.

At the end of 1957 Shmuel Zusmann and Moshe Schechter left Stanislawow with permission from the Soviet authorities. S. Zusmann arrived in Israel in 1958. He relates:

Before leaving, I was in Bursztyn, I wanted to take a look at the town. Have a glimpse at the few remaining Jewish houses, at the synagogue and the religious house of study, which remain intact, said goodbye to the lone Jew who remained in Bursztyn.

How does our town appear now?

How does the place in which we first

[pp. 397-398]

saw God's light [i.e., the light of day], spent our youth, enjoyed ourselves, laughed?

Right after Hitler's downfall, when the Soviets took over our regions, when the Bursztyn Jews were at that time no longer living, they soon ruined most of the Jewish houses, and left behind only those that were in good condition.

The remnants of the [Jewish] cemetery

Until today, the synagogue and the study house still stand. From the two prayer houses the Russians made grain storehouses.

The [Jewish] cemetery was desecrated and destroyed by the Gentiles. They tore out the headstones, and from the burial grounds, made a vegetable garden.

The Jewish houses on the street with the courthouse have remained intact. In the marketplace stands the pharmacy, the houses of Zelig Hammer, Chaim Nachwalger, Davidzshe Breiter, and others. On the street of the Christian cemetery stands the house of Elka Halpern.

The palace of Prince Jablonowski was ruined and razed. In a ruin that remained in that spot lives the only remaining Bursztyn Jew, Ulke the

[pp. 399-400]

Shoemaker. He frequently gets drunk and is made the laughingstock of the Bursztyn Gentiles.

There are a few Jews from Russia living in Bursztyn; those are the pharmacist, the physician, and so forth.

How do the Gentiles in the town live now without Jews? Are those who satiated themselves with the robbed possessions happy? Are they content, those who watched and helped annihilate their one-hundred-years'-long neighbors? In general, they hate to speak of that time, but once one is already talking, they all relate, without exception, that they helped and rescued Jews.

The older generation is not content and not happy, "It seems to me that were someone to take them back to those old times – even with the Jews! – they would be content."

[pp. 401-402]

From the Few That Survived

Y. F.

Maltche Feffer

One alone, the remnant of an established Jewish family in Bursztyn, she survived death, living on Aryan papers.

For a certain [period of] time she hid in the village of Kozari, in which the largest number of Jew killers in the region, lived. From there, many young and old peasants embarked on the "Jagd" [i.e., chase], catching Jews, handing them over to the Gestapo, or murdering them with their very own hands. How much boldness this Jewish girl must have had to move about among these very murderers, under the purchased [acquired] name, Helena Matkowska.

Maltche Erdstein-Feffer

When the ground began to burn under our feet, she left to do labor in Germany. There, too, lurked danger at every step, until she lived to see the liberation, the end of the war, and came to Poland, married her cousin, Loncia Feffer, and left for America, where they do not forget until this very day the horrible destruction of their many-branched family.

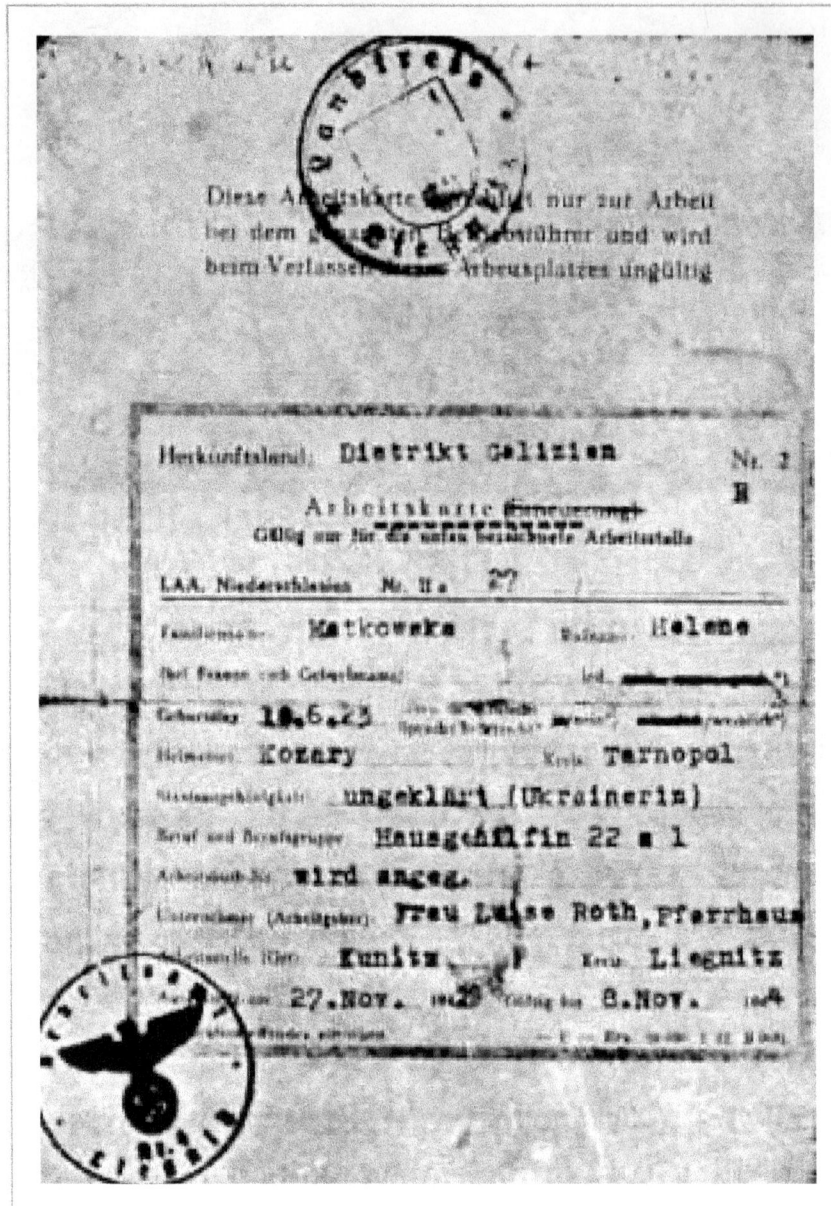

The German Ausweiss [i.e., identity card] of Maltche Feffer

[pp. 403-404]

Yocheved Rudy

Yocheved Rudy[1] is the child of a distinguished family in Bursztyn. Her grandfather, R' Yankl [Rude/Rudy], belonged to the Jewish landowners, had fields, and was esteemed for his honesty, not only among the Jews, but also, among the Polish and Ukrainian peasants of the region. Her father, R' Berl Rudy, went down the same paths of honest efforts and sincere, friendly relations with the people with whom he came in contact.

Yocheved Rudy

Yocheved had the "fortune" of having an Aryan face, and with the help of a fake document, she survived all the horrible hells. The Aryan document did not remove from her the feeling that she was a harassed animal that could not forget the dangers that lurked [in wait] for her. She is the only one who survived from an entire family with whose genuine Jewish feeling she still lives in America.

Translator's Footnote:

      1.   This surname has been spelled alternatively, elsewhere in this text, as "Rude/Rudy," and may also be spelled "Rudi."

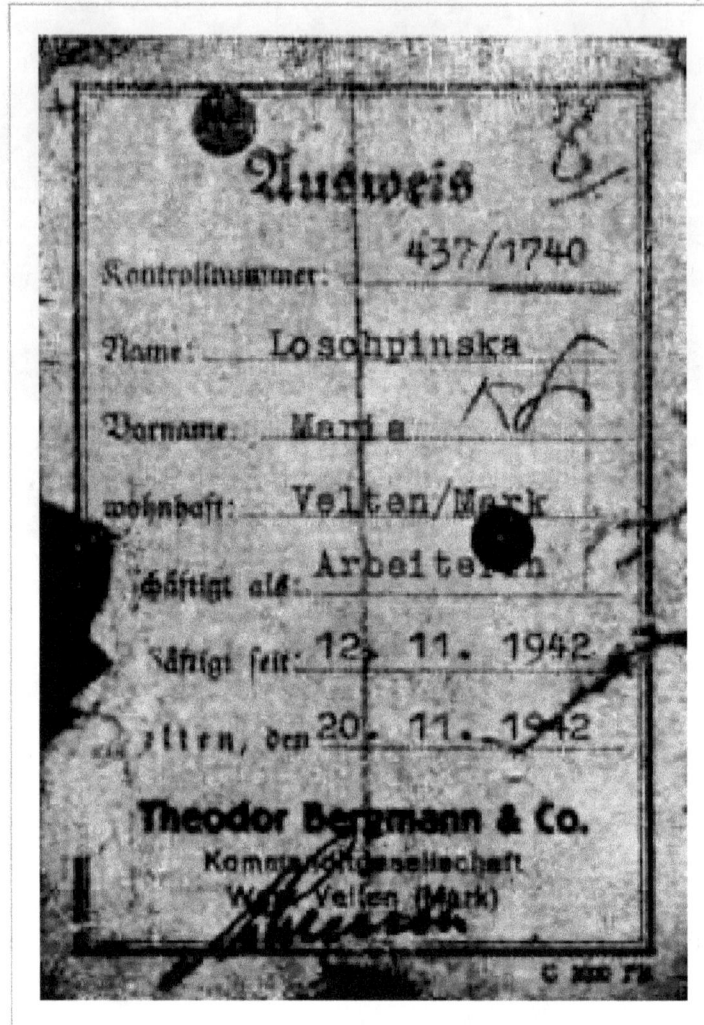

The German "Ausweiss"

[pp. 405-406]

The Rescued Torah Scroll

Pinye Haber, the son-in-law of Avrahamtze Yossel Yonah, hailed from Bohorodyczyn. When he moved to Bursztyn, he brought with [him] a Torah scroll, and donated the Torah scroll to the Stratyner synagogue. That was where he prayed.

When the Hitler bands began, just after their entering the town, to plunder, rob, clean out, and desecrate the religious study houses and all that was holy for Jews, Pinye Haber hid the scroll; where? – Nobody knew.

After the liberation of Bursztyn by the Russians in 1944, when the few surviving Jews came out of their hiding places, they came to the town and cried over the ruins.

Bedecked Torah scroll

Once, an old Ukrainian woman came to Yaakov Feldman, and said: I want to tell you a secret. And related to him that at the end of 1941 Pinye Haber and Mordechai Bernstein had handed over [to her] a Torah scroll to hide. They knew the old woman; she was a "Subotnik" [i.e., a Christian, Saturday Sabbath observer, or Seventh Day Adventist]. She was called the "Stepanka."[1] She took the scroll from them, made a special bunker, and therein hid the Torah scroll, surrounded by hay, so that it would not be touched by any dampness. The old woman asked Feldman that he put on a cap [possibly a yarmulke or kippah] and go with her.

The scroll was in the hiding place, just as she had related. The woman gave the scroll to Yankl Feldman, at the time, the husband of Dosia, the daughter of Pinye Haber, who had given the scroll to the old, good woman, to hide.

Following long wanderings, Dosia and Yankl Feldman arrived in Israel in 1948; they brought with them the rescued Torah scroll.

The scroll is located today in the best condition in the synagogue in which Feldman prays.

[pp. 407-408]

They Died En Route to Israel

Yitzchak Cohen was the son of the well-known merchant of manufactured goods, Malka Cohen. He returned to the town following the end of the First World War. Along with his wife, Reizel, both of them lived quietly and modestly. Over time, Itzig was considered to be one of the wealthiest merchants in Bursztyn.

But not only was Yitzchak Cohen absorbed in merchandise and purely personal matters. He distributed his time broad-handedly among various communal and philanthropic establishments.

Even before the First World War, Yitzchak Cohen joined the Chovevei-Tzion movement. Right after the war, he, as a religious Jew, was elected to the position of chairman of the national-religious party, "Mizrachi." In the later years [prior to World War II], he was particularly active in the local institutions.

Some of his activities within the institutions are worth mentioning:

Yitzchak Cohen stood at the head of the committee, whose task it was to build the great religious house of study. The study house was completed, and Yitzchak was elected one of the trustees. Being in this position until the outbreak of the Second World War, he was always only concerned with beautifying, improving, and making the religious house of study more comfortable.

He placed himself at the head of the Talmud Torah Committee and ran it. This institution was concerned with and enabled children of poor parents, or orphans, to learn free-of-charge.

In addition, his philanthropic work was multi-hued. So, for example, he always, along with other proprietors, joined the Kimcha d'Pischa [literally, "flour for Passover"] action, [which was] a fund that had to ensure that not a single Jew in the town, heaven forbid, would remain without Matzot, wine, and so forth, during the holiday [i.e., Passover].

In our region there was a pressing problem [concerning] caring for the impoverished populace with heating materials. For this purpose, Yitzchak Cohen established a special fund, whose task it was to provide poor people with wood to heat [their homes] during the winter months.

He did not mind dedicating his time to all of this, so as to represent the Jewish populace and various general institutions. In this manner, he was, for example, elected several times as an associate of the Magistrate, where he worked for the populace's good. At the same time, Yitzchak Cohen belonged to the administration of the People's Bank.

Yitzchak's wife, Reizel, helped him a great deal in his communal activities; she stood out for her good-hearted character and readiness to help [others]. She did this modestly and discretely.

When the Soviet Army entered the town, one strike after another was meted out against the Cohen family. Munye, their only son, was immediately arrested for Zionist

[pp. 409-410]

activity. Later on, Yitzchak was also arrested, and his property was confiscated. His wife, Reizel, was sent to Uzbekistan.

Following the war, fate reunited Yitzchak with his wife. They returned together to Bursztyn and found the town entirely destroyed. A few other Jews also returned. Together, all of them went to Poland with the repatriation stream, and settled in the Lower Silesian town, Richbach, whose name was later changed to Dzierzoniow.

Already at that time, they received news from their only son, Munye, that he was living somewhere, under arrest, in Siberia. They were permeated with the hope that little by little he would be returning, and the entire family would leave for Israel.

Yitzchak Cohen, having received the long dreamt of telegram from his only son, Munye, that he was returning and was already on his way, could not withstand the immense joy, and while holding the telegram in his hand, expired. [He] did not merit seeing his only son and did not live to make Aliyah to Israel. Tragic! Reizel, his wife, a broken and defeated woman waited for her only comfort, her son, Munye, who in the meantime returned, and together, they made their way to Israel. But her fate was also a bitter one: Along the way, Reizel took ill and died in Vienna.

There are no remaining pictures of this noteworthy pair. There are only two headstones along the way to the fatherland, which they did not merit to see.

Yitzchak was buried in Richbach, in Poland.

Reizel Cohen – in Vienna, Austria.

List of the Holy Ones

Who fell at the hands of the Nazis as martyrs during the Holocaust period*

Transliterated by Ann Harris

Edited by Yocheved Klausner

| A | B | C | D | E | F | G | H | I | J | K | L | M |
| N | O | P | Q | R | S | T | U | V | W | X | Y | Z |

Family name(s)	First name(s)	Maiden name	Gender	Marital status	Father's name	Mother's name	Name of spouse	Additional family	Remarks	Page
			M					children	SCHNEEWEISS, husband of Mali's first daughter	417
			M					children	SCHNEEWEISS, husband of Mali's second daughter	417
		MANDELBERG	F	Married	Itshe		Nadel			414
		SCHNEEWEISS	F			Mali		children	Mali's first daughter	417
		SCHNEEWEISS	F			Mali		children	Mali's second daughter	417
		SCHWARTZ	F	Married				husband & children	sister of Yashe SCHWARTZ	413
	Devora		F		Hershele				Hershele STRELISKER [Hershele from Strelisk]	415
	Eidel	KLIRSFELD	F	Married	Yisrael	Perl		husband		423
	Kunye		M					family		426
	Libe		F	Married			Moshe Leibele	children		420
	Moshe Leibale		M	Married			Libe	children		420
	Moshe Natan		M		Efraim			family		422
	Nadel		M	Married					MANDELBERG	414

Family name(s)	First name(s)	Maiden name	Gender	Marital status	Father's name	Mother's name	Name of spouse	Additional family	Remarks	Page
ABRAHAM	Chaya		F	Married			Avraham		family relation according to POT	420
ABRAHAM	Roza		F		Avraham	Chaya			family relation according to POT	420
ADLER	Daniel		M	Married			Roize			419
ADLER	Rozia		F	Married			Daniel			419
ADLER	Sane		M		Daniel	Roize				419
ANDERMANN	Itzik		M					family		424
AUSTER	Chana		F	Married				husband	could be different surname	418
AUSTER	Leib		M					family		424
AUSTER	Shimon		M					family		424
AUSTER	Shimon		M					family		426
AUSTER	Yankel		M					family		426
BACKER	Hersh Mendel		M					family		420
BANNER			F	Married			Urie			413
BANNER	Urie		M	Married						413
BAUER			F	Married			Shmuel			417
BAUER	Ettel		F						listed as male	417
BAUER	Freide		F	Married			Mendil			421
BAUER	Goshi									417
BAUER	Mendil		M	Married			Freide			421
BAUER	Sheindel		F		Mendil	Freide				421
BAUER	Shmuel		M	Married						417
BEIN	Meier		M					family		425
BERNSTEIN	Ezra		M		Leib	Sheindel				423
BERNSTEIN	Koppel		M		Leib	Sheindel				423
BERNSTEIN	Leib		M	Married			Sheindel			423
BERNSTEIN	Lotti		F		Leib	Sheindel			family relation by estimation	423
BERNSTEIN	Mordechai		M					family		419
BERNSTEIN	Sali		F		Leib	Sheindel			family relation by estimation	423

Family name(s)	First name(s)	Maiden name	Gender	Marital status	Father's name	Mother's name	Name of spouse	Additional family	Remarks	Page
BERNSTEIN	Shaya		M					family		419
BERNSTEIN	Sheindel		F	Married			Leib			423
BERNZWEIG			M	Married					son-in-law of Dr. Zeev SCHMURAK/ SCHMUREK	422
BERNZWEIG		SCHMARAK	F	Married	Zev					422
BIEN		MEHRBERG	F	Married	Efraim	Rechil	Baruch	children		416
BLECHER	Isser		M					family		426
BLEIBERG	Adel		F	Married			Moshe	children		413
BLEIBERG	Brani		F	Married			Kuba			413
BLEIBERG	Kuba		M	Married			Brani			413
BLEIBERG	Moshe		M	Married			Adel	children		413
BLUTREICH	Yosef		M					family		425
BRADMANN	Beile		F	Married			Zigmund	3 children		413
BRADMANN	Zigmund		M	Married			Beile	3 children		413
BRAND			M		Eliahu	Ettil			first son of Eliahu & Etel BRAND	417
BRAND			M		Eliahu	Ettil			second son of Eliahu & Etel BRAND	417
BRAND	Eliahu		M	Married			Ettil			417
BRAND	Ettil		F	Married			Eliahu			417
BRANDWEIN			F	Married			Moshe		rabbi's wife	417
BRANDWEIN			M		Moshe				first son of rabbi Moshe BRANDWEIN	417
BRANDWEIN			M		Moshe				second son of rabbi Moshe BRANDWEIN	417
BRANDWEIN			M		Moshe				third son of rabbi Moshe BRANDWEIN	417
BRANDWEIN	Rabbi Moshe		M	Married					Rabbi	417
BREITBART			M		Hersh	Chana				416
BREITBART	Chana		F	Married			Hersh			415
BREITBART	Dr. Wilhelm		M						from Nastaszcyn	418
BREITBART	Dzuniu		M						from Nastaszcyn	417
BREITBART	Hersh		M	Married			Chana			415

Family name(s)	First name(s)	Maiden name	Gender	Marital status	Father's name	Mother's name	Name of spouse	Additional family	Remarks	Page
BREITER			M		Shlomo	Shertche				420
BREITER			M		Shlomo	Shertche				420
BREITER			M		Shlomo	Shertche				420
BREITER	Avraham		M	Married			Eidel			413
BREITER	Bertshe (Ber)		M		Avraham	Eidel		family		413
BREITER	Blume		F	Married				husband & children	could be different surname	426
BREITER	Eidel		F	Married			Avraham			413
BREITER	Mechel		M		Avraham	Eidel				413
BREITER	Moshe		M	Married	Avraham	Eidel		family		413
BREITER	Sara		F	Married				husband & children	perhaps different family name	420
BREITER	Shertche		F	Married			Hersh			420
BREITER	Shlomo		M	Married			Sortsi			420
BREITER	Yosef		M					family		425
BRIER	Moshe		M					family		424
BRIKNER/ BRUCKNER	Hinde	BAUER	F	Married		Ettel	Yekutiel			417
BRIKNER/ BRUCKNER	Yekutiel		M	Married			Hinde			417
DEICHSLER			F		Leizer	Peshe				417
DEICHSLER	Chaim		M					family		417
DEICHSLER	Leizer		M	Married			Peshi			417
DEICHSLER	Peshi		F	Married			Leizer			417
DIER	Hersh		M					family		418
DOV	Leib		M					family		419
DRIMMER	Mechil		M					family		424
DRUCKER	Itzik Hersch		M					family		419
DRUCKER	Menashe		M					family		419
DRUCKER	Menie		M							419
DRUCKER	Yakov		M					family	tailor	424
EBERHAAR	Maltsche		F	Married			Yisrael			418
EBERHAAR	Yisrael		M	Married			Maltsche	family		418

Family name(s)	First name(s)	Maiden name	Gender	Marital status	Father's name	Mother's name	Name of spouse	Additional family	Remarks	Page
EBERT	Yoel		M							425
EHRLICH	Moshe		M					family		426
EHRLICH	Yona		M					family		419
EHRNBERG/ EHRENBERG			F	Married			A.			420
EHRNBERG/ EHRENBERG			F		A.					420
EHRNBERG/ EHRENBERG			M		A.					420
EHRNBERG/ EHRENBERG	A.		M	Married						420
EIRES	Henie		F					children		420
ERDSTEIN			M		Yosef	Heli				416
ERDSTEIN			F		Avraham					418
ERDSTEIN	Avraham		M							418
ERDSTEIN	Heli		F	Married			Yosef			416
ERDSTEIN	Yosef		M	Married			Heli			416
FEIER	Meier		M					family		423
FELDBAU			M					family		418
FELDBAU			F	Married			Zalman			424
FELDBAU	Avraham		M		Zalman			family		424
FELDBAU	Benyamin		M		Krantsche					422
FELDBAU	Berl		M					family		416
FELDBAU	Berl		M					family		419
FELDBAU	Efraim		M	Married			Etti	family		418
FELDBAU	Eidel		F	Married			Ziskind			416
FELDBAU	Eidel		F	Married			Ziskind			418
FELDBAU	Etti		F	Married			Efraim			418
FELDBAU	Hersh		M		Moshe			family		416
FELDBAU	Hersh		M		Koppel			family		419
FELDBAU	Krantsche		F							422
FELDBAU	Meier		M		Moshe			family		415
FELDBAU	Shimon		M		Zalman					424

Family name(s)	First name(s)	Maiden name	Gender	Marital status	Father's name	Mother's name	Name of spouse	Additional family	Remarks	Page
FELDBAU	Yossel		M		Krantsche					422
FELDBAU	Yossil		M			Krantsche		family		420
FELDBAU	Zalman		M	Married						424
FELDBAU	Ziskind		M	Married			Eidel	family		416
FELDBAU	Ziskind		M	Married			Eidel	family		418
FELDBAU	Ziskind		M					family		422
FELDKLEIN	Avraham		M		Zisshe			family		423
FELDMAN			M		Yakov	Peshe				426
FELDMAN	Beile		F							426
FELDMAN	Genie		F			Perl				426
FELDMAN	Itzie		M			Perl				426
FELDMAN	Perl		F							426
FELDMAN	Pesie		F	Married			Yakov		listed as wife of Yakov FELDMAN	426
FENSTER	Beile		F	Married			Y. L.			417
FENSTER	Teibele		F		Y. L.	Beile				417
FANZER	Shlomo		M	Married				family	vinegar manufacturer	418
FISCHER			M					family	from Kuropatniki	423
FISCHER	Aizik		M					family		421
FISCHMANN			M		Yehuda Hersh	Sara Zissel				413
FISCHMANN			M		Eli	Berte				416
FISCHMANN	Berta		F	Married			Eli			416
FISCHMANN	Betti		F		Yehuda Hersh	Sara Zissel				413
FISCHMANN	Eidel		F	Married			Yona			418
FISCHMANN	Eli		M	Married			Berta			416
FISCHMANN	Feige		F							420
FISCHMANN	Geni		F		Yehuda Hersh	Sara Zissel				413
FISCHMANN	Mundtsche		M		Yona	Eidel				418
FISCHMANN	Sara Genendl		F							420

Family name(s)	First name(s)	Maiden name	Gender	Marital status	Father's name	Mother's name	Name of spouse	Additional family	Remarks	Page
FISCHMANN	Sara Zissel		F	Married			Yehuda Hersh			413
FISCHMANN	Simche		M							420
FISCHMANN	Yeruber		M						Yarober first name	420
FISCHMANN	Yona		M	Married			Eidel			418
FLESCHER	Avraham		M					family		419
FRANKEL	Sara		F					family		426
FRECHTEL			F			Keile				420
FRECHTEL	Keile		F							420
GELLER	Shlomo		M					family		422
GINSBURG/ GINZBURG	Chaim		M		Yoel					417
GINSBURG/ GINZBURG	Gershon		M		Yoel					417
GINSBURG/ GINZBURG	Rabbi Yoel		M					family	Rabbi	417
GINSBURG/ GINZBURG	Zissel		F		Yoel					417
GLANZBERG/ GINZBURG	Brantsche		F					family		420
GLIKSMANN/ GLUCKSMANN	Nutta		M					family		424
GLOTZER			F	Married			Moshe			423
GLOTZER			F	Married			Yossil Yona			426
GLOTZER	Aharon		M		Yossil Yona					426
GLOTZER	Baruch Shmuel		M					family		424
GLOTZER	Berl		M							425
GLOTZER	Chaim David		M					family		421
GLOTZER	Ester		F		Yisrael	Ettel			family relation according to pages of Testimony (POT)	414
GLOTZER	Ettel		F	Married			Yisrael		family relation according to pages of Testimony (POT)	414

Family name(s)	First name(s)	Maiden name	Gender	Marital status	Father's name	Mother's name	Name of spouse	Additional family	Remarks	Page
GLOTZER	Godel		M					family		425
GLOTZER	Itzik Hersch		M					family		422
GLOTZER	Mechil		M					family		416
GLOTZER	Meier		M					family		419
GLOTZER	Meier		M						tailor	420
GLOTZER	Moshe		M		Nutta			family		422
GLOTZER	Moshe		M	Married		Slave			listed as Slave's	423
GLOTZER	Moshe		M		Yossil Yona					426
GLOTZER	Rachel		F							419
GLOTZER	Roza		F		Yisrael	Ettel			family relation according to pages of Testimony (POT)	414
GLOTZER	Sara Fradl		F	Married			Yitzchok			421
GLOTZER	Shimon		M	Married				family	butcher	420
GLOTZER	Shmuel		M					family		425
GLOTZER	Shmuel		M		Yossil Yona					426
GLOTZER	Simche		M						tailor	420
GLOTZER	Simche		M		Moshe			family		423
GLOTZER	Wolf		M		Yona Leib			family		425
GLOTZER	Yehuda		M					family		424
GLOTZER	Yehuda Hershke		M					family		426
GLOTZER	Yisrael		M	Married			Ettel		family relation according to pages of Testimony (POT)	414
GLOTZER	Yitzchok		M	Married	Berki		Sara Fradel	family	listed as Berke's	421
GLOTZER	Yona		M					family		419
GLOTZER	Yukil		M							419
GLOTZER MACHNICKI	Yossil Yona		M							418
GOLDSTEIN	Avraham		M					family		421

Family name(s)	First name(s)	Maiden name	Gender	Marital status	Father's name	Mother's name	Name of spouse	Additional family	Remarks	Page
GRANWITTER	Aharon		M		Wolf	Sara			perhaps his mother's first name was different	414
GRANWITTER	Sara		F	Married			Wolf		perhaps her first name was different	414
GRANWITTER	Sara		F		Wolf	Sara				414
GRANWITTER	Wolf		M	Married			Sara		perhaps first name of wife was different	414
GRINBERG/ GRUNBERG	Efraim		M	Married			Rivke	father-in-law		415
GRINBERG/ GRUNBERG	Geni		F		Efraim	Rivke				415
GRINBERG/ GRUNBERG	Moshe Leib		M					family	from Sarniki	423
GRINBERG/ GRUNBERG	Rivka+G107		F	Married			Efraim			415
GRINBERG/ GRUNBERG	Yakov		M		Efraim	Rivke				415
GRINBERG/ GRUNBERG	Yetti		F		Efraim	Rivke				415
GUTSTEIN	David		M					family		421
GUTSTEIN	Leah		F	Married				husband	could be different family name	421
GUTSTEIN	Meier		M	Married			Roize	3 children		421
GUTSTEIN	Perl		F		Meier	Roize				421
GUTSTEIN	Rivke		F		Meier	Roize				421
GUTSTEIN	Rozia		F	Married			Meier	3 children		421
GUTSTEIN	Sale		F		Meier	Roize				421
GUTSTEIN	Tisane		F	Married			Yossil			421
GUTSTEIN	Yossil Yona		M	Married			Tsani	husband		421
GUTTENPLAN	Leizer		M					family		419
GUTTENPLAN	Leizer		M					family		421
HABER			M	Married			Rivke			415
HABER			F		Itshe	Sara				418
HABER			F	Married			Nachum	children		420
HABER	Chana		F							416

Family name(s)	First name(s)	Maiden name	Gender	Marital status	Father's name	Mother's name	Name of spouse	Additional family	Remarks	Page
HABER	Itshe		M	Married	Moshe		Sara			418
HABER	Leah		F			Sara				422
HABER	Motel		M							416
HABER	Nachum		M					family		419
HABER	Nachum		M	Married				children	from SWISTELNIK	420
HABER	Reizel		F			Sara				422
HABER	Rivke		F	Married			Pinie			415
HABER	Rozia		F		Pinie	Rivke				415
HABER	Sara		F	Married			Itshe			418
HABER	Sara		F	Married			Mates			422
HABER	Shaul		M					family		423
HABER	Sheva		F			Sara				422
HABER	Shmuel		M					family	son-in-law of David KLIRSFELD	423
HABER	Yitzchok		M		Bendit			family		425
HALPERN	Chana		F			Elke			family relation according to POT	420
HALPERN	Dania		F			Elke			family relation according to POT	420
HALPERN	Elke		F							420
HALPERN	Hersh		M			Elke			family relation according to POT	420
HALPERN	Shmuel		M					family		421
HAMMER	Chayale		F							426
HAMMER	Hershke		M							426
HAMMER	Beile		F							421
HAMMER	Benyamin		M	Married			Dobrish			422
HAMMER	Binia		F	Married			Itzi			416
HAMMER	Dorbish		F	Married			Benyamin			422
HAMMER	Ester		F							415
HAMMER	Itzi		M					family		421
HAMMER	Leah		F	Married			Matti	3 children		415

Family name(s)	First name(s)	Maiden name	Gender	Marital status	Father's name	Mother's name	Name of spouse	Additional family	Remarks	Page
HAMMER	Moti		M	Married			Leah	3 children		415
HAMMER	Munie		F							421
HAMMER	Rivke		F							421
HAMMER	Shprintsche		F							421
HAMMER	Yossil		M							424
HANDSCHUH	Shlomo		M					family		417
HORNIK	Leibish		M					family		422
HAUPTMANN	Berish		M		Moshe	Chana				414
HAUPTMANN	Chana		F	Married			Moshe			414
HAUPTMANN	Fishel		M		Moshe	Chana				414
HAUPTMANN	Moshe		M	Married			Chana			414
HAUPTMANN	Yudel		M		Moshe	Chana				414
HELLER	Leon		M					family		416
HOCHBERG	Chaim		M	Married			Ettil			415
HOCHBERG	Ester		F		Chaim	Ettil		family	with the TANNE family	415
HOCHBERG	Ettil		F	Married			Chaim			415
ITTES?	Hersh		M					family	Itzies could be "son of Itzie", not surname	426
JAMPEL	Itte		F					family		424
JAMPEL	David		M					family		415
JAMPEL	Yisrael		M					family		415
JONAS/JANAS	Velvel		M					family		416
JONAS/JANAS	Yankel		M					family		416
JUDENFREUND			F	Married			Nachum			425
JUDENFREUND	Nachum		M	Married						425
JUPITER	Chaim Zvi		M	Married			Libe			415
JUPITER	Ettil		F							424
JUPITER	Libe		F	Married			Chaim Tzvi			415
KAHANE	Antshel		M					family		425
KAHANE	David		M						cantor	425

Family name(s)	First name(s)	Maiden name	Gender	Marital status	Father's name	Mother's name	Name of spouse	Additional family	Remarks	Page
KAHANE	Natan Shomer		M		Yosef Mordechai	Roize				422
KAHANE	Rozia		F	Married			Yosef Mordechai			422
KAHANE	Yosef Mordechai		M	Married			Roize			422
KAHN	Itzik		M	Married			Reizel			414
KAHN	Reizel		F	Married			Itzik			414
KANFER	Efraim		M	Married			Sara	family		416
KANFER	Sara		F	Married			Efraim			416
KATZ	Dr. Shmuel		M							413
KLARBERG	Dzshunie									422
KLARREICH	Ettil		F	Married			Shimon			415
KLARREICH	Reizel		F		Shimon	Ettil				415
KLARREICH	Sane		M		Shimon	Ettil				415
KLARREICH	Shimon		M	Married			Ettil			415
KLARREICH	Yudel		M					family		415
KLEIN	Devora		F	Married			Moshe			413
KLEIN	Moshe		M	Married			Devora			413
KLEINFELD	Daniel		M					family		425
KLEINFELD	Eidel		M					family		422
KLEINFELD	Hersh		M					family		425
KLIRSFELD	Arye Leib		M		Yisrael	Perl				423
KLIRSFELD	Chana		F		Yisrael	Perl				423
KLIRSFELD	Ester		F		Yisrael	Perl				423
KLIRSFELD	Feige		F		Yisrael	Perl				423
KLIRSFELD	Kula		F		Yisrael	Perl				423
KLIRSFELD	Mintsche		F		Yisrael	Perl				423
KLIRSFELD	Perl		F	Married			Yisrael			423
KLIRSFELD	Yisrael		M	Married			Perl			423
KLETTER	Meier		M					family		420

Family name(s)	First name(s)	Maiden name	Gender	Marital status	Father's name	Mother's name	Name of spouse	Additional family	Remarks	Page
KLUGMANN	Dr.		M					family		422
KROCHMAL	Golde Yocheved		F	Married				husband	perhaps different family name	420
KRUMMHOLZ	Dr.		M					family		426
KIMMEL			F	Married			Avraham			413
KIMMEL			M		Moshe	Elke				422
KIMMEL			M		Moshe	Elke				422
KIMMEL	Avraham		M	Married	David					413
KIMMEL	Avraham		M	Married			Sheindel	3 children		416
KIMMEL	Baruch		M					family		421
KIMMEL	Elke		F	Married			Moshe			422
KIMMEL	Itshe		M	Married			Peshe			415
KIMMEL	Kunye		M						son-in-law of Itche KIMMEL	415
KIMMEL	Leib Hersh		M	Married	Yosef	Sheva	Roize			414
KIMMEL	Leibish		M							423
KIMMEL	Moshe		M	Married			Elke			422
KIMMEL/ KUMMEL	Moshe		M		Leibish					423
KIMMEL	Peshe		F	Married			Itshe			415
KIMMEL	Regina		F		Itshe	Peshe				415
KIMMEL	Roize		F	Married			Leib Hersh			414
KIMMEL	Sheindil		F	Married			Avraham	3 children		416
KIMMEL/ KUMMEL	Sheva		F	Married			Yosef			414
KIMMEL	Urie		M					family	from Kuropatniki	423
KIMMEL	Yeti		F		Itshe	Peshe				415
KIMMEL	Yodel		M		Leibish					423
KIMMEL	Yona		M						not clear whether he is son of Leib Hersh & Roize or Yosef & Sheva	414
KIMMEL	Yosef		M	Married			Sheva			414
KIMMEL	Yosef		M		Itshe	Peshe				415

Family name(s)	First name(s)	Maiden name	Gender	Marital status	Father's name	Mother's name	Name of spouse	Additional family	Remarks	Page
LAKER			M		Meier	Leah				418
LAKER			M		Meier	Leah				418
LAKER			M		Meier	Leah				418
LAKER	Leah		F	Married			Meier			418
LAKER	Meier		M	Married			Leah			418
LANDAU	Hele		F							416
LANDAU	Lotzka		M							416
LANDAU	Rabbi Hertzel		M					family	Rabbi	417
LANDNER			F	Married			Leibtsche			415
LANDNER			M		Itzi	Feige				415
LANDNER	Berl		M							415
LANDNER	Feige		F	Married			Itzi			415
LANDNER	Itzi		M	Married			Feige			415
LANDNER	Leibtsche		M	Married						415
LANDNER	Leizer		M							415
LANDNER	Natan		M							415
LAUFER	Adel		F	Married			Yossil	family		417
LAUFER	Naftali		M					family		417
LAUFER	Yossil		M	Married			Adel	family		417
LEIDER	BenZion		M	Married			Yutta	family		416
LEIDER	Yutta		F	Married			BenZion			416
LEIES	Taube Gitl		F					family	Leyes could be "son of Leah", not surname	426
LEITER	Hersh		M					family		416
LERNER			F						mother of Leizer LERNER	423
LERNER			F						sister of Leizer LERNER	423
LERNER	Leizer		M							423
LEWITER	Feige		F							416
MANDELBERG	Lipe		M					family		413
MANDELBERG	Perl		F	Married			Yitzchok			414

Family name(s)	First name(s)	Maiden name	Gender	Marital status	Father's name	Mother's name	Name of spouse	Additional family	Remarks	Page
MANDELBERG	Shlomo		M							423
MANDELBERG	Yitzchok		M	Married			Perl			414
MARKFELD	Hersh		M	Married			Rivke	family		416
MARKFELD	Rivka		F	Married			Hersh			416
MEHRBERG	Avraham Yakov		M					family		424
MEHRBERG	Efraim		M	Married			Rechil			416
MEHRBERG	Leizer		M					family		425
MEHRBERG	Moshe		M					family		425
MEHRBERG	Rechil		F	Married			Efraim			416
MELLER	Antshel		M					family		420
MELAMED	Yudel		M					family		417
MELLER	Baruch		M					family	brother of Chaim MATEST	419
MINTZ	Yosef		M							414
MASTEL	Bracha		F	Married			David	children		421
MASTEL	David		M	Married			Bracha	children		421
MASTEL	Perl		F	Married			Shmuel	4 children		414
MASTEL	Shmuel		M	Married			Perl	4 children		414
MUTTERMILCH	Beile		F	Married			Shmuel	2 children		415
MUTTERMILCH	Shmuel		M	Married			Beile	2 children		415
NACHWALGER	Chaim		M	Married			Maltsche			413
NACHWALGER	Maltsche		F	Married			Chaim			413
NACHWALGER	Sale		F		Chaim	Maltsche				413
NACHWALGER	Yantsche		M		Chaim	Maltsche		family		413
NADLER	Yehudit		F							419
NEIBERGER/ NEUBERGER	David		M							423
NEMETH	Moshe		M					family		422
NEMETH	Yisrael		M					family		424
OSTROWER			M					family		415
OSTROWER	Berl		M		Simche	Hentsche				426

Family name(s)	First name(s)	Maiden name	Gender	Marital status	Father's name	Mother's name	Name of spouse	Additional family	Remarks	Page
OSTROWER	Berte		F		Simche	Hentsche				426
OSTROWER	Hentsche		F	Married			Simche			426
OSTROWER	Moshe		M		Simche	Hentsche				426
OSTROWER	Simche		M	Married			Hentsche			426
OSTROWER	Tchize		F							421
OSTROWER	Velvel		M			Tshize				421
PELZ	Avraham		M			Hentsche				416
PELZ	Hentsche		F							416
PELZ	Velvel		M			Hentsche		family		416
PERLMUTTER	Hersh		M					family	Trustee of the Community	414
PFEFFER			M		Ishe	Rachel				414
PFEFFER	Rachel		F	Married			Ishe			414
PFEFFER	Shlomo		M					family		415
PFEFFER	Yashe		M	Married			Rachel			414
PFEFFER	Chaike		F	Married			Itshe			418
PFEFFER	Itshe		M	Married			Heike			418
PFEFFER	Moshe		M					family	from Sarniki	423
PFEFFER	Shimon		M		Itshe	Heike				418
PIAKER	Chava		F							419
PIAKER	Sima		F			Chava				419
PIAKER	Brantsche		F	Married			Kalman			423
PIAKER	Dani		F	Married			Wolf	3 children		418
PIAKER	Kalman		M	Married			Brantsche			423
PIAKER	Pesach		M					family		418
PIAKER	Sane		M		Kalman	Brantsche				423
PIAKER	Wolf		M	Married			Dani	3 children		418
PILPEL	Yakov		M					family		423
PINELES			M					family	pharmacist	421
RAPS	Brantsche		F	Married			Eliash	children		425
RAPS	Eliash		M	Married			Brantsche	children		425

Family name(s)	First name(s)	Maiden name	Gender	Marital status	Father's name	Mother's name	Name of spouse	Additional family	Remarks	Page
RATFELD	Shlomo		M					family		419
RATZEN	Dr.		M					family		423
RIBLER	Leah		F	Married			Leib Shlomo			422
RIBLER	Leib Shlomo		M	Married			Leah	family		422
RIBLER	Shalom		M					family		418
REICHMANN	Mote		M					family		416
REICHMANN	Petachia		M					family		414
REICHMANN	Yakov		M					family		420
REINES	Mechil		M					family		416
REIS	Avraham		M					family		421
REIS	Moshe		M					family		425
REISMANN	Chaim		M					family		422
RIBLER	Devora		F					children		417
RIBLER	Ester		F					children		417
RIBLER	Elke		F							415
ROHER	Aharon		M							415
ROHER	Avraham		M							415
ROHER	Avraham David		M							415
ROHER	Chava Mintche		F							415
ROHER	Devora		F							415
ROHER	Mendel		M							415
ROHER	Reizil		F							415
ROHER	Roize		F							415
ROHER	Ruchtshe		F							415
ROHER	Yankel		M							415
ROHER	Yechezkel		M							415
ROSENBAUM	Moshe		M					family		422
ROSENBLATT			F	Married			David			424
ROSENBLATT			F						mother of Moshe ROSENBLATT	424

Family name(s)	First name(s)	Maiden name	Gender	Marital status	Father's name	Mother's name	Name of spouse	Additional family	Remarks	Page
ROSENBLATT	David		M	Married						424
ROSENBLATT	Moshe		M							424
ROSENBLATT	Yodel		M							424
ROTTENSTREICH	Prof. Fishel		M					family		422
RUDE/RUDY			F			Taube				419
RUDE/RUDY			F	Married			Yakov			421
RUDE/RUDY	Berl		M					family		417
RUDE/RUDY	Liftche		F	Married			Yosef Shlomo			419
RUDE/RUDY	Taube		F							419
RUDE/RUDY	Yakov		M	Married						421
RUDE/RUDY	Yosef Shlomo		M	Married			Liftsche			419
ZAGER			M	Married						417
ZAGER			F	Married						417
ZAGER	Bumek		M			Sara				421
ZAGER	Nunie		M			Sara				421
ZAGER	Sara		F							421
SAUER	Ing.		M						Engineer; SCHEUER is first name or surname	419
SCHAFFER	Avraham		M						from Sarniki	423
SCHAFFER	Nachum		M					family	from Sarniki	423
SCHECHTER	Ira		M					family		419
SCHENKLER	Sheina Golde		F	Married			Shlomo			424
SCHENKLER	Shlomo		M	Married			Sheina Golde			424
SCHENKLER	Yitzchok		M		Shlomo	Sheina Golde				424
SCHENKLER	Yossl		M		Shlomo	Sheina Golde				424
SCHLESINGER	Brania		M							425
SCHLOSSBERG	Freide		F					children		417
SCHLUSSBERG	Freide		F					children		418

Family name(s)	First name(s)	Maiden name	Gender	Marital status	Father's name	Mother's name	Name of spouse	Additional family	Remarks	Page
SCHMURAK/ SCHMUREK			F	Married					mother of Dr. Zeev SCHMURAK/ SCHMUREK	422
SCHMURAK/ SCHMUREK			F	Married			Zev			422
SCHMURAK/ SCHMUREK	Avraham		M					family		422
SCHMURAK/ SCHMUREK	Dr. Eliezer		M							422
SCHMURAK/ SCHMUREK	Dr. Zev		M	Married						422
SCHNAPP			F	Married			Mattie		family of Avrahamtzie SCHNAPP	425
SCHNAPP	Arahamtsche		M							425
SCHNAPP	Beile		F						family of Avrahamtzie SCHNAPP	425
SCHNAPP	Dulie		F						family of Avrahamtzie SCHNAPP	425
SCHNAPP	Henie		F						family of Avrahamtzie SCHNAPP	425
SCHNAPP	Mattie		M	Married					family of Avrahamtzie SCHNAPP	425
SCHNAPP	Shevach		M						family of Avrahamtzie SCHNAPP	425
SCHNAPP	Shmuel		M						family of Avrahamtzie SCHNAPP	425
SCHNAPP	Yitzchok		M						family of Avrahamtzie SCHNAPP	425
SCHNEEWEISS	Aharon		M	Married			Brane			421
SCHNEEWEISS	Brana		F	Married			Aharon			421
SCHNEEWEISS	Fitshe		M					family		421
SCHNEEWEISS	Mali		F	Married						417
SCHNEEWEISS	Moshe		M			Mali				417
SCHNEEWEISS	Rivke		F							421
SCHNEEWEISS	Soshe									417
SCHNEIDER			F	Married			Efraim	children		417
SCHNEIDER	Asher		M					family		426

Family name(s)	First name(s)	Maiden name	Gender	Marital status	Father's name	Mother's name	Name of spouse	Additional family	Remarks	Page
SCHNEIDER	Efraim		M	Married				children		417
SCHNEIDER	Fishel		M					family		420
SCHNEIDER	Hersh		M					family		417
SCHNEIDER	Itzik		M					family		425
SCHNEIDER	Leib Shlomo		M					family		426
SCHOR	Moshe		M					family		425
SCHUMER	Bilah		F							421
SCHUMER	Elke		F							421
SCHUMER	Gitale		M							421
SCHUMER	Sara		F							421
SCHURKMANN	Aharon		M		Wolf	Chava				422
SCHURKMANN	Chava		F	Married			Wolf			422
SCHURKMANN	Eli Moshe		M					family		415
SCHURKMANN	Eliahu Moshe		M					family		418
SCHURKMANN	Koppel		M					family		422
SCHURKMANN	Shmuel		M					family		422
SCHURKMANN	Wolf		M	Married			Chava			422
SCHURKMANN	Yekil		M					family		421
SCHWADRON			M					family	son-in-law of Itche DIBOKS, wife's maiden name DIBOKS	421
SCHWALB	Moshe		M					family		423
SCHWARTZ	Chaya		F							425
SCHWARTZ	David		M					family		426
SCHWARTZ	Eidel		F	Married			Sane			413
SCHWARTZ	Eli		M					family		418
SCHWARTZ	Gedalia		M					family		424
SCHWARTZ	Itzik		M					family		426
SCHWARTZ	Meni		M							413
SCHWARTZ	Nissan Wolf		M					family		424
SCHWARTZ	Reize		F			Chaya				425

Family name(s)	First name(s)	Maiden name	Gender	Marital status	Father's name	Mother's name	Name of spouse	Additional family	Remarks	Page
SCHWARTZ	Sane		M	Married			Eidel			413
SCHWARTZ	Sane		M		Yudele					414
SCHWARTZ	Sara		F			Chaya				425
SCHWARTZ	Shaya		M					family		423
SCHWARTZ	Yakov		M					family		424
SCHWARTZ	Yona		M					family		413
SCHWARTZ	Yosi		M							413
SCHWARTZ	Zeide		M			Chaya				425
SILBER	Hersh Leib		M	Married					ritual slaughterer	416
STANDER			F	Married			Leib			416
STANDER	Leib		M					family	son-in-law of Moshe FELDBAU	416
STANDER	Leib		M	Married					public bathhouse attendant	416
STEGMANN			F		Nachum	Yutta				419
STEGMANN	Nachum		M	Married			Yutta			419
STEGMANN	Yuta		F	Married			Nachum			419
STEINBERG			F			Bashe				416
STEINBERG	Bashe		F							416
STEINBERG	Yona		M					family		426
STOLAR	Meier Wolf		M					family		424
STOLAR	Velvel		M					family		425
STREGER	Benyamin		M					family		423
STREGER	Sara		F					family		423
STREGER	Yisrael		M					family		415
STRYZOWER	Chaim		M	Married			Leah	2 children		413
STRYZOWER	Leah		F	Married			Chaim	2 children		413
TEITLER			F	Married			Moshe			418
TEITLER	Benyamin		M					family		418
TEITLER	Moshe		M	Married						418
TOBIAS			F	Married		Chana	Mendel			417
TOBIAS			F	Married			Shmuel			418

Family name(s)	First name(s)	Maiden name	Gender	Marital status	Father's name	Mother's name	Name of spouse	Additional family	Remarks	Page
TOBIAS	Chana		F							417
TOBIAS	Hinde		F	Married			Mina			417
TOBIAS	Liftsche		F							417
TOBIAS	Malke		F			Liftsche				417
TOBIAS	Mina		M	Married			Hinde			417
TOBIAS	Moshe Yosef		M					family		420
TOBIAS	Shmuel		M	Married						418
TRAUGOTT	David		M	Married			Sasha			424
TRAUGOTT	Sasha		F	Married			David			424
UNGER	Benyamin		M					family		420
WAGSCHALL	David		M						son-in-law of Shalom BAUMRIND	414
WALFISCH	Aizik		M			Elke Perl		family		426
WALFISCH	Elke Perl		F						mother of Aizik WALFISCH	426
WALTER			M			Rasha				414
WALTER	Rashe		F	Married						414
WATTENBERG	Dr. Adolf		M							422
WEINERT	Abba		M					family		413
WEINERT	Leah		F							413
WEINERT	Peshi		F							413
WEINLES	Rivale		F							425
WEINREB	Yisachar		M					family	Hebrew teacher	420
WEISSMANN	Leah		F	Married			Moshe Aharon			418
WEISSMANN	Moshe Aharon		M	Married			Leah			418
WEITZ	Abba		M						melamed [teacher of young children in Talmud Torah school	417
WEITZ	Yisrael		M		Abba					417
WIESELBERG	Minke		F							420
ZIERING	Dr. Avraham		M					family		422

Family name(s)	First name(s)	Maiden name	Gender	Marital status	Father's name	Mother's name	Name of spouse	Additional family	Remarks	Page
ZIESER	Avraham		M	Married			Chaya		family relation according to POT	420
ZIMMER			M		Leib	Tzshani				423
ZIMMER	Leib		M	Married			Tzshani			423
ZIMMER	Tzani		F	Married			Leib			423
ZORN	Leib		M					family		425
ZUSMANN / SUSSMANN	Yerachmiel		M					family		424
ZUSMANN / SUSSMANN	Aizik		M					family		414
ZUSMANN / SUSSMANN	Yehuda		M					family		418

This list was compiled from information received and is incomplete.

[pp. 433-434]

Yizkor[1]

For Eternal Commemoration

[pp.435-436]

Klara Weingel

remembers her parents,

Mottie the candelabrum maker, and **Esther Bluma**

Died in America, 5703 (1943)

R' Leibush Elya of the brickyard and his wife

Chune Hammer, Leibush, Elya's son,

remembers his parents,

Leibush Elya, [and] his wife, **Ettel**

Aharon Kimmel

remembers

his mother, **Faige**, sister, **Chava**, and **Perl Schwartz** and three children, **Devorah** and **Yidl Reis** and two children

As a holy commemoration

of my parents,

Wolf Podhajcer and **Bluma Roize**,

their children,

Chaim and **Elka**

Yoel Korn

Klara Mazul,

Bertha remember their parents,

Yidl and **Chaya Schwartz**

As an eternal commemoration

My parents, **Devorah** and **Notte**, my in-laws, **Esther** and **Leib Auster**, two child martyrs, **Drezi** and **Notte**

Yaakov Glotzer

[pp.437-438]

Wolf Weinberg (Volke Hersh Mendel's)

remembers: his parents,

Hersh Mendel and **Faige**

Their children: **Aharon, Henich, Bracha, Yisroel**

Moshe Klirsfeld-Haber

remembers:

his parents, **David** and **Chana**; his sisters: **Syule, Rivka, Rochel Chaya**; his brothers, **Shmuel** and **Mordechai Mordechai** died in Israel on 1.5.1958

In commemoration

of my parents

Hersh and **Chantshe-Rive Feldbau**

Buntshe Bien

Mrs. Tichover (Chaim Yidel's daughter)

from Nastaszczyn remembers:

her father, **Chaim Yidel Bigel**

Hersh Weissmann (Yisroel Auster's grandchild)

remembers his parents,

Moshe Aharon and **Chava**; his sisters and brothers: **Moyshele, Eli-Simcha, Mendel-Leibush, Chaya-Devorah, Sarah Sheindel, Yisroel Shmelki**

Bertha, Moshe, and **David Bauer**

remember their parents,

Mendel and **Freida**, daughter of **Moshe Misser**, and their daughter, **Sheindel**

Mendel and **Freida Bauer**

[pp. 439-440]

For eternal memory

My parents

Hersh Leib and **Krosi**

My uncle, **Yisroel-Hersh (Kolechnik)**

Adolph Schwartz

As an eternal commemoration

of my father, **Yisroel Isser Frantsoyz** My mother, **Roize**, and her second husband, **Yosef Mordechai Cohen**, and my brother, **Nute Leibush Schumer**

Dr. Lipa Schumer

As a holy commemoration of

My wife's parents, **Zelik** and **Reizel Glotzer**, their children: **Yaakov, Gittel Rivka**, and **Avraham-Itzik**

Shimon Zager

As an eternal commemoration

of our parents,

Michael and **Libe Kimmel,**

their daughter and her husband, **Hersh Nechemias**, their grandchild, **Libe-Elka** and her husband, **Chaim Hersh Jupiter Koppel** and **Ire Kimmel**

In commemoration

of my parents, **Zisl** and **Berl**, my sisters, **Bronia** and **Chana**, and her child, my grandparents, **Yaakov** and **Chaya-Faige Rude [or Rudy]**, and their children: **Elka, Leah, Esther, Bluma**, and **Ruchtshe**

Yocheved Wein-Rudy

In commemoration

of

my wife, **Shoshana**, children: **Chaya-Mintshe**, and **Avraham**; my parents, **Yechezkel** and **Elka** and their children

Yitzchak Roher

[pp. 441-442]

Molly Kleiman

remembers:

Her parents, **Avraham** and **Fannie**,

sister, **Chaya Leah**, brother, **Daniel**, **Chaim Lieb**, and **Yaakov**

Yitzchak Kimmel

remembers his parents

Shlomo Kimmel and wife, his brother, **Ira Kimmel**, and two children, sister, **Peppy Steinberg**, brother-in-law, **Moshe**, and three children, sister, **Toibe Sheindel**, her husband, **Srulke**, aunt, **Esther**, and daughter, **Rivka**, **Leibush Kimmel**, and three children, uncle, **Yaakov Kimmel**, **Charne Feldklein**, and three children

---

Chaim Ebert, Yoel the Red's son

remembers:

His parents, **Yoel** and **Toibe**; his wife's parents, **Chana**, **Reuven** the butcher's daughter, and her husband, **Aharon Lieb**, their children: **Yoel**, **Yaakov**, **Yosef**, **Chaya**

Yosef Glotzer, Velvele,
Yonah Lieb's son,

remembers his parents,

Velvl and **Eidel**,

their children: **Chava**, **Peppy**, **Shmuel Henech**, and **Esther**

Shmuel and Moshe Drucker

remember

their parents, **Bluma** and **Chaim**, their murdered sister, **Rani**, **Eidel**, and **Faige**

We sob for these

The Henich Family

remembers

R' Moshe Haber and wife, their children: **Berl**, **Mattes**, **Itshe**, and **Yaakov**

Velvl Henich's father-in-law, **R' Yossel Laufer**, and wife, **Hudel**, and their son, **Naftali** and family, **Harry Henich's** father-in-law, **Mendel Podhajcer**, [and] his wife, **Rivka**

Natan and Drezia Ribler

remember:

Yehudah Yitzchak and his wife, **Chana**, their children: **Moshe**, **Shimon**, **Yaakov**, **Krantzye**, **Devorah**, **Shmuel**, **Shalom**, **Ita**, **Lieb Shlomo**

Drezia's parents, **David** and **Rochel Weinstock**, their children: **Toibe-Rivka**, **Liba**, **Itzik-Yoel**, **Avrahamtshe**

Shmuel Schapira

remembers his father,

R' Hershele Strelisker, his mother, **Esther**, his sister, **Chaya Devorah**, and her husband, **David Rosenkrantz**

[pp. 443-444]

A candle for the martyrs

My parents,

Ephraim and **Chana Zager**,

and my brother,

Avraham Tzvi

Yitzchak Zager

Lipa Landau

remembers his parents,

Shlomo Rores and **Chasia**

David Treiber

remembers his parents,

Eli and **Roize**,

his wife and child,

Sasha Ita and **Shoshana**

Murdered by the hands of the Hitlerist murderers

Yosef Goldstein

remembers his parents,

Menni Mindales and **Leib**,

his brother, **Yitzchak-Hersh** and **Akiva**,

his wife's parents, **Yosef** and **Chava Liblich**, and their daughter, **Faige**

In commemoration

Of my parents,

Berka and **Faige**,

their children,

Antiel and **Leah**

Wolf Weinberg

In commemoration

of our parents,

Chaya and **Itche** and brother, **Shimon**

From **Avraham** and **Peppy Erdstein** and their daughters, **Mintche** and **Rochel Leah**

Hersh and Loncia Feffer

[pp. 445-446]

He Shall Avenge Their Vengeance and Remember Their Self-Sacrifice

Rochel Schwartz,
1926-1937, the daughter of **Yosef** and **Gittel**

Yosef and Yukev [Yaakov] Schwartz
remember:

Hershele Gedaliah's, his wife, **Rochel,** and family:

Yisroel, Chaya – children: **Sarah, Ratze, Meir**

Gedaliah, Toibe – children: **Krantzye, Faige, Pessie, Yisroel, Naftali**

Elya, Liftshe – children: **Sarah, Yaakov, Hentshe, Yosef, Toibe, Ovadiah**

Yehoshua, Sarahtshe – children: **Natanel, Yaakov Henoch, Maltshe, Naftali, Freida, Golda. Rechil, Ephraim, Sarah**

Krantzye, her mother, **Toibe,**
the elderly grandmother, and **Ita Liba**

As a holy commemoration
of

Baila and Taibele Fenster

Yisroel

Berl Feldbau
remembers his parents,

Ziskind and Eidel; their children: **Avrahamtzi, Hersh Meir, Sarah-Rivka.** His grandparents: **Moshe and Rashe,** their children: **Meir, Shmuel-Mordechai, Aryeh-Lieb, Hersh, Binyamin, Esther** and husband, **Nute** and **Ettel**

From the right: **Yisroel Schwartz, Avrahamtzi Feldbau, Itche Bigel,** and **Yankl Mehrberg's son** Z"L

[pp. 447-448]

In memory
Of the family
Itche Kimmel
(from the brickyard)

Rosa Haber Z"L
Pinye Haber's daughter

Gedaliah Kitner
remembers:

His parents, **Mendel** and **Faige,**
His wife and child,
His brother and family

Baruch Bien
remembers:

his wife, **Sarah,** and children: Yehudah David.

His parents, **Meir** and **Eidel**

Meir and Eidel Bien

In memory of
Minka Wieselberg

Her children,
Chava and Aryeh

Yosef Bigel
remembers:

His parents, **Avrahamtze** and **Chasia,**
his sister and brother

[pp. 449-450]

In commemoration
of **Buntshe Meller**
And his wife, **Baila**

Zalmen Singer
remembers his parents:
Ben Tzion Wolf, Singer's son-in-law, and his wife, Esther. Moshe Natan Singer, his wife, Perl, their children: Rivka, Mordechai David, Hersh, Wolf, Pessie, and Gittel

In commemoration
Of our mother,
Perl Feldman

Her sons,
Yankl, **Meir**, and **Moshe**

In memory
of
Chana Rudy-Tobias

Shmerl Pelz
remembers
his mother, his brothers, Velvil and Avraham

Hentche Pelz

In commemoration
Of
Shimon Klarer and wife,
his children
killed by the German murderers

[pp. 451-452]

As an eternal commemoration
Of our mother,
Golda Krochmal

Our sisters:
Yocheved and her husband, **Pesha** and her husband, **Letzer Deichsler**,
and the child of **Miriam Matess**, **Taibel** and **Chaim Yidl Krochmal**

Translator's footnote:

1.   Yizkor literally means "remember," and is also used here as an allusion to the memorial service recited by someone who is mourning the loss of a parent or other close one. The following section is comprised of photographs and names of Bursztyn Jews who perished during the Holocaust/Second World War.

[pp. 455-458]

Typed up by Genia Hollander

Book Committee:

**Dr. M. Haber, S. Schapira (New York), Moshe Cohen,
M. Nachwalger, Chaim Matesses, Bine Breiter, Ben Menachem,
Sara Kessler, Yona Bernstein**

To the Young Generation
To our American-born Children

You have been privileged to be born in a free country, the United States of America. The past of your parents is unknown to you. The name of their old hometown might even seem strange to you.

Our Memorial Book, to which your parents have contributed, tells us everything connected with our hometown, Bursztyn, a townlet now far from Stanislaw, Galicia. It was a typical townlet, like hundreds of other tiny communities in Poland. Life was so simple, so primitive, but in spite of all, it had a beauty of its own.

The Bursztyn Jews were religious and their life centred around their synagogue. The holy Sabbath made them forget their daily cares and worries. There were many scholars and men of intellect in Bursztyn. The education given to the children was traditional. The boys were taught in a "Heder", and some of them afterwards continued their studies in a "Yeshiva" or "Beth-Midrash". The girls learned the prayers and some of them took Hebrew and German or Polish lessons from the local teacher. Some of the young people, however, were not satisfied with this primitive way of life, in which they saw no future or chance of making good in such a small town. Both merchants and workers tried hard to make a living. The merchants traded with the gentile farmers in the surrounding villages, and while struggling for commercial success, they remained true to their moral precepts.

The Jews of Bursztyn were renowned for their hospitality. They gladly shared their meals with the hungry and poor way-farers. They gave to the utmost of their ability to charitable causes, and everyone was willing to help a friend in need.

The first cultural institution, a library, was established together with a Zionist organization, at the beginning of the 20th century, by a group of progressive Zionist youth. The library became the centre of their life. Newspapers in many languages, including the Hebrew daily "Hatzefira" and the Hebrew weekly, "Hamitzpa", were subscribed to by the organization. The young people longed for educational progress. Their lives were always full of dreams of Zion.

During the period between the two World Wars, the Jews of Bursztyn, like elsewhere in Poland, were undergoing a cultural revolution. Up to 1914, almost the entire population was religious and the children started their education in the "Heder". The youth wore long coats ("kapotes") and did not shave. Only in rare cases could Jewish parents afford to give their children a modern education. In those circles, attention was seldom paid to Jewish problems.

World War I violently shook the slumbering Jewish population of Bursztyn. The youth began to feel a tremendous thirst for education, and to evince a desire to look like their fellow-citizens, while remaining intensely Jewish. Certain Jewish circles were greatly inspired by socialist ideology and saw redemption only in this movement.

The majority, however, achieved some degree of knowledge, not in the regular schools, but by painstaking self-education. The Peretz library, which had by then been founded, was the source of the education of an entire generation.

In this matter, a large number of young people graduated, while being supported by their parents during their studies. However, the qualified advocates, philosophers and other professionals remained jobless, because of the anti-Semitic bias which then prevailed in Poland. Their only hope lay in being able to emigrate to Palestine, America and other countries. But the Nazi occupation in 1939 put an end to their dreams.

With the annihilation of the millions of our brothers and sisters, our own community was also destroyed, and almost the entire 2,500 inhabitants of Bursztyn perished. The handful of survivors tell us in our Memorial Book of the terrible sufferings undergone by our martyrs. They describe the lives of our dear families in the ghettos of Bursztyn, Bakachewitz and Rohatyn, and the final journey with its merciless end in Maidanek and Auschwitz.

Our Memorial Book is a documentary record of the life of a Diaspora townlet, of which there will never be any continuation.

We have written this Book especially for the young generation, for our children in Israel and for those of you in America. The Bursztyn Memorial Book is also yours.

Honour it and read it!

The Committee

NAME INDEX

Jamper, 49
Jampol, 78, 83
Janas, 218
Jankiv, 32, 33
Jawsrewska, 176
Jonas, 218
Joseph I, 46
Joseph II, 41, 42
Judenfreund, 218
Jupiter, 43, 97, 218, 232

K

Kahane, 218, 219
Kahn, 219
Kaminska, 84
Kanfer, 219
Katz, 8, 27, 186, 219
Kaufman, 87
Kessler, 6, 18, 236
Kielman, 233
Kimmel, 11, 46, 80, 113, 130, 220, 231, 232, 233, 234
Kimmels, 114
Kirshen, 18
Kitner, 80, 234
Klarberg, 48, 219
Klarer, 19, 235
Klarreich, 219
Klarreichs, 113, 114
Klein, 219
Kleinfeld, 48, 73, 130, 144, 219
Kletter, 9, 13, 58, 132, 143, 192, 193, 196, 219
Klirsfeld, 4, 18, 112, 208, 217, 219, 232
Klugmann, 8, 141, 220
Klysz, 182
Kobak, 49
Kochman, 32, 155
Kolechnik, 232
Komariatsky, 23, 182
Kopchinski, 161, 163, 165, 166, 167
Koppel, 232
Kortasz, 130
Krantz, 140
Krigel, 11
Krochmal, 12, 63, 65, 78, 220, 235
Krummholz, 220
Kurkis, 49, 50
Kuropatniki, 40, 56, 113, 130, 166, 188, 189, 191, 213, 220
Kurtasz, 115

Kutner, 72

L

Laker, 221
Landau, 8, 22, 39, 43, 48, 84, 106, 160, 181, 221, 233
Landner, 49, 63, 83, 84, 87, 118, 124, 125, 155, 221
Lasberg, 102, 137
Lask, 29, 32
Laufer, 52, 113, 123, 221
Leibale, 8, 208
Leider, 221
Leies, 221
Leiter, 221
Leivick, 84
Lerner, 221
Lewiter, 221
Lindner, 16
Lorberbaum, 43
Lysicer, 103, 104

M

Mach, 127
Machnicki, 56
Malikows, 60
Maltz, 16, 48, 49, 50, 51, 52, 53, 75, 77, 79, 93, 135, 136, 149
Mandelbaum, 174
Mandelberg, 9, 18, 32, 80, 83, 114, 154, 167, 208, 221, 222
Marburg, 12
Maria Theresa, 41
Maricki, 33
Markfeld, 222
Mastel, 31, 34, 154, 156, 222
Matess, 235
Matesses, 236
Matest, 222
Matschke, 171, 172
Matsis, 5, 6
Mazul, 231
Mehrberg, 46, 210, 222, 234
Melamed, 222
Meller, 104, 222, 235
Meltzer, 12, 16
Menachem, 6, 16, 93, 236
Miller, 5
Milner, 187
Mindeles, 72

www.ingramcontent.com/pod-product-compliance
Lightning Source LLC
Chambersburg PA
CBHW050410110426
42812CB00006BA/1857